THE ADMINISTRATION OF CAMPUS DISCIPLINE:

Student, Organizational and Community Issues

Edited By
Brent G. Paterson and
William L. Kibler

The Higher Education Administration Series
Edited by Donald D. Gehring and D. Parker Young
COLLEGE ADMINISTRATION PUBLICATIONS, INC.

College Administration Publications, Inc.,
P. O. Box 9587, Asheville, N. C. 28815-0587

© 1998 College Administration Publications, Inc.,
All rights reserved. Published 1998
Printed in the United States of America

Library of Congress Cataloging-in-Publication Data

The administration of campus discipline : student, organizational and
community issues / edited by Brent G. Paterson and William L.
Kibler

    p.   cm. — (The higher education administration series)
Includes bibliographical references and indexes.
ISBN 0-912557-19-2 — Paperback Edition
ISBN 0-912557-22-2 — Hardback Edition
    1. College discipline—United States. 2. College students—United
States.—Discipline. 3. College students—Legal status, laws, etc.-
-United States. 4. Universities and colleges—Law and legislation-
-United States. I. Paterson, Brent G., 1957- . II. Kibler,
William L., 1954- . III. Series.
LB2344.A35 1997   97-39108
                                                    CIP

This publication is designed to provide accurate and authoritative information in regard to the subject matter covered. It is sold with the understanding that the publisher and author are not engaged in rendering legal,
accounting or other professional service. If legal advice or other expert
assistance is required, the services of a competent professional person
should be sought.
—*from a Declaration of Principles jointly adopted by a committee of the
American Bar Association and a committee of publishers.*

Table of Contents

Part Two: Student Conduct Issues • 75

IV. Adjudicating Campus Sexual Assault Cases • 77

V. Addressing Relationship Violence • 95

Part Five: Intervention Strategies • 225
XII. Increasing Campus Judicial Board Effectiveness • 227

XIII. Alternative Dispute Resolution: A New Look at Resolving Campus Conflict • 237

Foreword

For as long as there have been students in colleges there has been a need to address inappropriate student behavior. At colonial colleges, the trustees handled serious disciplinary matters while the college president often delegated less serious matters to faculty members (Dannells, 1988). Public confessions and ridicule, floggings, fines and expulsion were common punishments for student offenders.

The early 1900s saw the emergence of deans of men and deans of women on college campuses. These deans brought a new approach to student discipline—a holistic and humanistic approach that emphasized self-control. Court intervention and a push for student rights in the 1960s and 1970s caused many colleges and universities to adopt formal legalistic models to address student discipline. Some campuses established systems that closely resembled the court system. Today, virtually every college and university has a staff who specializes in student discipline. These student judicial affairs specialists must balance the educational aspects of student discipline with the expectations from attorneys, parents and others that attempt to turn student discipline into a criminal court proceeding.

Don Gehring, the first president of the Association for Student Judicial Affairs, coined the phrase, "besieged clan," to describe student judicial affairs officers. We often feel bombarded from all sides presidents, faculty, staff, parents, students, attorneys, and the media. There is little understanding of what we do as student judicial officers. Faculty and staff often think the process is too legalistic. They want the "inappropriate behavior" addressed, but would prefer not to be involved in the process except to tell you what punishment they expect. The president just wants the problem solved. Meanwhile, parents want to insure that their sons and daughters are being treated fairly. It seems today that students do not have a sense of responsibility for their actions. A familiar cry from students is "the system caused me to act in that manner." The system may be the environment in the residence hall or fraternity house, the lack of "adult supervision," the lack of explicit directions to not do something or the infamous "everyone else is doing it." We survive by sharing our experiences and learning from each other.

The attacks on student judicial affairs have not been limited to those directly involved in campus discipline. In the closing chapter of this book, Don Gehring predicts increasing involvement of the federal government in the operations of colleges and universities. In the last ten years, the Drug Free Schools and Communities Act, the Student Right-to-Know and Campus Security Act, the Violence Against Women Act, and revisions to the Family Educational Rights and Privacy Act have changed the way in which colleges and universities address conduct violations. The courts continue to redefine the student judicial process.

In Georgia, the state supreme court ruled that the Family Educational Rights and Privacy Act did not cover student judicial records. As a result, all student judicial records and student judicial hearings are open to the public at public institutions in Georgia. See chapter 3 "Student Judicial Records, Privacy and the Press's Right to Know" for more information.

At the time of this writing, Congress is considering the "Accuracy in Campus Crime Reporting Act of 1997" (ACCRA). While the intent is honorable, the act fails to realize the realities of campus discipline. U.S. Representative John Duncan, Jr., key sponsor of the act, in introducing the ACCRA to the media stated, "Many criminal actions have been channeled into campus disciplinary courts that are not open to public scrutiny. Many college administrators have simply wanted to avoid the bad publicity. There have been numerous cases nationwide in which students have graduated without even their parents knowing that their children had committed sexual assaults and other serious criminal acts. This bill will end the veil of secrecy surrounding such activities" (as cited in Lowery, 1997).

If ACCRA is enacted as currently written, the manner in which campus discipline is handled at colleges and universities, across the country, will change. First, campus officials from residence life staff to student counseling staff will be required to report statistics on campus incidents that could be defined as criminal offenses. Second, hearings for most discipline cases will be made open to the public, without restriction. Third, all campus disciplinary records will be open to public inspection. Needless to say, should this act become law, victims will fail to report incidents to campus officials for fear that their names and stories will be published on the front page of the campus newspaper. At the same time, police agencies will refrain from sharing police reports with student judicial officers until criminal charges are resolved. It appears that the ACCRA will have the opposite effect of its intent. Even if Congress does not approve the act, there will continue to be efforts to change how student discipline is handled by those who know very little about the process.

In the chapters contained in this book is valuable information on many topics of importance to student judicial officers and other student affairs staff. We chose these topics because they are issues that every student judicial officer faces sometime in his/her career, some more often than others.

The authors were selected for their expertise in the topic. Each has extensive experience with student judicial affairs as a practitioner or attorney advising colleges and universities on student judicial matters. Each of the authors has written journal articles on the topic and/or made presentations at national conferences and institutes on the topic. Student judicial affairs colleagues frequently seek their advice when dealing with a troubling situation on their campuses.

We want to thank the authors for their interest in this project and their dedication in producing the written work. Their efforts were made in the interest of helping others. They will receive no monetary benefit from the book. Instead, the authors and we, the editors, agreed to donate the royalties from sales of the book to the Association for Student Judicial Affairs to establish a conference scholarship for graduate students.

Special thanks to Dennis Gregory who always submitted his drafts before deadlines, who kept us on track when we became discouraged, and who agreed to edit the case study section at the last minute.

We hope that this book will be a regular reference source in your personal library.

> —Brent Paterson
> Bill Kibler
> College Station, TX

References

Dannells, M. (1988). Discipline. In A. L. Rentz & G. L. Saddlemire (Eds.), *Student affairs functions in higher education* (pp. 127-154). Springfield, IL: Charles C. Thomas.

Lowery, J. W. (1997). What ACCRA would do. *Synthesis: Law and policy in higher education, 8*(3), 611, 618.

About the Authors

TIMOTHY F. BROOKS is assistant vice-president and dean of students at the University of Delaware. He has been a dean of students for over fifteen years. He also serves on the faculty of education at the University of Delaware. Dr. Brooks is a past president of the Association for Student Judicial Affairs and has twice served as the director of the Donald D. Gehring Judicial Affairs Training Institute.

He has made over sixty national presentations and has written a number of publications on issues ranging from judicial systems, Greek affairs, institutional liability, and crisis management. Dr. Brooks received his B.A. from Bowdoin College, M.A. from Pacific Lutheran University, and Ed.D. from Oregon State University.

CHARLES CARLETTA is a member of the law firm of Pattison, Sampson, Ginsberg & Griffin, P.C. He is admitted to all of the courts of the State of New York, the United Sates Court of Military Appeals and the Supreme Court of the United States of America. His law firm is general counsel to Rensselaer Polytechnic Institute, The State Colleges, The Albany College of Pharmacy, the Faculty-Student Association of Hudson Valley Community College and the Hudson Mohawk Association of Colleges and Universities and is special counsel or consults with other private and public institutions of higher learning throughout the country.

He maintains membership in the National Association of College and University Attorneys, the National Association of College and University Business Officers, the College and University Personnel Association, The Association for Student Judicial Affairs and the International Association of Campus Law Enforcement Administrators and is frequently a guest lecturer at their meetings and contributing author to their publications.

He is the recent recipient of special recognition from the Stetson University College of Law and the Hudson Mohawk Association of Colleges and Universities for his contributions to higher education. Mr. Carletta received his B.A. from Manhattan College in 1966 and his J.D. from the Albany Law School of Union University in 1969.

DONALD D. GEHRING is professor of higher education and director of the Higher Education Administration Doctoral Program at Bowling Green State University. Prior to joining the faculty at Bowling Green, he was associate professor at the University of Louisville. In addition, Dr. Gehring has had extensive experience in student affairs administration. He earned a bachelor's degree in industrial management at Georgia Institute of Technology, a master's degree in mathematics education from Emory University, and a doctorate in higher education at the University of Georgia.

Dr. Gehring has earned distinction as a teacher, being cited for both innovation in teaching (Metroversity Grawmeyer Award finalist), and being nominated by his peers and students in the School of Education at the University of Louisville as the 1982 nominee for the University Distinguished Teaching Award. His publications are found in *The Journal of College and University Student Housing; Personnel and Guidance Journal; The Dental Educator, Surgery; Programming; The Journal of College Student Personnel* and *NASPA Journal*. He is the co-editor of *The College Student and the Courts*, co-author of *Alcohol on Campus* and has also contributed chapters on legal issues to a number of other books.

He is the founder and first president of the Association for Student Judicial Affairs (ASJA). Dr. Gehring has been honored with numerous awards for his contributions to higher education including the NASPA Award for Outstanding Contribution to Literature or Research, the Robert H. Shaffer Award for Excellence as a Graduate Faculty Member (NASPA), the Melvene Draheim Hardee Award for Outstanding Contribution to Student Affairs in Higher Education (Southern Association for College Student Affairs), Distinguished Service Award (Association of College and University Housing Officers-International), the D. Parker Young Award for Outstanding Scholarly and Research Contributions in areas of higher education law and judicial affairs (ASJA), and Senior Scholar (ACPA).

DENNIS GREGORY is currently serving as assistant vice-president for student development and student life at Francis Marion University in Florence, South Carolina. Prior to going to Francis Marion, Dr. Gregory served for two years as associate dean of students at the University of Tennessee–Knoxville and for eight years as director of residence life and housing and as an adjunct faculty member in counselor education at Wake Forest University. He holds the degree of Doctor of Education in Higher Education Administration as well as the Master of Education from the University of Virginia and a Bachelor of Science degree from James Madison University. Dr. Gregory has served in a variety of positions of professional leadership including conference chair and president of the Association for Student Judicial Affairs, and president of the North Carolina Housing Officers. He is a member of the AFA President's Commission on Greek Culture.

He served, in September 1994, as a member of a panel to discuss issues related to the Buckley Amendment and public release of student conduct records at the National Conference of the Society of Professional Journalists. In February 1995 he served as a panelist on the PBS television show, Freedom Speaks, which dealt with campus crime and the First Amendment implications of FERPA's protection of student conduct records.

Dr. Gregory has published articles in a variety of professional journals including the *NASPA Journal, The College Student Affairs Journal, The Journal of College and University Student Housing,* and the *Journal of Law and Education.* In April 1994, his article entitled "Misguided Campaigns for the Release of Students' Disciplinary Records" was published in *The Chronicle of Higher Education.*

WILLIAM L. KIBLER serves as the associate vice-president for student affairs and associate professor of educational administration at Texas A&M University. In addition to extensive experience in student judicial affairs, Dr. Kibler has had supervisory responsibilities for a variety of areas including student housing, disabled student services, student counseling services, student health services, and the student union. He has co-authored a book on academic integrity and has over ten professional articles in the areas of academic integrity, student judicial affairs and student affairs administration.

Dr. Kibler received the 1994 D. Parker Young Award from the Association for Student Judicial Affairs in recognition of outstanding scholarly and research contributions in the areas of higher education law and judicial affairs. He is a past president of the Association for Student Judicial Affairs and has served as the national conference chair for the National Association of Student Personnel Administrators. He was a founding member and served on the board of directors of the Center for Academic Integrity. Dr. Kibler received his bachelor's degree in economics and a master's degree and a specialist's degree in counselor education from the University of Florida. He earned a doctoral degree in educational administration from Texas A&M University.

GLENN MALONEY is associate dean of students at The University of Texas at Austin. Prior to joining the staff at the University of Texas, he served as activities coordinator at the University of Nebraska-Lincoln.

He received both his Bachelor of Science and Master of Arts degrees from Indiana University of Pennsylvania.

Mr. Maloney is the author of "Student Organizations and Student Activities" in *Student Services and the Law* (Barr and Associates, 1988). He has made numerous presentations on student organization legal issues and has received the Tracy R. Teele Memorial Award for outstanding contributions to the field of Judicial Affairs and Legal Issues given by ACPA's Commission XV.

Mr. Maloney has served on the directorate bodies of ACPA Commissions IV (Students, Their Activities and Community) and XV (Judicial Affairs and Legal Issues), as well as, a term on the ACPA executive council. He is also an active member of TACUSPA (Texas Association of College and University Student Personnel Administrators) and served as chair of the TACUSPA Legal Conference.

CAROLYN PALMER is associate professor of higher education and student affairs at Bowling Green State University. Prior to joining the faculty at Bowling Green State University, she served as a housing officer at the University of Illinois for fifteen years. She recently conducted a major research project on campus violence that resulted in her book entitled *Violent Crimes and Other Forms of Victimization in Residence Halls*. She is a frequent speaker on campus violence and victimization of women.

Dr. Palmer received her Ph.D. in quantitative and evaluative research methodologies at the University of Illinois. She holds a bachelor's degree from the University of Massachusetts and a master's degree from the University of Connecticut.

BRENT G. PATERSON is Director of Student Life at Texas A&M University where he has responsibility for adult and graduate student services; alcohol and drug education programs; gay, lesbian and bisexual student services; negotiation and mediation services; off-campus student services; parent programs; services for students with disabilities; student judicial services; student legal services; student life orientation; and women's programs. In addition, Dr. Paterson is an associate professor of educational administration. He has extensive experience in student judicial affairs as well as experience in housing and admissions at both public and private universities.

Dr. Paterson holds a bachelor's degree in elementary education from Lambuth College, a master's degree in counseling and personnel services from Memphis State University, and a Ph.D. in higher education from the University of Denver. He is certified as a mediator and neutral in compliance with the Texas Civil Practices and Remedies Code. Dr. Paterson has been active in the National Association of Student Personnel Administrators (NASPA), the Southern Association for College Student Affairs (SACSA), the Texas Association of College and University Student Personnel Administrators (TACUSPA), and the Association for Student Judicial Affairs (ASJA). Currently, he serves as an associate editor of *The College Student Affairs Journal*. He has co-authored a book on academic integrity and has authored several articles published in *The College Student Affairs Journal* and the *NASPA Journal*.

EDWARD N. STONER II is a partner in the law firm of Reed Smith Shaw & McClay. He received a bachelor's degree from DePauw University and his law degree from the University of Virginia, joining the firm of Reed Smith Shaw & McClay in Pittsburgh upon graduation.

Mr. Stoner has represented college and university clients not only in labor law matters, but also in general matters involving student life and discipline and faculty relations. He serves as outside counsel for Duquesne University and has also represented other local schools including Westminster College, and the University of Pittsburgh.

He is a member of the National Association of Student Personnel Administrators and the Association for Student Judicial Affairs. Mr. Stoner also is a member of the Board of Directors of the National Association of College and University Attorneys (NACUA). Mr. Stoner served for three years as the co-chairman of NACUA's section of athletics. Mr. Stoner is admitted to practice in Pennsylvania and is a member of the bar of the Supreme Court of the United States.

PATRICIA S. TERRELL is the vice-president for student services and dean of academic support services at Utah State University. She was previously the associate vice president for student affairs and dean of student life at Southern Methodist University for eight years and also held positions in student affairs administration at the University of Louisville. She has or has had responsibility for student judicial affairs at all three institutions.

Dr Terrell's professional involvement includes extensive previous service to the National Association of Student Personnel Administrators which includes NASPA Region III vice-president and chair of the 1990 NASPA Conference and the Southern Association for College Student Affairs. Dr. Terrell has published articles in the *NASPA Journal* and *The College Student Affairs Journal*. She is the immediate past president of the Golden Key National Honor Society and serves on the board of directors.

Dr. Terrell has a bachelor's degree in elementary education and a master's degree in student personnel from the University of Louisville. She received her doctorate in education from the University of Kentucky.

DIANE M. WARYOLD is the assistant dean of students for judicial programs and graduate adjunct professor at the University of North Carolina at Charlotte. Prior to joining the staff at the University of North Carolina at Charlotte, she held positions in student judicial affairs at the University of Georgia and the University of Florida. Dr. Waryold is a past president of the Association for Student Judicial Affairs (ASJA) and a charter member of the association. She was awarded the Don Gehring Award in recognition for sustained service to ASJA in 1993. Dr. Waryold received a Bachelor of Science degree in education from the State University College of New York at Cortland, a Master of Education degree from the University of Florida and a doctorate in educational leadership from Florida State University.

EUGENE (GENE) ZDZIARSKI is assistant director of student life at Texas A&M University. Mr. Zdziarski received his Bachelor of Science degree in business administration and personnel management from Oklahoma State University, and his Master of Science degree in educational leadership/college student personnel from the University of Tennessee at Knoxville. He is currently working on his Ph.D. in educational administration at Texas A&M University.

Mr. Zdziarski is certified as a mediator and neutral in compliance with the provisions of section 154.052 of the Texas Civil Practices and Remedies Code and does consulting with colleges and universities on establishing campus dispute resolution centers, as well as private mediation. He has also served as the central office manager for the Association for Student Judicial Affairs for the past five years.

Part One

Organizational and Legal Considerations

Chapter I

A Model Code for Student Discipline

Edward N. Stoner, II

INTRODUCTION

So! You have been given the assignment of creating a good student disciplinary code for your campus. Congratulations! You are about to embark on one of the most challenging and important tasks facing any student affairs professional. As you doubtless already are aware, the task will be challenging because there are numerous legal as well as student affairs issues involved in creating a good student code.

There is not a pat set of answers to these issues but, on the other hand, there are several "right" ways to address many of the issues. At the same time, the task is one of the most important you can do for your campus because the quality of the living learning environment on campus will reflect the standards you set in your student code and the degree of fairness and professionalism which it enables you to put into effect.

In order to assist you in this challenge there are several general points you ought to keep in mind and there are also some suggestions which may help you to make the drafting process itself more successful. Let's look first at the general points.

NO CRIMINAL LAW LANGUAGE IN YOUR STUDENT CODE

This is the first and great commandment of having an effective student code. If you get nothing else out of this chapter, or out of this entire book, please take this point with you. The reason for this principle is simply that a student code is not a criminal law code. No one will get a jail sentence or be subject to a criminal fine for failing to follow the college's rules. This is, perhaps, an elementary point but it bears repeating. Your student code is NOT a criminal law code. It does not intend to be, and it is not, a substitute for the criminal law.

3

Instead, it is the method by which the college establishes its educational values and creates a positive living learning environment on campus.

This point is not a secret one, known only to student affairs professionals, as is illustrated by the fact that, when Mr. Justice Blackmun was an appellate court judge, he observed exactly this point when he wrote, "School regulations are not to be measured by the standards which prevail for criminal law and for criminal procedure" (*Esteban v. Central Missouri State College*, 1969).

After you are finished drafting your code, put your computer on "spell check" and make sure criminal law words like "guilt," "prosecutor" and "defendants" do not appear in your code. Instead, you will have a process in which you determine whether a student violated the college's rules or is to be held "responsible." It will be comforting to know that, if you delete criminal law words from your code, there will be at least two other advantages. The first advantage is that it will help you to remember to treat everyone who comes before your board as "students" which is, after all, what they are. They are not "defendants" or "prosecuting witnesses"; they are students. Note I did not say they are "merely" students because we want to remember that, even though they may have violated the college's rules we want to treat all students as being very important—and this fact is simply not a a very important touchstone in the criminal law process.

The second advantage is that, if you delete these criminal law words from your code, you will not fall into the "trap" of incorporating criminal law legal concepts into your student code. This would, potentially, be a serious error. Student affairs professionals do not, usually, understand all the nuances of the criminal law because, generally, they are not lawyers. You do not want to suggest, to either a judge who might review your code or a lawyer for a student who has violated the code, that your institution intended to follow criminal law procedures because you used criminal law terms in your code.

A good example of this point is the standard which is commonly used in student codes to determine whether a student has violated the code. Unlike the criminal law, a college does not determine anything by the criminal law standard of "beyond a reasonable doubt." Instead, we use the standard of "more likely than not." This is the civil law standard appropriate to an administrative proceeding like a college disciplinary code and, if you use it, it will not cause you any problems because the standard is very familiar to lawyers and judges alike (Stoner & Cerminara, 1994, p.113).

Thus, no matter what else you do when you are drafting your student code, please remember not to use criminal law language.

REMEMBER TO TREAT ALL STUDENTS WITH
EQUAL FAIRNESS AND DIGNITY

This point is quite a bit different from the first one, but it is equally important. All provisions of your code should be evaluated against this standard. It is not as easy as it seems because there will be a lot of forces tugging at you to "tilt" things one way or the other. As to students who claim the code has been violated, it is very important to be fair to them and to treat them with dignity because we have created the standards in the code so that they will enjoy a positive living learning environment.

As to students who may have violated the code, we do not presume that they did violate the code. Because they are students to whom we have also made the commitment of a positive living learning environment, we want to treat them with fairness and dignity, even if we believe and determine that they have violated the college's rules.

This not only emphasizes how important students are to our academic community but also our commitment to treat all students with fairness and dignity at all times. It is a perfect example of what distinguishes the campus code system from a criminal law process. Our purposes are educational, not punitive, and we keep that in mind all of the time.

Here is one example that was brought to my attention by students at Duquesne University in Pittsburgh. It concerns the right to appeal. Our model code allowed only the student who violated the rules to appeal. When I explained this principle of treating all students with equal fairness and dignity, students challenged me to explain why student victims could not appeal, too, if they believed relevant witnesses had not been heard or the sanction was not right. I realized I had no good answer, so our next code revision allowed all students involved in the process the same rights to appeal.

This principle, treating all students with equal fairness and dignity, comes up frequently in all discipline situations so it is critical that it be a part of your code drafting process, as well.

KEEP IT FLEXIBLE

This principle applies not only to you, when you are drafting the code, but also to the provisions you put into the code. They must enable you to respond with a process that fits the circumstances. On the first point, you will want to provide for periodic review. This will keep your code current. Sometimes, the law changes and you will want your code to change when required. More likely, the educational environment will change and students will find new ways to misbehave. Computer offenses, unknown a decade ago, are a good example.

A second flexibility point is to allow, in your code, for items that are not contained in the code itself. For example, there will be forms that are used (e.g., notice of alleged violation of the college's rules, notice of date of hearing, notice of result of hearing). There will be a "script" which the hearing officer or panel chair will follow so that each important part of the hearing is accomplished and not overlooked. The code should allow for each of these and for them to be changed from time to time without going through the process of amending the code itself.

A final flexibility point is that the code should allow for different panels or persons to hear cases, as appropriate. You may elect to have a joint student/faculty/administrator panel hear most cases, for example, but you will want to preserve the option to assign a special panel or even a single person to hear a case in special circumstances. If your code reserves this flexibility, you will have it when you need it (Stoner & Cerminara, 1994, p. 96)

DO NOT QUOTE, OR INCORPORATE BY REFERENCE, STATE CRIMINAL LAW LANGUAGE

You will quickly see that this point is a corollary to the first one. But it, too, is important. State your college's standards in your college's language. Do not use criminal law language. For example, do not forbid "rape" because this is a criminal law word, with criminal law baggage. Define the conduct in simple, understandable language. On the other hand, do not incorporate state criminal law standards. For example, do not say that "hazing, as defined in state law" is forbidden. Use your own words so that you are not implying that the college can deal with hazing only if a criminal offense is first proved.

If you follow these four principles, you will be well on your way to coming up with a student code that will help you to create a positive living learning environment on campus.

The Drafters

The next step, after you have committed yourself to these four principles, is to decide who will do the drafting of your student code. As in any committee process, the larger the group, the harder it is to get the job done. So, try to keep the group small, but effective.

There are three persons, or groups, who should be involved in your drafting process. The first is the student affairs professional(s). They must be involved for they will define campus standards at the outset and, at the end of the day, are responsible for administering the code. The second is students. After all, this code is designed to create a good living learning environment for them. Thus, they must be involved. Select the students who will be involved carefully. A typical decision is to include students from the judicial system (again, so they can correctly administer the code and, also, so that their input can make the code run smoothly) and a student from the student government. Three, is a good number of students.

Finally, you must involve your campus attorney. My preference is that counsel be involved in the drafting process but at least your counsel must be involved before the code is finally adopted. There are several reasons for this. If your attorney is involved in the drafting, he or she will be better able to defend the college if it is sued for taking disciplinary action. In addition, the attorney will be able to explain to administrators who were not involved in the drafting why the judicial board's action was appropriate and in compliance with procedure. This is much better than having your attorney learn about your process for the first time in the middle of a heated debate involving parents, students, coaches, alums and other administrators!

Naturally, if your attorney was involved in the drafting he or she will be a better "defender" of your process, because he or she will have a proprietary interest in it as a drafter. Thus, your college attorney will, more likely, be an advocate on your side and not one of your critics if he or she is involved in the drafting stage.

At the risk of offending truly exceptional persons, I want to note that there are several categories of persons who may be interested but who should not be included on the drafting "team." These are faculty members, trustees and law professors. Most are not trained in student affairs and are not as directly connected to creating and defending a positive living learning environment on campus as are student affairs professionals, students and your campus counsel.

Law professors, especially ones who do not also practice law, typically are not good resources because they tend to forget our very first principle (this is not a criminal law code) and to err on the side of protecting rule violators at the expense of providing equal fairness to student victims and the rest of the community. In short, get your legal advice from the person who will be defending the code after it has imposed discipline in a "hard" case.

Now, you have in place your drafting team and guiding principles. What is the process you might use in drafting your code? Here are a number of suggestions.

The Drafting Process

Although this list of how to draft a student code may seem long, you will have a better final product if you consider each of these suggestions.

Read the current code. Your drafting process will flow from what is already in place. Although everyone thinks they know what the current code says, make sure everyone reads the code before the work begins. This seems elementary, but, often persons have definite opinions about student codes that come from hearsay and gossip, not from actually reading the code. So make sure that everyone on the drafting team, from the CSAO to the attorney and the students, actually reads the code first. Also, each person should be given copies of all forms and procedures currently in place—even if you intend to discard them.

The person in charge of the process should meet, one at a time, with key constituents to identify problems and issues which need to be considered in the drafting process. These key constituents will vary from campus to campus and it is, to some degree, a political decision. I would definitely include other student affairs professionals, prior student chairs of the judicial boards, the campus counsel or general counsel, and the president.

You may include others at this stage from the following list of persons who might, also, come before the entire drafting committee. One final person I would try to include, however, is the athletics director—not because he or she is an expert on student codes or student affairs but because student athletes do have special problems as students and also seem to get into more than their share of high profile "problems."

Those involved in the drafting need to understand the campus "social system." This may seem like a given, but you need to make sure that everyone is working from the same perspective. Your attorney, for example, may be new to your institution. This occasion will be a good time to let him or her know what life on campus really is like. In reviewing your "social system," I would also share a few good touchstones:

- **Do not simply "throw out" the old code** (unless it is "really bad"). Most codes reflect the campus social system and there may be good reasons why things work on your campus, even if they are not typical. Use your old code as a vehicle for understanding the campus social system.

- **Focus on the problems your campus has had with the prior code.** This will enable you to fix the problems by redrafting problem areas of the code. If you simply discard the whole prior code and start over you might create new problems without realizing it.

- **Be sure you know the history of student discipline and of "problem cases" which arose under it** whether you "throw out" the old code or not. Know the number of cases, the types of violations, the typical sanctions, the types of appeals and whether they were granted (by sending the matter back to the hearing panel to correct any error), and, finally, whether there were any lawsuits or adverse media coverage of your student discipline. All of this information will help you to focus properly on creating a good student code.

Invite input from other interested constituencies on campus. Although it is important to keep the drafting group small, it is equally important to include all parts of the campus in the code revision process. Here is a list of constituencies you might wish to include:

- **Others on the student affairs staff.** Everyone on the staff should be included. This can be done at a staff meeting, if you like, but it is critical to have input from all residence life staff members, as well as those who work directly with the student code hearing process because these persons know the problems first hand and will be the first line of persons charged with creating "solutions."

- **Everyone who has served on judicial boards in the last year (or two).** Here, I would invite input from literally everyone who has served on a recent judicial board: faculty members, administrators and students.

- **Faculty.** These critical members of our academic community must have input, even though they may not have served on a judicial board in the past. If their input in sought, they will be more willing to participate in the future when needed. More importantly, some code violations involve faculty and their perspectives on how to identify and deal with problems can be invaluable. For example, they are involved in plagiarism cases, as well as other misbehavior in the classroom.

- **Athletic Director.** As noted above, it is critical to involve the athletic director. It also would be wise to involve coaches. This is a great opportunity to have a dialog about student behavior and what is expected of students who happen to be athletes without having it occur in the emotion charged atmosphere of a situation in which a student athlete is believed to have committed a serious rules violation. You may not win any friends among the coaches but if they are involved they cannot later claim they were surprised and if they understand the principles applicable to all students they may make some extra effort to make sure that student athletes understand the college's standards.

- **Other persons who may be interested.** This will vary from campus to campus but it likely may include persons from campus police, the president's office and even a member of the board of trustees (such as the person in charge of the student affairs committee). At one campus, they sought input from the alumni affairs office and found it paid nice dividends with a good article in the alumni magazine about the new student code.

- **Students.** Naturally, I have saved the most important for last. It is important to include as broad a range of students as possible: for input, not for control of the process. Naturally, some students want no discipline. This is predictable but not acceptable. Still, listen to them and educate them. Perhaps, you will convince them that a good living learning environment is in their best interest, too. Surely, all will agree that the goals of treating all students with fairness, dignity, care and concern are appropriate. In any event, invite input from student government, the campus press, resident students, commuter students, non-traditional students, and any other students you think would be appropriate.

Use models. Any model code should be used as a checklist—not as something to copy. The model code came about as a result of revisions to the codes of a number of colleges. It contains a number of options on various issues, and that is how you want to use any model —as a source of alternative approaches to establishing a workable student code system. There are other good models, too. The best model to use is an actual code from an institution like yours: public or private, whichever you are; about your size; if your school has a religious affiliation, use a code from an institution of the same faith for their values should be reflected in their code; and look for a code from a school which has the similar student mix as you do (commuter/ residential or four-year versus community college).

Remember your audience. Although you are writing a student code, remember that you have many audiences. These include students, faculty, administrators, parents, future students, alumni, opposing attorneys, your own attorneys, trustees, and even coaches. Keep it simple so that all of these persons will understand it!

Remember your goals. It is important to identify the goals you are trying accomplish so that, when you finish your code revision, you have the best chance of having accomplished your goals. Each campus' goals in revision its code may be different, but here are some possible goals:

• **Make is easier to deal with problem cases.** Toward this goal, please have only one student code. Some people, with the best of intentions, have come up with different processes or different offenses. This is a nightmare because actual conduct does not fit into convenient cubbyholes, so that you may find that a single incident falls under multiple processes. For example, you may have an allegation of a date rape involving an interracial couple where it is alleged that some violence occurred with racial epithets. If you have one process for physical abuse, another for sexual violence and a third for racially motivated offenses, your entire process will grind to a halt as you try to unravel your processes and as you try to comply with the procedures required by different codes. So, please, have only one code.

• **Identify problem cases and make sure your code makes it possible to deal with them effectively.** For example, I would suggest using a hypothetical sexual violence case and walking it through your new process, to make sure that the "typical" issues can be resolved intelligently.

- **One of my goals is always to make sure that, whatever result is reached, the result reached can be effectively defended** if the college is sued in protest to the discipline. The most basic protection is to make your procedures clear and understandable, and then to follow them.
- **Another goal might be to involve your college counsel in your student code process.** If this is difficult, you might do so by asking him or her what recent state law (or other) there is which you should observe in writing the new code. And, sometime when it is not critical, invite your counsel to observe a hearing. Then, when a crisis does erupt, he or she will be better able to defend you because he or she will understand exactly how the process does work.
- **Other goals might include reducing the number of cases which go to hearings** (include effective mediation!) or eliminating sanctions which are ineffective (e.g., writing an essay). Whatever your goals are, list them and you will be more likely to achieve them.

Now, you are ready to write! With these tips, you should be able to write a good student code. Unfortunately, that is the easy part because deciding what the students did and how best their spirit of insubordination can be channeled into something positive remains ahead of you. Good luck!

The following article is reprinted from *The Journal of College and University Law*, volume 17, number 2, pages 89-121, with the permission of the authors, the National Association of College and University Attorneys (NACUA), and *The Journal of College and University Law*.

HARNESSING THE "SPIRIT OF INSUBORDINATION": STUDENT DISCIPLINARY CODE

Edward N. Stoner II and Kathy L. Cerminara

The article of discipline is the most difficult in American education. Premature ideas of independence, too little repressed by parents, beget a spirit of insubordination, which is the great obstacle to science with us and a principle cause of its decay since the revolution. I look to it with dismay in our institution, as a breaker ahead, which I am far from being confident we shall be able to weather.
Thomas Jefferson
Letter to Thomas Cooper, Nov. 2, 1822
The Works of Thomas Jefferson (1884)

Since the days Thomas Jefferson wrote to Mr. Cooper,[1] institutions of higher education have struggled with the responsibility of disciplining students. This task has been made more difficult because the legal relationship between a college or a university and its students has never fit neatly within one legal doctrine.[2] During the first part of the twentieth century, the concept of in loco parentis[3] predominated. Under this doctrine, courts viewed institutions as standing in the place of students' parents. Courts tended to give colleges and universities a great deal of discretion when they viewed the institutions as standing in loco parentis[4] to the students.

During the 1960s, however, courts began to move away from the concept of in loco parentis. Instead, courts viewed the relationship between student and institution as contractual. Under this view, institutions enter into contracts with their students to provide them with educational services in exchange for students' paying certain fees and obeying certain rules.[5] In addition, beginning with the landmark case of *Dixon v. Alabama Board of Education*,[6] in 1961, courts have required public institutions of higher learning to afford students due process[7] before taking disciplinary action.[8]

Although courts no longer merely rubber-stamp college or university decisions, as they once may have done under the doctrine of in loco parentis, principles from all three views appear in student disciplinary cases. Courts afford institutions of higher education a great deal of discretion.[9] At the same time, however, they require colleges and universities to honor the contracts they make and to provide fair procedures.

Colleges and universities thus operate within a volatile environment. In order to ensure smooth administration, yet still to fulfill their responsibility of maintaining discipline within an educational environment, colleges and universities are well-advised to establish written student disciplinary codes.[10] For a public college or university, such a written code provides constitutionally-required notice to students, faculty and administrators concerning the institution's policies and procedures. It may also ensure against charges of unconstitutional arbitrary action—for example, allegations that the school singled out one student for particularly unfair treatment.

The private institution too may avoid charges of arbitrary or unfair treatment by implementing a written student disciplinary code.[11] A written student code can benefit both public and private institutions, as well as students, by clearly setting forth the terms of the "contract" between the student and the school with respect to disciplinary matters.[12]

What follows is a model student code which college or university counsel and administrators may use in creating their own written student disciplinary code. Of course, decisions with regard to certain topics will depend upon the preference of each individual college or university. Such topics include choosing a person at the institution to administer student-code policies and procedures; establishing a minimum amount of notice of the alleged violation; setting a maximum period between the time students are notified of charges against them, and the day on which those charges are heard; and deciding who will determine sanctions. Nevertheless, the following model is a sound beginning upon which to build a student disciplinary code.

College or university counsel and administrators should keep a few principles in mind when drafting their own student disciplinary codes. First, the institution, whether public or private, should try to follow the general dictates of due process. Due process, roughly translated, means ensuring that procedures are fair to the accused student.[13] If an institution is public, it is required to grant due process.[14] If the institution is private, constitutional due process may not be required,[15] but the institution's actions may appear fairer and more reasonable to a court if it gives students as much procedural protection as would a public institution.

Second, although college discipline is sometimes seen as the "criminal law of university government,"[16] student disciplinary codes need not be drafted with the specificity of criminal statutes.[17] In fact, to avoid indicating that it expects its student code to be treated like a criminal statute, a college or university should avoid language implying that criminal standards apply.[18] Any code promulgated by a college or university should, however, be sufficiently specific to make the rules clear.[19]

Third, student code drafters should be aware that, as in any generic document, the principles set forth in the model student code represent the generally prevailing law. In some instances, courts disagree.[20] In others, administrators hold opposing views.[21] In these cases, the model either offers the drafters alternative choices or advocates the position taken by the majority of courts or schools, while noting that the position taken is not unanimously held. As with any formal document, college or university counsel should review case law in his or her own jurisdiction to ensure that the institution is not bound by opposing precedent.

Finally, although such a section is not included in this model student code, the college or university should try to emphasize, in addition to its prohibitions, rights which it recognizes. This can be included in a preamble to the student code[22] or in the college or university handbook.[23] The institution thereby assures its students that it does not intend to take away rights,[24] but intends merely to control action going beyond the exercise of such rights. The institution can thus help to insulate itself from student attacks based upon allegations that the student code violates some constitutional right.[25]

The following model student code is organized so that all concerned students, administrators and faculty members can understand the concepts embodied therein. It progresses from a general definition section to a section outlining the authority of the institution's judicial bodies, a description of misconduct covered by the code, an outline of the procedures for bringing charges of misconduct, holding hearings and deciding appeals and, finally, a section on interpretation and revision of the code. The commentary following each section sets forth not only the practical reason for including each section within the code, but also the legal support for each provision, and, in some cases, suggestions on how the college or university attorney could approach certain situations.

In the final analysis, even the adoption of a sound student code, coupled with enlightened administration, will not eliminate the "spirit of insubordination" which Thomas Jefferson saw as such a significant problem for higher education nearly a century-and-three-quarters ago. Indeed, as Mr. Jefferson recognized, such insubordination results, in part, from the "ideas of independence" which are the backbone of our liberties, not only in higher higher education, but also in the world at large.

To the captains of our ships of higher education, therefore, the calm waters of consistently proper student behavior are unlikely ever to be reached. Instead, as Mr. Jefferson feared, the challenges of student discipline are likely always to loom as breakers ahead. Nevertheless, a sound student code following this model, like a sound ship under a sailing captain of old, will enable college and university administrators to navigate confidently past the dangers of insubordination, even when those dangers are accompanied, as they often are, by storm clouds of public concern and campus unrest.

MODEL STUDENT CODE

Article I: Definitions[26]

1. The term [College/University] means [name of institution].

2. The term "student" includes all persons taking courses at the [College/University], both full-time and part-time, pursuing undergraduate, graduate, or professional studies and those who attend post-secondary educational institutions other than [name of institution] and who reside in [College/University] residence halls. Persons who are not officially enrolled for a particular term but who have a continuing relationship with the [College/University] are considered "students."

> *Commentary: This definition is intended to include persons not enrolled for a particular term but who enroll for courses from time to time, perhaps toward a degree. Such persons would be expected to honor the Student Code even between periods of their actual enrollment.*

3. The term "faculty member" means any person hired by the [College/University] to conduct classroom activities.

4. The term "[College/University] official" includes any person employed by the [College/University], performing assigned administrative or professional responsibilities.

5. The term "member of the [College/University] community" includes any person who is a student, faculty member, [College/University] official or any other person employed by the [College/University]. A person's status in a particular situation shall be determined by [title of appropriate college or university administrator].[27]

6. The term "[College/University] premises" includes all land, buildings, facilities, and other property in the possession of or owned, used, or controlled by the [College/University] (including adjacent streets and sidewalks).

7. The term "organization" means any number of persons who have complied with the formal requirements for [College/University] [recognition/registration].

8. The term "judicial body" means any person or persons authorized by the [title of administrator identified in Article I, number 13][28] to determine whether a student has violated the Student Code and to recommend imposition of sanctions.

> *Commentary: A "judicial body," sometimes called a "hearing board," need not be comprised of any particular number of persons. Concerns recur about the composition of such bodies. An impartial decision-maker is essential to due process.[29] Courts have recognized, however, that in the college or university context it is often impossible to assemble a group of people who have not in some way heard of the charges at issue or who do not know the person(s) involved.[30] Frequently, "judicial bodies" which determine whether the Student Code has been violated include both students and fac-*

ulty members or administrators. In this model, the code administrator defines the composition of hearing boards, but if the history or social system on campus dictates otherwise, the composition may be defined in more detail in the student code.

9. The term "judicial advisor" means a [College/University] official authorized on a case-by-case basis by the [title of administrator identified in Article I, number 13] to impose sanctions upon students found to have violated the student code. The [title of administrator identified in Article I, number 13] may authorize a judicial advisor to serve simultaneously as a judicial advisor and the sole member or one of the members of a judicial body. Nothing shall prevent the [title of administrator identified in Article I, number 13] from authorizing the same judicial advisor to impose sanctions in all cases.

Commentary: Just as courts have recognized that persons comprising a judicial body may have prior knowledge of the events at issue or the person(s) involved, they have recognized that it is sometimes impossible on a college campus to avoid having one person occupy two roles with respect to disciplinary proceedings.[31] While it is not improper, whenever possible the college or university should avoid putting someone in the position of "wearing two hats."

If the size of the institution's staff permits, it is decidedly preferable to have the functions of informal investigating and/or mediating separated from that of determining whether a violation has occurred and setting the sanction. Admittedly, such separation can be achieved more easily at large institutions. Thus, this model recognizes the advisability of separating the functions when possible, while preserving the flexibility to combine functions which usually will be a fact of life at smaller institutions. A student challenging a hearing board's decision on the grounds of bias must, in order to win the case, prove actual bias or that the board acted improperly.[32] This model anticipates that a college or university official will determine sanctions after a violation has been found. In some systems sanctions are set by students.

10. The term "appellate board" means any person or persons authorized by the [title of administrator identified in Article I, number 13] to consider an appeal from a judicial body's determination that a student has violated the student code or from the sanctions imposed by the judicial advisor.

11. The term "shall" is used in the imperative sense.

12. The term "may" is used in the permissive sense.

13. The [title of appropriate administrator] is that person designated by the [College/University] president to be responsible for the administration of the student code. The term "policy" is defined as the written regulations of the [College/University] as found in, but not limited to, the student code, residence life handbook, and graduate/undergraduate catalogs.

The Administration of Campus Discipline . . .

Commentary: Listed herein is a sampling of the types of other sources of rules and regulations governing colleges or universities.

14. The term "cheating" includes, but is not limited to: (1) use of any unauthorized assistance in taking quizzes, tests, or examinations; (2) dependence upon the aid of sources beyond those authorized by the instructor in writing papers, preparing reports, solving problems, or carrying out other assignments; or (3) the acquisition, without permission, of tests or other academic material belonging to a member of the [college/university] faculty or staff.

15. The term "plagiarism" includes, but is not limited to, the use, by paraphrase or direct quotation, of the published or unpublished work of another person without full and clear acknowledgment. It also includes the unacknowledged use of materials prepared by another person or agency engaged in the selling of term papers or other academic materials.

Commentary: Cheating and plagiarism are the two most common types of academic misconduct.[33] The courts' views about institutional decisions regarding such academic misconduct will be discussed in greater detail hereinafter.[34]

Article II: Judicial Authority

1. The judicial advisor shall determine the composition of judicial bodies and appellate boards and determine which judicial body, judicial advisor and appellate board shall be authorized to hear each case.

2. The judicial advisor shall develop policies for the administration of the judicial program and procedural rules for the conduct of hearings that are not inconsistent with provisions of the student code.

3. Decisions made by a judicial body and/or Judicial Advisor shall be final, pending the normal appeal process.

4. A judicial body may be designated as arbiter of disputes within the student community in cases that do not involve a violation of the student code. All parties must agree to arbitration, and to be bound by the decision with no right of appeal.

Article III: Proscribed Conduct

A. Jurisdiction of the [college/university]

Generally, [college/university] jurisdiction and discipline shall be limited to conduct which occurs on [college/university] premises or which adversely affects the [college/university] community and/or the pursuit of its objectives.

Commentary: The college or university should state in general terms the conduct which the institution intends to reach. A college or university has jurisdiction to punish a student for activities which take place off-campus when those activities adversely affect the interests of the college or univer-

sity community. School officials have wide latitude in determining whether an activity adversely affects the interests of the university community.[35]

Under this model student code, when an activity occurs off-campus, it would be the responsibility of the administrator designated in Article I, number 13, to determine whether college or university jurisdiction should be asserted.[36] *Utilizing this procedure on a case-by-case basis allows the institution to consider the unique facts of each situation without the impossible problem of drafting language to cover every possible situation.*

B. Conduct Rules and Regulations

Any student found to have committed the following misconduct is subject to the disciplinary sanctions outlined in Article IV:

1. Acts of dishonesty, including but not limited to the following:
    a. Cheating, plagiarism, or other forms of academic dishonesty.
    b. Furnishing false information to any [college/university] official, faculty member or office.
    c. Forgery, alteration, or misuse of any [college/university] document, record, or instrument of identification.
    d. Tampering with the election of any [college-/university-] recognized student organization.

2. Disruption or obstruction of teaching, research, administration, disciplinary proceedings, other [college/university] activities, including its public-service functions on or off campus, or other authorized non- [college/university] activities, when the act occurs on [college/university] premises.

3. Physical abuse, verbal abuse, threats, intimidation, harassment, coercion and/or other conduct which threatens or endangers the health or safety of any person.[37]

4. Attempted or actual theft of and/or damage to property of the [college/university] or property of a member of the [college/ university] community or other personal or public property.

5. Hazing, defined as an act which endangers the mental or physical health or safety of a student, or which destroys or removes public or private property, for the purpose of initiation, admission into, affiliation with, or as a condition for continued membership in, a group or organization.[38]

6. Failure to comply with directions of [college/university] officials or law enforcement officers acting in performance of their duties and/or failure to identify oneself to these persons when requested to do so.

7. Unauthorized possession, duplication or use of keys to any [college/university] premises or unauthorized entry to or use of [college/university] premises.

8. Violation of published [College/University] policies, rules or regulations.

9. Violation of federal, state or local law on [College/University] premises or at [College/University] sponsored or supervised activities.

10. Use, possession or distribution of narcotic or other controlled substances except as expressly permitted by law.

11. Use, possession or distribution of alcoholic beverages except as expressly permitted by the law and [College/University] regulations, or public intoxication.

12. Illegal or unauthorized possession of firearms, explosives, other weapons, or dangerous chemicals on [College/University] premises.

13. Participation in a campus demonstration which disrupts the normal operations of the [College/University] and infringes on the rights of other members of the [College/University] community; leading or inciting others to disrupt scheduled and/or normal activities within any campus building or area; intentional obstruction which unreasonably interferes with freedom of movement, either pedestrian or vehicular, on campus.

14. Obstruction of the free flow of pedestrian or vehicular traffic on [College/University] premises or at [College-/University-] sponsored or supervised functions.

15. Conduct which is disorderly, lewd, or indecent; breach of peace; or aiding, abetting, or procuring another person to breach the peace on [College/University] premises or at functions sponsored by, or participated in by, the [College/University].

16. Theft or other abuse of computer time, including but not limited to:
    a. Unauthorized entry into a file, to use, read, or change the contents, or for any other purpose.
    b. Unauthorized transfer of a file.
    c. Unauthorized use of another individual's identification and password.
    d. Use of computing facilities to interfere with the work of another student, faculty member or [College/University] Official.
    e. Use of computing facilities to send obscene or abusive messages.
    f. Use of computing facilities to interfere with normal operation of the [College/University] computing system.

17. Abuse of the judicial system, including but not limited to:
    a. Failure to obey the summons of a judicial body or [College/University] official.
    b. Falsification, distortion, or misrepresentation of information before a judicial body.

c. Disruption or interference with the orderly conduct of a judicial proceeding.

d. Institution of a judicial proceeding knowingly without cause.

e. Attempting to discourage an individual's proper participation in, or use of, the judicial system.

f. Attempting to influence the impartiality of a member of a judicial body prior to, and/or during the course of, the judicial proceeding.

g. Harassment (verbal or physical) and/or intimidation of a member of a judicial body prior to, during, and/or after a judicial proceeding.

h. Failure to comply with the sanction(s) imposed under the student code.

i. Influencing or attempting to influence another person to commit an abuse of the judicial system.

Commentary: Colleges or universities are, of course, free to include in their lists of misconduct as many types of acts as they choose, within certain limitations. The list of acts of misconduct which constitute violations of the student code should give students fair notice of the types of conduct which may result in sanctions. The college or university should, however, be careful to emphasize that the list is not all-inclusive. Otherwise, the college or university may be held to a contract, inadvertently created, to punish only misconduct listed, and none other.[39]

Courts tend to give college and university officials much greater freedom concerning purely academic decisions than they do concerning purely disciplinary decisions.[40] *Academic-misconduct cases involving cheating or plagiarism, for example, present a unique hybrid of academic and disciplinary decisions.*[41] *Because several courts have categorized cases of academic misconduct as disciplinary, rather than academic,*[42] *the authors suggest that institutions classify such "academic misconduct," as requiring the same procedures as cases involving purely disciplinary matters.*[43] *Academic misconduct may also be grounds for academic sanctions, such as the imposition of a lower grade.*

This system must be dove-tailed with the institutional process for student review of academic sanctions. Even if a faculty member imposes an academic sanction for an academic offense, the authors recommend that the student have the right to have the conduct reviewed under the student code. If these procedures produce a conclusion that the misconduct occurred, the student code procedures can uphold, increase, or reduce the sanction. If no violation is found, the sanction imposed by the faculty member must be lifted.

Concerning items number three, thirteen, fifteen and seventeen, the college or university must ensure that regulations which may infringe upon the right of free speech do not violate the first amendment because of over breadth or vagueness.[44] *They must also ensure that it is not an abuse of the judicial system (i.e., a violation of item number sixteen) for persons to attend the hearing but to refuse to testify by asserting their fifth-amendment right not to incriminate themselves.*[45] *A person may assert the privilege against self-incrimination as to possible criminal exposure during a civil proceeding.*[46]

In the college disciplinary setting, the student may remain silent, and such silence should not be used against the student,[47] *but a violation of the student code may nevertheless be found based upon the other evidence presented.*

C. Violation of Law and [College/University] Discipline

1. If a student is charged only with an off-campus violation of federal, state, or local laws, but not with any other violation of this code, disciplinary action may be taken and sanctions imposed for grave misconduct which demonstrates flagrant disregard for the [college/university] community. In such cases, no sanction may be imposed unless the student has been found guilty in a court of law or has declined to contest such charges, although not actually admitting guilt (e.g., "no contest" or *no lo contendere*).

   Commentary: The college or university may punish off-campus violations of the law if such misconduct affects the college or university community.[48]

2. [Alternative A]

   [College/university] disciplinary proceedings may be instituted against a student charged with violation of a law which is also a violation of this student code, for example, if both violations result from the same factual situation, without regard to the pendency of civil litigation in court or criminal arrest and prosecution. Proceedings under this student code may be carried out prior to, simultaneously with, or following civil or criminal proceedings off-campus.

   [Alternative B]

   If a violation of law which also would be a violation of this student code is alleged, proceedings under this student code may move forward against an offender who has been subjected to civil prosecution only if the [College/University] determines that its interest is clearly distinct from that of the community outside the [College/University]. Ordinarily, the [College/University] should not impose sanctions if public prosecution of a student is anticipated, or until law enforcement officials have disposed of the case.[49]

   Commentary: A college or university may take student disciplinary action before criminal charges arising out of the same facts are resolved.[50] *There are two basic approaches to the recurring dilemma of how a college or university should proceed when a student is accused not only of violating school regulations, but also of breaking the law. Alternative A is the pro-active approach, in which the institution has reserved the authority to take action under the student code in all such situations. A college or university may choose this approach because it does not wish to trivialize its code.*

To postpone the use of its disciplinary code and system of hearings and appeals in those cases involving criminal conduct would lead, in the words of one court, to an "absurd situation:" A student who violated a rule or regulation short of committing a crime receives immediate discipline, while a student who committed a more serious offense is entitled to attend school without immediate disciplinary action.[51] Alternative B illustrates the other approach. Although such an approach is not often admitted explicitly, it is not uncommon. It does, however, lead to a student code which deals only with minor offenses. The authors recommend Alternative A.

3. When a student is charged by federal, state or local authorities with a violation of law, the [college/university] will not request or agree to special consideration for that individual because of his or her status as a student. If the alleged offense is also the subject of a proceeding before a judicial body under the student code, however, the [college/university] may advise off-campus authorities of the existence of the student code and of how such matters will be handled internally within the [college/university] community.

The [college/university] will cooperate fully with law enforcement and other agencies in the enforcement of criminal law on campus and in the conditions imposed by criminal courts for the rehabilitation of student violators. Individual students and faculty members, acting in their personal capacities, remain free to interact with governmental representatives, as they deem appropriate.

Commentary: Counsel for the college or university should establish a solid relationship with the local prosecuting attorney in anticipation of such situations. The college or university attorney should educate the prosecuting attorney about the institution's student code and its general philosophy regarding discipline. By doing this, the institution may better coordinate its efforts with that of the prosecuting attorney when a disciplinary problem overlapping criminal charges arises. In addition, the prosecuting attorney who understands that the college or university will handle matters appropriately may bypass intervention, choosing instead to allow the institution to handle the situation.

Finally, familiarizing the prosecuting attorney with the student code before an incident arises helps avoid media errors, subsequent retractions and negative publicity when an incident arises. This area requires a delicate balance, good judgment, and an appreciation of the separate rules of student discipline and law enforcement. college officials must take care not to attempt, or appear to attempt, to influence prosecutorial decisionmaking. Although the campus and criminal systems must remain distinct, with neither dictating to the other, it is nevertheless important to have a clear line of communication.

Besides working with the prosecuting attorney, the college or university attorney should establish a relationship with the attorney for the accused student. This is important because the university attorney can help the defense attorney make an informed decision as to whether the accused student should submit to the school's disciplinary proceedings. For example, if the accused student is found to have violated university rules, university, not criminal, sanctions will be imposed. These sanctions most likely will be less severe than criminal sanctions.

Complainants who feel vindicated and satisfied with the result of the institutional disciplinary hearing may be inclined to drop the criminal charges. In any case, the institution's representative must be mindful of a fair result for both the student who has alleged a violation of the student code and the alleged violator. This in turn will alleviate the burden on the prosecuting attorney, whose offices are traditionally understaffed and overworked. Moreover, the student "victim" will be able to present testimony in an atmosphere less antagonistic than criminal court.

Article IV: Judicial Policies

A. Charges and Hearings

1. Any member of the [college/university] community may file charges against any student for misconduct. Charges shall be prepared in writing and directed to the judicial advisor responsible for the administration of the [college/university] judicial system. Any charge should be submitted as soon as possible after the event takes place, preferably within [specified amount of time].

   Commentary: This section not only describes who may file charges, but also requires that such charges be in writing and that they all be submitted to the same person. Such measures are desirable because: (1) they ensure that college or university officials can immediately assess the gravity of each complaint; and (2) they serve to provide notice in an orderly fashion.[52] The use of a standard form for charges will ensure the receipt of all the necessary information.[53]

   Practice varies widely concerning the length of limitations periods. For example, at Westminster College complainants are asked to file charges within forty-eight (48) hours.[54] At Pratt Institute, charges of discriminatory treatment must be submitted within twenty-eight (28) days of the date the complainant first attempted to resolve the matter, which must be done within ninety (90) days of the incident.[55] Finally, at Northwestern University, complainants have one year during which to file charges.[56]

2. The judicial advisor may conduct an investigation to determine if the charges have merit and/or if they can be disposed of administratively by mutual consent of the parties involved on a basis acceptable to the judicial advisor. Such disposition shall be final and there shall be no subsequent proceedings. If the charges cannot be disposed of by mutual consent, the judicial advisor may later serve in the same matter as the judicial body or a member thereof.

   Commentary: As noted previously,[57] courts have recognized that it is not possible in the college or university setting to ensure that the participants in the disciplinary process have not had prior contact with the student(s) involved or prior knowledge of the events which are the subject of the pro-

ceeding. Where staffing permits, it is preferable to separate the administrative and judicial functions.

3. All charges shall be presented to the accused student in written form. A time shall be set for a hearing, not less than five nor more than fifteen calendar days after the student has been notified. Maximum time limits for scheduling of hearings may be extended at the discretion of the judicial advisor.

   Commentary: Notice and an opportunity to be heard are essential to all student disciplinary proceedings, at least in the public college and university settings.[58] Requiring that the accused student receive written notice of the charge ensures that the accused student receives adequate notice of the alleged violations. Such notice should be "reasonably calculated, under all the circumstances, to apprise interested parties of the pendency of the action and afford them an opportunity to present their objections."[59]

   Further, there is no bright-line rule governing how far in advance of a hearing notice should be given.[60] Indeed, some courts have indicated that notice of charges may be given at the same time the student has an opportunity to defend against those charges.[61] Nevertheless, it seems fairer to give some reasonable amount of time to allow accused students to prepare their defenses. Proper notice may benefit the institution if a student challenges its actions.[62] The institution must, however, be sure to follow its own rules once it establishes an amount of time which is to pass between notice and the hearing.[63]

   Granting the judicial advisor discretion to extend the maximum time limits permits the institution flexibility in cases in which examination periods, breaks and holidays disrupt the time at which hearings would otherwise be scheduled. Some institutions may wish to deal with break and/or holiday issues more explicitly by providing in their codes for dates certain to be used in such situations. For example, a college or university may wish to provide that, in cases in which an examination period or break intervenes between the time of notice and the hearing date, hearings always will be held on the first day on which classes are again in session.

4. Hearings shall be conducted by a judicial body according to the following guidelines:

   a. Hearings normally shall be conducted in private. At the request of the accused student, and subject to the discretion of the chairperson, a representative of the student press may be admitted, but shall not have the privilege of participating in the hearing.

   b. Admission of any person to the hearing shall be at the discretion of the judicial body and/or its judicial advisor.

   c. In hearings involving more that one accused student, the chairperson of the judicial body, in his or her discretion, may permit the hearings concerning each student to be conducted separately.

   d. The complainant and the accused have the right to be assisted by any advisor they choose, at their own expense. The advisor

The Administration of Campus Discipline ...

may be an attorney. The complainant and/or the accused is responsible for presenting his or her own case and, therefore, advisors are not permitted to speak or to participate directly in any hearing before a judicial body.

e. The complainant, the accused and the judicial body shall have the privilege of presenting witnesses, subject to the right of cross-examination by the judicial body.

f. Pertinent records, exhibits and written statements may be accepted as evidence for consideration by a judicial body at the discretion of the chairperson.

g. All procedural questions are subject to the final decision of the chairperson of the judicial body.

h. After the hearing, the judicial body shall determine (by majority vote if the judicial body consists of more than one person) whether the student has violated each section of the student code which the student is charged with violating.

i. The judicial body's determination shall be made on the basis of whether it is more likely than not that the accused student violated the student code.

Commentary: The law requires no particular form of hearings.[64] For two reasons, however, the institution should establish guidelines pursuant to which hearings are to be conducted. First, doing so will ensure that the institution always treats students accused of misconduct evenhandedly. That is, a college or university can feel safe in knowing that, as long as the student disciplinary board follows the procedures set forth in its code, each accused student will receive the same treatment. Thus, there is less opportunity for any student to complain of unequal treatment. Second, establishing such guidelines in advance will avert snap decisions concerning such issues as whether to permit a student to have counsel or whether the hearing should be public.

This compendium of hearing guidelines incorporates the following legal principles: First, the hearing need not be open to the public.[65] Second, neither the Federal Rules of Evidence nor any state's rules of evidence apply in student disciplinary proceedings.[66] Third, although the courts are split on the issue,[67] a student need not be permitted to be represented by counsel at most student disciplinary hearings.[68]

There are two possible exceptions to this rule: First, a public institution's disciplinary board may be considered a state agency in some situations. Being deemed a state agency may bring into play certain state administrative agency laws, which may require representation by an attorney.[69] Second, if criminal charges are either pending or potential, the college or university must permit the student to have counsel.[70] Even in these cases, however, counsel may be restricted to an advisory role.[71] It is not required that either students or counsel be given the opportunity to cross-examine witnesses. Cross-examination by the disciplinary hearing board is sufficient.[72]

A smaller school may wish to institute either an arbitration or a mediation requirement prior to reaching the hearing stage.[73] Such an option is acceptable because the concept of due process is flexible, requiring no more than is necessary to provide fair notice and an opportunity to be heard.[74] In other words, in some cases a hearing is not required; a meeting between the students involved and college administrators suffices, as long as accused students are informed of the charges and given an opportunity to tell their side of the story.

By contrast, larger schools may not want to require such an initial meeting because such meetings could consume all the administrator's time with little benefit. Local experience will dictate whether it is effective to attempt to resolve alleged student code violations through such a meeting. This model student code advocates using a "more likely than not" or "preponderance of the evidence" standard for disciplinary decision-making. This is because the "beyond a reasonable doubt" standard applied in criminal cases is too demanding for college disciplinary proceedings.[75]

Courts review disciplinary decisions of colleges or universities under a "substantial evidence" standard. In doing so, courts generally examine whether there was enough evidence at the hearing to demonstrate that it was "more likely than not" that the accused student violated the student code, or whether a "preponderance of the evidence" demonstrated such violation—the same standard applied in most civil cases.[76] Some codes use a "clear and convincing" standard, but such a standard is not common.[77]

5. There shall be a single verbatim record, such as a tape recording, of all hearings before a judicial body. The record shall be the property of the [college/university].

Commentary: The purpose of this provision is twofold. First, it assures all parties that a record will be made of the hearing.[78] Second, it establishes that such record is the property of the institution. In some cases, a student may request permission to make a record of the proceedings.[79] An institution may not wish to permit a student to do so because, for example, it may not want its students replaying tapes of college disciplinary proceedings as a form of entertainment. The college or university may grant student requests to make a record of the proceeding if it wishes, perhaps on the condition that the tape nevertheless become the school's property and not be removed from its control. In any event, a provision requiring that a record be kept can shield the institution from liability should it refuse the student's request.[80]

6. Except in the case of a student charged with failing to obey the summons of a judicial body or [college/university] official, no student may be found to have violated the student code solely because the student failed to appear before a judicial body. In all cases, the evidence in support of the charges shall be presented and considered.

Commentary: *Judgment by default* is a rather harsh penalty to impose upon a student accused of violating the disciplinary code. It is also a good way to ask for a lawsuit.

B. Sanctions
1. The following sanctions may be imposed upon any student found to have violated the student code:
   a. Warning: A notice in writing to the student that the student is violating or has violated institutional regulations.
   b. Probation: A written reprimand for violation of specified regulations. Probation is for a designated period of time and includes the probability of more severe disciplinary sanctions if the student is found to be violating any institutional regulation(s) during the probationary period.
   c. Loss of Privileges: Denial of specified privileges for a designated period of time.
   d. Fines: Previously established and published fines may be imposed.
   e. Restitution: Compensation for loss, damage or injury. This may take the form of appropriate service and/or monetary or material replacement.
   f. Discretionary Sanctions: Work assignments, service to the [college/university] or other related discretionary assignments (such assignments must have the prior approval of the judicial advisor).
   g. Residence Hall Suspension: Separation of the student from the residence halls for a definite period of time, after which the student is eligible to return. Conditions for readmission may be specified.
   h. Residence Hall Expulsion: Permanent separation of the student from the residence halls.
   i. [College/University] Suspension: Separation of the student from the [college/university] for a definite period of time, after which the student is eligible to return. Conditions for readmission may be specified.
   j. [College/University] Expulsion: Permanent separation of the student from the [College/University].[81]

Commentary: colleges and universities may, within certain limitations,[82] authorize as many types of sanctions as they wish. This section gives the institution maximum flexibility by permitting the judicial advisor to impose any sanction for any infraction of the student code. An alternative approach is to enumerate those offenses carrying more serious sanctions (i.e., expulsion and suspension), and to allow the Judicial Advisor to choose among the remaining sanctions in punishing other offenses.[83]

2. More than one of the sanctions listed above may be imposed for any single violation.
3. Other than [college/university] expulsion, disciplinary sanctions shall not be made part of the student's permanent academic record,

but shall become part of the student's confidential record. Upon graduation, the student's confidential record may be expunged of disciplinary actions other than residence-hall expulsion, [college/university] suspension or [college/university] expulsion, upon application to the judicial advisor. Cases involving the imposition of sanctions other than residence-hall expulsion, [college/university] suspension or [college/university] expulsion shall be expunged from the student's confidential record [insert preferred number] years after final disposition of the case.

Commentary: The maintenance of student records is regulated by the Buckley Amendment.[84] *The Buckley Amendment does not mandate that records of disciplinary action be treated as this section provides, but if a college or university already has a policy concerning such records, school officials may wish to incorporate that policy into the student code. Drafters of student codes should investigate their own state's laws to determine whether any privacy acts affect this issue.*[85]

When determining the institution's preferred course of action, student-code drafters should realize that disclosure of severe disciplinary actions could affect the student's ability to enter other institutions.[86] *This would occur only if such news "imposed on [the students] a stigma or other disability that foreclosed his freedom to take advantage of other . . . opportunities."*[87] *Whether any sanction short of expulsion should appear on an academic transcript and, even then, whether the reason for expulsion should appear, are issues meriting careful consideration.*

4. The following sanctions may be imposed upon groups or organizations:

   a. Those sanctions listed above in Section B 1, a through e.

   b. Deactivation: Loss of all privileges, including [college/university] recognition, for a specified period of time.

Commentary: When a student organization engages in some act of misconduct, the college or university may take action not only against the student(s) involved, but also against the organization itself. This procedure does not violate the double jeopardy clause of the Constitution[88] *for two reasons. First, the double jeopardy clause applies only to criminal, not civil, proceedings.*[89] *Proceedings under a school's student code are not criminal proceedings.*[90] *Furthermore, the actors [student(s) and organization] are separate offenders. Punishing each of them for the same act is not punishing the same offender twice for one act of misconduct.*[91] *Similarly, it does not violate the double jeopardy clause for the same student to be subjected to both criminal and student-code (civil) sanctions for the same misconduct.*[92]

5. In each case in which a judicial body determines that a student has violated the student code, the sanction(s) shall be determined and imposed by the judicial advisor. In cases in which persons other than or in addition to the judicial advisor have been authorized to serve as the judicial body, the recommendation of all members of the judicial body shall be considered by the judicial advisor

The Administration of Campus Discipline . . .

in determining and imposing sanctions. The judicial advisor is not limited to sanctions recommended by members of the judicial body. Following the hearing, the judicial body and the judicial advisor shall advise the accused in writing of its determination and of the sanction(s) imposed, if any.

Commentary: Imposition of sanctions by the judicial advisor ensures some consistency among the sanctions meted out over time. A college or university may choose to allow students, rather than a college or university official, to impose sanctions in each case.@÷ Such a choice is not unusual. It may be more equitable, however, to have the judicial advisor choose the punishment in all situations, so as to avoid putting students who sit on the judicial body in the awkward position of imposing a harsh punishment on a peer.

C. Interim Suspension

In certain circumstances, the [title of administrator identified in Article I, number 13], or a designee, may impose a [college/university] or residence-hall suspension prior to the hearing before a judicial body.

1. Interim suspension may be imposed only: (a) to ensure the safety and well-being of members of the [college/university] community or preservation of [college/university] property; (b) to ensure the student's own physical or emotional safety and well-being; or (c) if the student poses a definite threat of disruption of or interference with the normal operations of the [college/university].

2. During the interim suspension, students shall be denied access to the residence halls and/or to the campus (including classes) and/or all other [college/university] activities or privileges for which the student might otherwise be eligible, as the [title of administrator identified in Article I, number 13] or the judicial advisor may determine to be appropriate.

Commentary: It is permissible to impose an interim suspension in certain instances.[94] The requisite notice and hearing process, however, should follow as soon as is practicable.[95]

D. Appeals

1. A decision reached by the judicial body or a sanction imposed by the judicial advisor may be appealed by accused students or complainants to an appellate board within five (5) school days of the decision. Such appeals shall be in writing and shall be delivered to the judicial advisor or his or her designee.

Commentary: This is another point at which it may be wise to grant students more rights than they might otherwise have. Although there is some authority for the proposition that students need not be given the right to appeal from a decision rendered as a result of a hearing,[96] providing an appellate process promotes an image of fairness. Further enhancing the image of fairness, this model affords not only the accused student but also the complainant a right to appeal. Particulars, such as the amount of time within which to permit appeals, may vary from school to school.

2. Except as required to explain the basis of new evidence, an appeal shall be limited to review of the verbatim record of the initial hearing and supporting documents for one or more of the following purposes:

   a. To determine whether the original hearing was conducted fairly in light of the charges and evidence presented, and in conformity with prescribed procedures giving the complaining party a reasonable opportunity to prepare and present evidence that the student code was violated, and giving the accused student a reasonable opportunity to prepare and to present a rebuttal of those allegations.

   b. To determine whether the decision reached regarding the accused student was based on substantial evidence, that is, whether the facts in the case were sufficient to establish that a violation of the student code occurred.

   c. To determine whether the sanction(s) imposed were appropriate for the violation of the student code which the student was found to have committed.

   d. To consider new evidence, sufficient to alter a decision or other relevant facts not brought out in the original hearing, because such evidence and/or facts were not known to the person appealing at the time of the original hearing.

   Commentary: The appellate body should review the hearing board's decision in order to determine whether it was supported by substantial evidence.[97] Substantial evidence is "more than a mere scintilla. It means such relevant evidence as a reasonable mind might accept as adequate to support a conclusion."[98] In making such a determination, the appellate board should not substitute its judgment for the judgment of the judicial body. Instead, it should review the judicial body's determination only to see whether there was evidence before the judicial body which supported the result reached below.[99]

3. If an appeal is upheld by the appellate board, the matter shall be remanded to the original judicial body and judicial advisor for re-opening of the hearing to allow reconsideration of the original determination and/or sanction(s).

   Commentary: A smaller institution may wish to permit yet another step in the appeal process by providing that a person disagreeing with the decision of the appellate board may appeal to the president or other top-ranking official. In such cases, the institution may want to provide that the decision of the president shall be "final and binding."[100] Doing so would open the door to arguing that, as in labor disputes in which the parties have agreed that disputes be submitted to binding arbitration, the decision of the president as "arbitrator" should not be disturbed by a court as long as it is reasonable and derives its essence from the student code.[101]

The Administration of Campus Discipline . . .

4. In cases involving appeals by students accused of violating the student code, review of the sanction by the appellate board may not result in more severe sanction(s) for the accused student. Instead, following an appeal, the [title of administrator identified in Article I, number 13] may, upon review of the case, reduce, but not increase, the sanctions imposed by the judicial advisor.

Commentary: Providing that an appeal may result in decreased, but not increased, sanctions ensures that accused students will feel free to exercise their rights of appeal. students may be deterred from appealing if they fear that sanctions may be increased as a result. Granting a right of appeal under conditions which actually deter such appeals only serves to lessen the perception of fairness in the process.

5. In cases involving appeals by persons other than students accused of violating the student code, the [title of administrator identified in Article I, number 13] may, upon review of the case, reduce or increase the sanctions imposed by the judicial advisor or remand the case to the original judicial body and judicial advisor.

Commentary: To grant a complaining student a right of appeal would be of little value without this provision. In cases in which a complaining student appeals a decision in which no violation was found, this provision is not necessary. In cases in which a complaining student is appealing only the sanction imposed against a student found to have violated the student code, however, the complaining student presumably believes that a stiffer sanction should be imposed.

In most cases in which the administrator believes that the appeal of a person other than the accused student should be granted, the remedy should be to remand the case to the original judicial body and judicial advisor. That body or person may further consider the evidence and either render a new decision or better explain the basis for the original decision.

Article V: Interpretation and Revision

A. Any question of interpretation regarding the student code shall be referred to the [title of administrator identified in Article I, number 13] or his or her designee for final determination.

B. The student code shall be reviewed every [__] years under the direction of the judicial advisor

Commentary: Every student code should be reviewed periodically, at least every three years. Specifying some "normal" period for review may help ensure that such a review is done.

Endnotes

1. Thomas Cooper was the second president (1820-1835) of South Carolina College, later renamed the University of South Carolina. Mr. Jefferson was the founder of the University of Virginia.

2. National Association of College and University Attorneys, STUDENT LEGAL ISSUES: ARTICLES RECOMMENDED BY THE NACUA SECTION ON STUDENT AFFAIRS at vii (1989). For a good historical overview, see generally Fowler, The Legal Relationship Between the American College Student and the College: An Historical Perspective and the Renewal of a Proposal, 13 *J. L. & EDUC*. 401 (1984).

3. Literally, "in the place of a parent." *Black's Law Dictionary* 708 (5th ed. 1979).

4. See *Gott v. Berea College*, 156 Ky. 376, 161 S.W. 204 (1913); Kaplin, Law on the Campus 1960-1985: Years of Growth and Challenge, 12 J.C.U.L. 269, 272 (1985); Note, Reasonable Rules, Reasonably Enforced Guidelines for University Disciplinary Proceedings, 53 MINN. L. REV. 301, 310 (1968).

5. See, e.g., *Dartmouth Review v. Dartmouth College*, No. 88-E-111, slip op. d 13 (N.H. Super. Ct. Jan. 3, 1989); *Prusack v. State*, 117 A.D.2d 729, 498 N.Y.S.2d 455 (1986); *Corso v. Creighton Univ.*, 731 F.2d 529 (8th Cir. 1984); *Cloud v. Trustees of Boston Univ.*, 720 F.2d 721 (1st Cir. 1983). See also Jennings, Breach of Contract Suits by Students Against Postsecondary Education Institutions: Can They Succeed?, 7 *J.C.U.L.* 191 (1981).

6. 294 F.2d 150 (5th Cir. 1961), cert. denied, 368 U.S. 930, 82 S. Ct. 368 (1961). For a discussion of the importance of *Dixon*, see Reidhaar, The Assault on the Citadel: Reflections on a Quarter Century of Change in the Relationships Between the Student and the University, 12 *J.C.U.L.* 343, 346 (1985); Wright, The Constitution on Campus, 22 *VAND. L. REV.* 1027, 1031-32 (1969).

7. The fourteenth amendment to the United States Constitution provides in part: "No State shall . . . deprive any person of life, liberty or property, without due process of law." U.S. CONST. amend. XIV, 1.

8. Although *Dixon* has been referred to as a "landmark" decision, see *Goss v. Lopez*, 419 U.S. 565, 576 n.8, 95 S. Ct. 729, 737 n.8 (1975). A court as early as 1887 spoke in terms of a college student having certain rights to notice and a hearing before being dismissed from school. Commonwealth ex ref. *Hill v. McCauley*, 3 Pa. County Ct. 77 (1887).

Only public schools, or private schools which have the requisite amount of interaction with the state to constitute "state action," have been required to provide due process for their students. See *Dartmouth Review*, slip op. at 12; *VanLoock v. Curran*, 489 So.2d 525, 528 (Ala. 1986). See generally Silets, Of Students' Rights and Honor: The Application of the Fourteenth Amendment's Due Process Strictures to Honor Code Proceedings at Private Colleges and Universities, 64 *DEN. U.L. REV.* 47 (1987); Thigpen, The Application of Fourteenth Amendment Norms to Private Colleges and Universities, 11 *J. L. & EDUC.* 171 (1982); Annotation, Action of Private Institution of Higher Education as Constituting State Action or Action Under Color of Law for Purposes of the Fourteenth Amendment and 42 U.S.C.S. 1983, 37 A.L.R. FED. 601 (1978).

Students at private colleges and universities, however, have attempted to bring due process and other constitutional cases against private institutions. See, e.g., *Albert v. Carovano*, 851 F.2d 561 (2d Cir. 1988); *Cummings v. Virginia School of Cosmetology*, 466 F. Supp. 780 (E.D. Va. 1979); *Miller v. Long Island Univ.*, 85 Misc. 2d 393, 380 N.Y.S.2d 917 (N.Y. Sup. Ct. 1976). In addition, it should be noted that Dickinson College, the institution at issue in *McCauley*, is a private school, and the court still imposed "notice and hearing" requirements. 3 Pa. County Ct. 77. For a comprehensive recent discussion of the state of the law with regard to whether due process applies to private college and university disciplinary proceedings, see *Boehm v. University of Pa. School of Veterinary Medicine*, 392 Pa. Super. 502 (1990).

9. See *Dartmouth Review,* slip op. at 12; *Schulman v. Franklin & Marshall College,* 538 A.2d 49, 52 (Pa. Super. Ct. 1988).

10. Indeed, some courts have required a written disciplinary code. In *Soglin v. Kauffman,* 418 F.2d 163 (7th Cir. 1969), for example, the court ruled that the University of Wisconsin had acted unconstitutionally in sanctioning students for "misconduct" when no rules specifically defined what the university viewed as "misconduct." The court ruled that while a university had the power to punish misconduct, it had to promulgate rules describing such misconduct to avoid punishing students on the basis of unconstitutionally vague, overbroad criteria. 418 F.2d at 166-67. "Pursuant to appropriate rule or regulation, the university has the power to maintain order by suspension or expulsion of disruptive students. Requiring that such sanctions be administered in accordance with preexisting rules does not place an unwarranted burden upon university administrations." Id. at 168.

11. Wise policy may sometimes involve granting students more rights than the Constitution requires. Wright, supra note 6, at 1035. See also W. KAPLIN, *THE LAW OF HIGHER EDUCATION* at 294, 312-14 (2d ed. 1985).

12. There is one negative aspect to the promulgation of a written student code. "Although the trend toward written codes is a sound one, legally speaking, because it gives students fairer notice of what is expected from them and often results in a better-conceived and administered system, written rules also provide a specific target to aim at in a lawsuit." W. KAPLIN, supra note 11, at 292.

For this reason, the institution should be aware that if it chooses to have a written student disciplinary code, it must follow the dictates of that code. *Tedeschi v. Wagner College,* 49 N.Y.2d 652, 658-60, 404 N.E.2d 1302, 1305-06 (1980); *VanLoock v. Curran,* 489 So.2d at 528; W. KAPLIN, supra note 11, at 302. See *Warren v. Drake Univ.,* 886 F.2d 200, 202 (8th Cir. 1989).

13. See, e.g., *Clayton v. Trustees of Princeton Univ.,* 608 F. Supp. 413, 435-36 (D.N.J. 1985).

14. See supra note 8; Miles, The Due Process Rights of Students in Public School or College Disciplinary Hearings, 48 *ALA. LAW.* 144, 146 (1987) ("It is a good idea for a school or college to grant as much due process as it thinks is allowable, given a balance between the circumstances, the educational mission of the school and the rights of the student."); W. KAPLIN, supra note 11, at 302-07.

15. See supra note 8.

16. Comment, Private Government on the Campus Judicial Review of University Expulsions, 72 *YALE L.J.* 1362, 1364 (1963).

17. Note, Due Process Rights in Student Disciplinary Matters, 14 *J.C.U.L.* 359, 367 n.43 (1987).

18. A college or university would not want to use terms such as "guilty" or "beyond a reasonable doubt," for example. Nor would it want to describe its hearings as "trials;" the persons presenting the evidence of violations as "prosecutors;" or the students who are alleged to have violated the code of conduct as "defendants."

19. Picozzi, University Disciplinary Process: What's Fair, What's Due, and What You Don't Get, 96 *YALE L.J.* 2132, 2155 (1987) (written rules ensure that both the administrator and the student know what process is due an accused student).

On the other hand, a college or university often wants to draft its student code without too much specificity in order to preserve as much flexibility as possible.

20. See, e.g., infra notes 68 and 72.

21. See, e.g., infra notes 50-51 and accompanying text.

22. See, e.g.: University of Pittsburgh Student Code of Conduct and Judicial Procedures at 3-5; The George Washington University Guide to Student Rights and Responsibilities at 1 (both available from NACUA).

23. See, e.g., Policy Statement, University of Michigan Interim Policy on Discrimination and Discriminatory Conduct by Students in the University Environment at 1 (available from NACUA).

24. See *Tinker v. Des Moines Indep. School Dist.*, 393 U.S. 503, 89 S. Ct. 733 (1968) (first amendment applies in public high school context). Because of cases such as Tinker, public institutions must ensure that their students are guaranteed, *inter alla*, First-Amendment rights.

25. Stating that students are guaranteed such rights, however, will not always ensure that the school will not be attacked. In *Doe v. University of Mich.*, 721 F. Supp. 852 (E.D. Mich. 1989), the university was careful to provide in the preamble to its Interim Policy on Discrimination and Discriminatory Conduct by Students in the University Environment that it promoted: "a strong commitment to the principle of freedom of speech guaranteed by the First Amendment to the United States Constitution . . . The University is dedicated to allowing students vigorous and open academic discourse and intellectual inquiry, including speech that espouses controversial or even offensive ideas."

Such pronouncements did not protect the university from a ruling holding invalid its policy which prohibited, inter alla, "threats or verbal slurs, invectives or epithets referring to an individual's race, ethnicity, religion, sex, sexual orientation, creed, national origin, ancestry, age or handicap made with the purpose of injuring the person to whom the words or actions are directed and that are not made as a part of a discussion or exchange of an idea, ideology or philosophy." The court found that the policy was both overbroad in that it prohibited some speech protected by the first amendment and so vague that it deprived students of due process.

Of course, private universities are not required to ensure that their students receive first-amendment freedoms. See, e.g., *Doe v. University of Mich.*, 721 F. Supp. 852, 867. Nevertheless, the private college or university should endeavor to ensure such protections. Confusion often arises over whether the First Amendment applies in cases involving private institutions. Assuming that it does for purposes of assuring students of the institution's good intentions will make the institution's actions appear more reasonable in the face of a challenge.

26. The authors recommend that, as in every good legal document, a student code should contain a section in which the code's drafters define all the terms of art that will appear throughout the code. Following is a partial list of definitions recommended for use with a college or university's student code. Definitions of some terms will, of course, vary with the type of disciplinary system established, and with the institution's traditional definitions of certain concepts (plagiarism or cheating, for example).

27. The college or university must designate a person within its administration to oversee the operation of the student code and to be responsible for its administration. See infra Article 1, number 13. The person designated should be the same person assigned under Article V, Section A, to resolve other questions of interpretation.

28. The person who authorizes the judicial body should be the same one designated to be responsible for the administration of the student code. See infra Article 1, number 13.

29. Friendly, Some Kind of Hearing, 123 *U. PA. L. REV.* 1267, 1279 (1975).

30. "Members of the college community, including students, usually comprise the hearing board. Given the nature of the academic community, members of the hearing board may know the student outside the context of the disciplinary proceedings." Note, supra note 17, at 371. See *Nash v. Auburn Univ.,* 812 F.2d 655, 666 (11th Cir. 1987) (participation of a student justice with prior knowledge of the charge did not indicate bias); *Gorman v. University of R.I.,* 837 F.2d 7, 15 (1st Cir. 1988). But see Note, supra note 17, at 372 ("[w]hile a board member has no constitutional obligation of recusation, fundamental fairness may suggest this action as in the best interest of both parties").

31. *Winnick v. Manning,* 460 F.2d 545, 548 (2dCir. 1972); *Gorman,* 837 F.2d at 15; *Hillman v. Elliott,* 436 F. Supp. 812, 816 (W.D. Va. 1977). Cf. *Megill v. Board of Regents,* 541 F.2d 1073, 1079 (5th Cir. 1976); *Duke v. North Tex. State Univ.,* 469 F.2d 829, 834 (5th Cir. 1972); *Alex v. Allen,* 409 F. Supp. 379, 387-88 (W.D. Pa. 1976).

32. "[T]he law indulges the presumption that school authorities act reasonably and fairly and in good faith in exercising the authority with which it clothes them, and casts the burden on him who calls their conduct into question to show that they have not been activated by proper motives." *Barker v. Hardway,* 283 F. Supp. 228, 237 (S.D. W. Va. 1968), aff'd 399 F.2d 638 (4th Cir. 1968), cert. denied, 394 U.S. 905, 89 S. Ct. 1009 (1969). See also *Dartmouth Review v. Dartmouth College,* No. 88-E-111, slip op. at 18 (N.H. Jan. 3, 1989); *Jenkins v. Louisiana State Bd. of Educ.,* 506 F.2d 992, 1003 (5th Cir. 1975); *Winnick,* 462 F.2d at 548. Cf. *Levitt v. University of Tex.,* 759 F.2d 1224, 1228 (5th Cir. 1985).

33. Fox, Due Process and Student Academic Misconduct, 25 *AM. BUS.* L.J. 671, 671- 72 (1988).

34. See infra text accompanying notes 40-43.

35. See Wright, The Constitution on the Campus, 22 *VAND. L. REV.* 1027, 1068 (1968). In *Kusnir v. Leach,* 64 Pa. Commw. 65, 439 A 2d 223 (1982), a college disciplinary board suspended a student for two semesters for participating in misconduct at a private party at a private off-campus residence. The student asserted, in part, that the college lacked jurisdiction to punish students for off-campus misconduct.

The court disagreed, saying the argument had "no merit:" "Obviously, a college has a vital interest in the character of its students, and may regard off-campus behavior as a reflection of a student's character and his fitness to be a member of the student body." *Kusnir,* 64 Pa. Commw. at 69, 439 A.2d at 226. See also *Esteban v. Central Mo. State College,* 415 F.2d 1077, 1088-89 (8th Cir. 1969); *Hart v. Ferris State College,* 557 F. Supp. 1379 (W.D. Mich. 1983); *Sohmer v. Kinnard,* 535 F. Supp. 50 (D. Md. 1982); *Wallace v. Florida A & M Univ.,* 433 So.2d 600 (Flat App. 1983); Annotation, Misconduct of College or University Student on Campus As Grounds for Expulsion, Suspension, or Other Disciplinary Action, 28 *A.L.R.* 4th 463 (1984).

36. See infra Article V, Section A.

37. A provision such as this one would bring within the Student Code incidents of alleged date rape. Despite the sensitive nature of this subject, institutions may wish to consider incidents of alleged date rape to be within the provisions of their Student Codes because doing so may afford an avenue of redress to com-

plainants who feel uncomfortable pressing charges in court. See Wing, Student Court to Judge Campus Date Rape Cases, U., Nov. 1989, at 2, col. 1.

While this language is appropriate for a private university or college which need not worry unduly about due-process requirements under federal or state law, persons drafting a code at a public institution may wish to review with their institutional counsel whether more specific language is required in their situation.

For example, the University of Michigan's Interim Policy on Discrimination and Discriminatory Conduct by Students in the University Environment was found to be unconstitutionally vague when it prohibited "[p]hysical acts or threats or verbal slurs, invectives or epithets referring to an individual's race, ethnicity, religion, sex, sexual orientation, creed, national origin, ancestry, age or handicap made with the purpose of injuring the person to whom the words or actions are directed and that are not made as part of a discussion or exchange of an idea, ideology or philosophy." See Doe v. University of Mich., 721 F. Supp. 852 (E.D. Mich. 1989). That language is considerably more broad than the language proposed in this Model Student Code. See generally, Hodulik, Prohibiting Discriminatory Harassment by Regulating Student Speech: A Balancing of First Amendment and University Interests, 16 J.C.U.L. 573 (199D).

38. See PA. STAT. ANN. tit. 24, 5352 (Purdon 1990 Supp.). In Pennsylvania, the legislature has promulgated an Antihazing Law, PA. STAT. ANN. tit. 24, 5351-5354 (Purdon logo Supp.), which requires that all public or private institutions of higher education adopt a written anti-hazing policy and establish rules for enforcement of the policy and punishment of offenders. As part of this law, the legislature has defined what it considers to be hazing. See also ALA. CODE 16-1-23 (1978) (defining hazing and classifying it as a Class C misdemeanor); In. REV. STAT. ch. 144, pare. 222 (1989) (defining hazing); OHIO REV. CODE ANN. 2903.31 (Baldwin 1986) (making hazing a fourth-degree misdemeanor). Student code drafters would be well-advised to determine whether applicable state law provides a definition of hazing and, if so, to incorporate such definition into their code in order to make the provision self-executing, i.e., to provide that, whenever a student is charged with hazing under state law, such actions would also constitute hazing under the student code.

39. It is a maxim of statutory interpretation that expressio unius est exclusio alterius, or to mention certain circumstances, implies that the drafter meant to exclude all others. See BLACK'S LAW DICTIONARY 521 (5th Ed. 1979).

40. See Regents of Univ. of Mich. v. Ewing, 474 U.S. 214, 106 S. Ct. 507 (1985); Board of Curators v. Horowitz, 435 U.S. 78, 98 S. Ct. 948 (1978). The dichotomy has developed because "disciplinary determinations are based on objective findings of fact so that hearings are useful and appropriate in this context. However, academic determinations are quite different because they are more subjective and evaluative." Levin, "Constitutional Law Due Process of Law," 47 U. CIN. L. REV. 514, 517 (1978). See Horowitz, 435 U.S. at 87-91, 98 S. Ct. at 953-56. See generally Wilhelm, Academic or Disciplinary Decisions: When is Due Process Required?, 6 U. BRIDGEPORT L. REV. 391 (1985); Fournet, Due Process and the University Student: The Academic/Disciplinary Dichotomy, 37 LA. L. REV. 939 (1977); W. KAPLIN, supra note 11, at 307-12.

41. Fox, Due Process and Student Academic Misconduct, 25 AM. Bus. L.J. at 672

42. See, e.g., Jaksa v. Regents of Univ. of Mich., 597 F. Supp. 1245, 1248 n.2 (E.D. Mich.), aff'd per curiam, 787 F.2d 590 (6th Cir. 1986); Hall v. Medical College of Ohio, 742 F.2d 299, 308-09 (6th Cir. 1984). But see Corso v. Creighton Univ., 731 F.2d 529,

532 (8th Cir. 1984) ("[c]heating on exams is clearly an academic matter"); Garsh-
man v. Pennsylvania State Univ., 395 F. Supp. 912, 921 (M.D. Pa. 1975) ("a determination as to the academic honesty of a student is ... peculiarly within the
discretion of a college administrator"); McDonald v. Board of Trustees, 375 F. Supp.
95, 104 (N.D. Ill.) aff'd, 503 F.2d 105 (7th Cir. 1974). See also Roberts, Public University Responses to Academic Dishonesty: Disciplinary or Academic, 15 J.L.&
EDUC. 369 (1986) (cases cited at footnotes 16 through 32 therein).

43. Incidents of cheating and plagiarism generally involve some degree of fact-
finding. "If the academic dishonesty matter includes factual disputes, university
officials should grant the student the same procedural safeguards as those in a
disciplinary matter." Note, supra note 16, at 364. See also Roberts, supra note 42,
at 384 ("even if a public university classifies the punishment of cheating as an
academic matter, the courts may not hold the same view").

44. Regulation of speech is an intricate area of the law. See generally Hodulik,
supra note 36. In Doe v. University of Mich., 721 F. Supp. 852 (E.D. Mich. 1989),
the United States District Court for the Eastern District of Michigan, Southern Division, invalidated a portion of the University of Michigan's policy on discrimination and discriminatory conduct because the sweeping provisions of that policy
could be, and in fact had been, used to punish students for activity protected by
the first amendment. See supra note.

But see Students Against Apartheid Coalition v. O'Neil, 838 F.2d 735 (4th Cir.
1988) (University of Virginia's regulation prohibiting temporary structures on the
south side of rotunda in order to preserve integrity of upper lawn, a historical
architectural area, did not violate the first amendment because it was content-
neutral, narrowly tailored to meet a significant government interest and left open
other avenues of communication).

After extensive study and debate, the University of Wisconsin System recently
adopted administrative rules aimed at prohibiting discriminatory harassment. See
Hodulik, supra note 36, at 574-75. The rules (in part) provide as follows: UWS
17.06 Offenses defined. The university may discipline a student in nonacademic
matters in the following situations:
... (2)

(a) For racist or discriminatory comments, epithets or other expressive behavior
    directed at an individual or on separate occasions at different individuals,
    or for physical conduct, if such comments, epithets, other expressive behavior
    or physical conduct intentionally:

    1. Demean the race, sex, religion, color, creed, disability, sexual orientation,
       national origin ancestry or age of the individual or individuals; and

    2. Create an intimidating, hostile or demeaning environment for education,
       university-related work, or other university-authorized activity.

(b) Whether the intent required under par. (a) Is present shall be determined by
    consideration of all relevant circumstances.

(c) In order to illustrate the types of conduct which this subsection is designed
    to cover, the following examples are set forth. These examples are not meant
    to illustrate the only situations or types of conduct intended to be covered.

    1. A student would be in violation if:

       a. He or she intentionally made demeaning remarks to an individual based
          on that person's ethnicity, such as name calling, racial slurs, or "jokes"; and

b. His or her purpose in uttering the remarks was to make the educational environment hostile for the person to whom the demeaning remark was addressed.

2. A student would be in violation if:

a. He or she intentionally placed visual or written material demeaning the race or sex of an individual in that person's university living quarters or work area; and

b. His or her purpose was to make the educational environment hostile for the person in whose quarters or work area the material was placed.

3. A student would be in violation if he or she seriously damaged or destroyed private property of any member of the university community or guest because of that person's race, sex, religion, color, creed, disability, sexual orientation, national origin, ancestry or age.

4. A student would not be in violation if, during a class discussion, he or she expressed a derogatory opinion concerning a racial or ethnic group. There is no violation, since the student's remark was addressed to the class as a whole, not to a specific individual. Moreover, on the facts as stated, there seems no evidence that the student's purpose was to create a hostile environment.

Compare University of California Student Conduct, Policies Applying to Campus Activities, Organizations and Students (Part A), 51.00 (pertinent portion available from NACUA).

The Wisconsin rule has been challenged in federal district court. See *UWM Post v. Board*, No. 90-C-0328, slip op. (E.D. Wis. 1990). The plaintiffs contended that Rule 17.06 violated the first and fourteenth amendments to the United States Constitution and article I, sections 1 and 3, of the Wisconsin Constitution. Hodulik, supra note 37, at 573. This challenge is sure to add to the complexity of first amendment jurisprudence in this area. See generally, T. HUSTOLES & W.B. CONNOLLY, JR., *REGULATING RACIAL HARASSMENT ON CAMPUS: A LEGAL COMPENDIUM* (NACUA 1990). See also Outlines presented in Concurrent Session, 1990 NACUA Conference, "Racial Harassment and the First Amendment" (available from NACUA).

45. The fifth amendment provides in part that "[n]o person shall . . . be compelled in any criminal case to be a witness against himself." U.S. CONST. amend. V.

46. See *Picozzi v. Sandalow*, 623 F. Supp. 1571, 1582 (E.D. Mich.) aff'd, 827 F.2d 770 (6th Cir. 1987); Note, supra note 17, at 377-79.

47. See *Hart v. Ferris State College*, 557 F. Supp. at 1384-85. Cf. *Garrity v. New Jersey*, 385 U.S. 493, 87 S. Ct. 616 (1967).

48. See supra note 35 and accompanying text.

49. The University of Kansas, You and the University of Kansas, Student Handbook, 1988-89, as quoted in Richmond, Students' Right to Counsel in University Disciplinary Proceedings, 15 *J.C.U.L.* 289, 312 n.166 (1989].

50. *Gabrilowitz v. Newman*, 582 F.2d 100, 104 (1st Cir. 1978); *Hart*, 557 F. Supp. at 1384; *Furutani v. Ewigleben*, 297 F. Supp. 1163 (N.D. Cal. 1969); *Goldberg v. Regents of Univ. of Cal.*, 248 Cal. App.2d 867, 57 Cal. Rptr. 463 (1967); *Nzuve v. Castleton State College*, 133 Vt. 225, 335 A.2d 321 (1975). Cf. *Peiffer v. Lebanon School Dist.*, 848 F.2d 44 (ad Cir. 1988). See, e.g., *Warren v. Drake Univ.*, 886 F.2d 200 (8th Cir. 1989).

51. *Johnson v. Board of Educ.*, 62 Misc.2d 929, 310 N.Y.S.2d 429, 433 (1970).

52. See Picozzi, University Disciplinary Process: What's Fair, What's Due, and What You Don't Get, 96 *YALE L.J.* 2132, 2157 n.107 (1987).

53. See, e.g., Office of Student Affairs, Westminster College, Student Handbook Bulletin 1989-90 at 14.

54. Id.

55. Pratt Institute Non-Discrimination Grievance Procedures at 1-2 (available from NACUA).

56. Northwestern University Offenses and Hearing Procedures at 24 (available from NACUA).

57. See supra notes 29-3Z and accompanying text. In *Nash v. Auburn Univ.*, 812 F.2d 655 (11th Cir. 1987) the court required evidence of actual bias on the part of a student justice, refusing to hold that the accused students had been denied a bias-free tribunal merely because one student justice knew of suspicions about the student and had had prior contact with potential witnesses. Id.

   See also, *Gorman v. University of R.I.*, 837 F.2d 7, 15 (1st Cir. 1988), where the court rejected the accused student's contention that a university administrator's function both as advisor to the disciplinary board and as a non-voting member of the board evidenced bias. Because there was no actual evidence of bias, the court noted that this argument "assumes too much." ("[I]n the intimate setting of a college or university, prior contact between the participants is likely, and does not per se indicate bias or partiality"); *Dartmouth Review v. Dartmouth College,* slip op. No. 88-E-111 at 18-20 (N.H. Jan. 3, 1989).

58. *Goss v. Lopez,* 419 U.S. 565, 95 S. Ct. 729 (1975). See generally *Cleveland Bd. of Educ. v. Loudermill,* 470 U.S. 532, 546, 105 S. Ct. 1487, 1495 (1985) (procedural due process for employee about to be terminated requires notice of charges, oral or written statement of employer's side and opportunity to rebut); *Goldberg v. Kelly,* 397 U.S. 254, 90 S. Ct. 1011 (1970). See also Cooper & Strope, Long-Term Suspensions and Expulsions After Loss, 57 *EDUC. LAW REP.* 29 (1989).

59. *Memphis Light, Gas & Water Div. v. Craft,* 436 U.S. 1, 13, 98 S. Ct. 1554, 1562 (1978), quoting *Mullane v. Central Hanover Trust Co.*, 339 U.S. 306, 314, 70 S. Ct. G52, 657 (1950). The court in *Goss* stated that the student must be told "what he is accused of doing and what the basis of the accusation is." 419 U.S. at 582. The court in *Dixon v. Alabama Bd. of Educ.* required "a statement of the specific charges and grounds." 294 F.2d 150, 158 (5th Cir. 1961).

60. See *Nash*, 812 F.2d at 661.

61. *Goss*, 419 U.S. at 582, 95 S. Ct. at 740.

62. Note, supra note 17, at 370.

63. See supra note 12.

64. *Goss*, 419 U.S. at 583-84, 95 S. Ct. at 740-41; *Dixon*, 294 F.2d at 158-59.

65. *Hart v. Ferris State College*, 557 F. Supp. 1379, 1389 (W. D. Mich. 1983).

66. *Nash v. Auburn Univ.*, 812 F.2d 655, 665 (Fifth Cir. 1987); *Boykins v. Fairchild Bd. of Educ.*, 492 F.2d 697, 701 (5th Cir. 1974).

67. See Blaskey, University Students' Right to Retain Counsel for Disciplinary Proceedings, 24 *CAL. W.L. REV.* 65, 65-66 (1988); Note, supra note 17, at 372-73.

68. Compare *Marin v. University of P.R.*, 377 F. Supp. 613, 623-24 (D.P.R. 1974); *Givens v. Poe*, 346 F. Supp. 202 (W.D.N.C. 1972); *Esteban v. Central Mo. State College*, 277 F. Supp. 649, 651 (W.D. Mo.), l'd, 415 F.2d 1077 (8th Cir.), cert. denied, 398 U.S. 965, 90 S. Ct. 21 (1970); *French v. Bashful*, 303 F. Supp. 1333, 1337 (E.D. La. 1969) (all recognizing a right to have counsel present at college or university dis-

ciplinary proceedings, although the court in *French* limited its holding to cases involving retained, rather than appointed, counsel) with *Madera v. Board of Educ.,* 386 F.2d 778, 786-87 (2d Cir. 1967), cert. denied, 390 U.S. 1028, 88 S. Ct. 1416 (1968); *Everett v. Marcase,* 426 F. Supp. 397 (E.D. Pa. 1977) (attorney need not be permitted).

69. See, e.g., *Kusnir v. Leach,* 64 Pa. Commw. 65, 71-72, 439 A.2d 223, 226-27(1982).

70. *Gabrilowitz v. Newman,* 582 F.2d 100, 106 (1st Cir. 1978).

71. Id.

72. See *Nash v. Auburn Univ.,* 812 F.2d 655, 664 (filth Cir. 1987) (accused students' ability to submit questions to the disciplinary board, to be asked of the witnesses, held sufficient); *Wimmer v. Lehman,* 705 F.2d 1402, 1406 (4th Cir. 1983); *University of Houston v. Sabeti,* 676 S.W.2d 685, 689 (Text Ct. App. 1984); *Hart v. Ferris State College,* 557 F. Supp. 1379, 1386-87 (W.D. Mich. 1983) (probable value of cross-examination by student's counsel is minimal compared to significant burden it would impose); *Gorman v. University of R.I.,* 837 F.2d 7, 16 (1st Cir. 1988) (right to unlimited cross-examination not an essential requirement of due process).

But see *Speake v. Grantham,* 317 F. Supp.1253, 1258 (S.D. Miss.), aff'd per curium, 440 F.2d 1351 (5th Cir. 1971); *Dillon v. Pulaski County Special School Dist.,* 468 F. Supp. 54, 58 (E.D. Ark.), aff'd, 594 F.2d 699 (8th Cir. 1979); *Keene v. Rodgers,* 316 F. Supp. 217, 221 (D. Me. 1970) (student has right to confront and cross-examine witnesses against him or her).

73. See, e.g., Office of Student Affairs, Westminster College, Student Handbook Bulletin 1989-90 at 15 (detailing a required pre-hearing conference, at which a student may request an administrative hearing rather than a hearing before the college judicial board).

74. *Mathews v. Eldridge,* 424 U.S. 319, 348-49, 96 S. Ct. 893, 909 (1976); *Joint Anti-Fascist Refugee Comm. v. McGrath,* 341 U.S. 123, 71 S. Ct. 624 (1951) (Frankfurter, J., concurring); *Henson v. Honor Comm. of Univ. of Va.,* 719 F.2d 69, 74 (4th Cir. 1983).

75. *Sill v. Pennsylvania State Univ.,* 462 F.2d 463, 467 (ad Cir. 1972); *Speake,* 317 F. Supp. at 1281-82; *Jones v. State Bd. of Educ.,* 407 F.2d 834, 836 (6th Cir. 1969); *Keene,* 316 F. Supp. at 221; *Esteban,* 415 F.2d 1077, 1088-90 (8th Cir. 1969).

But see *Smyth v. Lubbers,* 398 F. Supp. 777, 797-99 (W.D. Mich. 1975) (recommending use of a "clear and convincing" standard and ruling that a "substantial evidence" standard was constitutionally inadequate in a case involving an alleged violation of a student code which would also constitute a crime); Long, The Standard of Proof in Student Disciplinary Cases, 12 *J.C.U.L.* 71 (1985) (advocating use of a "clear and convincing" standard).

76. See infra notes 90-92 and accompanying text.

77. See supra note 75.

78. At least one court has required that a transcript be made of student disciplinary hearings. See *Marin v. University of P.R.,* 377 F. Supp. 613, 623 (D.P.R. 1973).

79. See, e.g., *Gorman v. University of R.I.,* 837 F.2d 7 (1st Cir. 1988).

80. See, e.g., *Gorman,* 837 F.2d at 16 (record of proceedings required by university manual constituted a sufficient record so that denial of student's request to tape-record the hearing was not so unfair as to violate due process).

81. A student who is expelled or suspended may ask a court to enjoin the discipline. Courts have held that suspension does not constitute irreparable harm so as to support a motion for injunctive relief. *Boehm v. University of Pa. School*

of Veterinary Medicine, 392 Pa. Super. 502 573 A.2d 575 (1990); *Schulman,* 371 Pa. Super. 345, 538 A.2d 49, 51-52.

But see *Dartmouth Review,* slip op. at 24; *Jones v. Board of Governors,* 557 F. Supp. 263 (W.D.N.C.), aff'd 704 F.2d 713 (4th Cir. 1983); *McLaughlin v. Massachusetts Maritime Academy,* 564 F. Supp. 809, 811 (D. Mass. 1983); *Gardenshire v. Chalmers,* 326 F. Supp. 1200, 1202 (D. Kan. 1971); *Stricklin v. Regents of Univ. of Wis.,* 297 F. Supp. 416, 422 (W.D. Wis. 1968).

82. The district court in *Gorman,* for example, found that the University of Rhode Island's sanction of compulsory psychiatric treatment was a "shocking extreme" and would violate the student's right to privacy. 646 F. Supp. 799, 814.

83. See, e.g., Pavela, Limiting the "Pursuit of Perfect Justice" on Campus: A Proposed Code of Student Conduct, 6 *J.C.U.L.* 137, 143 (1979).

84. Family Educational Rights and Privacy Act of 1974, Title V, 513, 88 Stat. 484, 571-574 (20 U.S.C. 1232g); as further amended by Pub. L. No. 93-568, 2, 88 Stat. 1855, 1858-1862 (20 U.S.C. 1232g).

85. Cf. *Cloud v. Trustees of Boston Univ.,* 720 F.2d 721, 726 (1st Cir. 1983).

86. Cf. *Bishop v. Wood,* 426 U.S. 341, 349-50, 96 S. Ct. 2074, 2079-80 (1976); *Board of Regents v. Roth,* 408 U.S. 564, 575, 92 S. Ct. 2701, 2708 (1972). See, e.g., *Greenhill v. Bailey,* 519 F.2d 57 (8th Cir. 1975) (school notifying Association of American Medical Colleges that it had dismissed student for poor academic standing due to "[l]ack of intellectual ability or insufficient preparation" deprived student of liberty interest in attending other schools).

87. *Roth,* 408 U.S. 564, 573, 92 S. Ct. 2701, 2707 (1972).

88. The fifth amendment to the United States Constitution provides in part: "[N]or shall any person be subject for the same offense to be twice put in jeopardy of life or limb." U.S. CONST. amend. V. This provision applies to the states through the fourteenth amendment. *Benton v. Maryland,* 395 U.S. 784, 794, 89 S. Ct. 2056, 2062 (1969).

89. *Paine v. Board of Regents,* 355 F. Supp. 199, 203 (W.D. Tex) off'd, 474 F.2d 1397 (5th Cir. 1973). Cf.; *Oliver v. United States Dept. of Justice,* 517 F.2d 426, 428 (2d Cir. 1975) (deportation proceedings following a criminal conviction do not violate double jeopardy clause); *United States v. Forty-Two Jars "Bee Royale Capsules,"* 160 F. Supp. 818, 821 (D.N.J. 1988) (double jeopardy does not apply to drug misbranding proceedings); *Attorney Grievance Comm. v. Andresen,* 281 Md. 152, 379 A.2d 159, 160 (1977) (double jeopardy clause does not apply to attorney disciplinary proceedings). See also Thomas, An Elegant Theory of Double Jeopordy, 4 *U. ILL. L. REV.* 827, 837 (1988).

90. See, e.g., *Nzuve v. Castleton State College,* 335 A.2d 321, 323 (Vt. 1975).

91. Cf. *United States v. Richmond,* 700 F.2d 1183, 1195 n.7 (8th Cir. 1983) (punishment of both a corporation and its officers does not constitute double punishment).

92. See *Paine,* 355 F. Supp. at 203.

93. See, e.g., Section VII, Northwestern University Offenses and Hearing Procedures (available from NACUA) (providing that a hearing board comprised of students and faculty will determine and impose sanctions). By way of further contrast, it should be noted that the University of Virginia's Honor Code provides for only one possible sanction—that of expulsion—for any violation. University of Virginia Honor Committee Constitution Art. II Duly 1986). In light of this severe, mandated sanction, the system utilizes a "beyond a reasonable doubt" standard.

"On my honor . . .": Philosophy and Guidelines of the Honor System, University of Virginia (1988).

94. This concept stems from a passage in *Goss v. Lopez*, 419 U.S. 565, 582-83, 95 S. Ct. 729, 740-41, which provides that "[s]tudents whose presence poses a continuing danger to persons or property or an ongoing threat of disrupting the academic process may be immediately removed from school. In such cases, the necessary notice and . . . hearing should follow as soon as practicable."

In *Cleveland Board of Educ. v. Loudermill*, 470 U.S. 532, 105 S. Ct. 1487 (1985), however, the Supreme Court indicated that in most cases an interim suspension without some sort of hearing beforehand is something to be avoided if possible. *Loudermill* was not a school case, but it indicated that, at least in the public employment context, a pre-termination hearing serves as "an initial check against mistaken decisions." *Id.* at 545, 105 S. Ct. at 1495.

95. *Goss*, 419 U.S. at 582-83, 95 S. Ct. at 740. See *Picozzi*, supra note 52, at 2158 n.111, in which the author indicates that judgments of whether the imminent danger necessary to justify an interim suspension is present should be left to the discretion of the administrator responsible for implementing the student code but that the administrator's decision should be reviewed as soon thereafter as is practicable.

96. See *Nash v. Auburn Univ.*, 621 F. Supp. 948, 957 (M.D. Ala.), aff'd, 812 F.2d 655 (fifth Cir. 1987).

97. *Speake v. Grantham*, 317 F. Supp. 1253, 1282 (S.D. Miss. 1971); *Jones v. State Bd. of Educ.*, 407 F.2d 834, 836 (6th Cir. 1969); *Givens v. Poe*, 346 F. Supp. 202, 209 (W.D.N.C. 1972); *Herman v. University of S.C.*, 341 F. Supp. 226, 231 (D.S.C. 1971), aff'd per curium, 457 F.2d 902 (4th Cir. 1972); *Center for Participant Educ. v. Marshall*, 337 F. Supp. 126, 136 (N.D. Fla. 1972). See also Note, supra note 17, at 379-80.

But see *Smyth v. Lubbers*, 398 F. Supp. 777 (W.D. Mich. 1975) (applying an original, not appellate, standard of proof of clear and convincing evidence); *McDonald v. Board of Trustees*, 375 F. Supp. 95, 103-04 (N.D. Ill. 1974), aff'd, 503 F.2d 105 (7th Cir. 1974); Long, supra note 75, at 81.

98. *Sill v. Pennsylvania State Univ.*, 318 F. Supp. 608, 621 (M.D. Pa.), aff'd, 462 F.2d 463 (ad Cir. 1972), [citing *Universal Camera Corp. v. NLRB*, 340 U.S. 474, 71 S. Ct. 456 (1951)].

99. Cf. *Mullins v. Secretary of Health & Human Services*, 680 F.2d 472 (6th Cir. 1982).

100. See, e.g., Compass, 1989 Student Handbook of Allegheny College, Judicial System Art. VI, 2 at p. 85.

101. See, e.g., *Baker v. Lafayette College*, 516 Pa. 291, 299-300, 532 A.2d 399, 403 (1987). See generally *United Paperworkers Int'l Union v. Misco, Inc.*, 484 U.S. 29, 108 S. Ct. 364 (1987); *United Steelworkers of Am. v. Enterprise Wheel & Car Corp.*, 363 U.S. 593 80 S. Ct. 1358 (1960).

References

Esteban v. Central Missouri State College, 415 F.2d 1077, 1088-1099 (8th Cir. 1969).

Stoner, E. & Cerminara, K. (1994). Harnessing the "spirit of insubordination": A model student disciplinary code. *The Journal of College and University Law*, 17(2), 89-121.

Chapter II

Distinctions Between
the Criminal Justice System and
the Campus Judicial Process:
Implications for Public and Private Institutions

Charles F. Carletta

INTRODUCTION

The campus judicial process differs both in purpose and function from the criminal process. The campus process is generally thought of as instructional in nature, whereas the criminal process is primarily designed as punitive, although some legal scholars believe it to be rehabilitative.

The procedural functioning of the criminal court system is weighted heavily in favor of protection of the accused's rights. Their rights are guaranteed by statutes, such as the state penal code and criminal procedure law and by the United States Constitution and those of the various states. Campus judicial systems are philosophically premised upon protection of the academic community. While judicial systems differ depending on whether the institution is public or private, the protections afforded the accused party are far less comprehensive than those of the criminal system. Likewise, the range of sanctions is much less severe and obviously does not involve incarceration.

PROCEDURAL DIFFERENCES

Evidence

One of the most important elements of any judicial process is the set of rules that delineate the evidentiary standards to be used. Criminal courts must adhere to a set of formal rules of evidence, which are codified in statute and quite burdensome to the prosecutor. While the state or federal rules of evidence need not be followed in a campus judicial proceeding, (*Esteban v.Central Missouri State College*, 1967)[1] hearsay evidence, an out of court statement offered to the court for its truth [Federal Rules of Evidence 801(c)], should not by itself be sufficient to suspend or expel a student because, among other reasons, it is nearly impossible to mount a cross-examination against it.

Burden of Proof

Additionally, different systems promulgate their own rules for establishing exactly how much must be proven before a favorable decision has been earned. This is called the "burden of proof." In a criminal court the charges against a defendant must be proven "beyond a reasonable doubt." If any reasonable doubt exists as to whether or not the defendant committed the crime, the defendant must be found to be not guilty of the offense charged; hence the need for unanimous verdicts for a finding of guilty in a criminal matter (*Winship*, 1970).

In campus judicial proceedings the charges against a student need only be proven by "substantial evidence"(*Slaughter v. Brigham Young University*, 1975). Substantial evidence is defined as "such evidence that a reasonable mind might accept as adequate to support a conclusion" (*Black's Law Dictionary*, 1990, p. 1428) Some commentators like to suggest the campus should go up a step: from substantial evidence to proving the facts by a "preponderance of the evidence."[2] Most experts advise not going beyond the standard of proving that it is "more probable than not that the incident occurred as alleged."

Assistance by Attorneys

The defendant in a criminal proceeding is unequivocally entitled to be represented by an attorney (*Gideon v. Wainwright*, 1963)[3]. A student, in a campus judicial proceeding, has no right to be represented by an attorney. In some instances, the student does, at least at a public university, have the right to have an attorney present to render advice, but not to present a defense or to conduct cross-examinations (*Gabrilowitz v. Newman*, 1978). There is no right to appointed counsel for an indigent student. Students ought to be advised by their own attorney in those situations in which they are already facing criminal charges for the same conduct that is the subject of the campus hearing. Counsel still may not participate in the campus process but may best serve the interests of the student by preventing an admission during the campus process that can be incriminating in the subsequent criminal trial.

Self-Incrimination

The constitutional right against self-incrimination dictates that no person shall be compelled in any criminal case to be a witness against himself (*Fisher v. United States*, 1976). In a similar vein, if a student's testimony in a campus disciplinary matter is considered compelled, it will not be admissible in a later criminal proceeding. Thus the 5th Amendment protection can apply in a campus judicial proceeding if, by the rules of the campus system, students are required to testify or if their silence will be held against them (*Furutani v. Ewigleben*, 1969).

The Administration of Campus Discipline . . .

The right not to be forced to incriminate oneself should be built into every system, public or private. Besides being a basic facet of fair play, it provides an appropriate educational opportunity for all students involved in the matter. It is important to recognize that some private colleges use honor codes which by their nature often negate this idea.

Other Differences

There are several other rights that are provided for in the United States Constitution and, indeed, in some state constitutions that simply do not apply to campus judicial processes because of the distinctions that have been mentioned earlier. These include accusation by the indictment process (U.S. Constitution, 5th amendment)[4], prehearing discovery of evidence (although I strongly recommend that all evidence being used against students that is in printed form be shared with them before any hearing), extensive use of adjournments, changes of venue, the right to a trial by jury (U.S. Constitution, 6th amendment)[5], the right to a public trial, and the right to be protected against double jeopardy (*Benton v. Maryland*, 1969).[6]

The double jeopardy rule confuses many administrators. The constitutional right regarding freedom from double jeopardy directs itself against being tried criminally more than once for the same offense. Since a campus judicial process is nothing more than an administrative process, the term is inappropriate. Administrators should refrain from referencing the term in any fashion except to explain why the term is inappropriate when applied to the campus judicial process, even when the same conduct on the part of the accused student can generate two procedures: an administrative hearing on campus and a criminal trial in a municipal court.

Some Similarities

Other facets of the criminal process can have replication in the campus judicial process simply by the campus system creating, publishing, and asserting such features. For instance, campus systems can have limited subpoena power if they allow themselves to do so. All hearings should involve the accused's right to confront and cross-examine adverse witnesses. This applies certainly in a criminal prosecution (U.S. Constitution, 6th amendment)[7] but should also apply in campus proceedings as one of the elements of fair play.

Furthermore, since both the criminal system (*Griffin v. Illinois*, 1956)[8] and the campus disciplinary process involve at least one element of appeal, there should be a free transcript of the evidentiary hearing available to the accused student. While most campus proceedings are taped, the taping should be done in a professional manner such that a typewritten transcript can be made from the tape and distributed as part of the appellate process.

PRIVATE VS. PUBLIC

Introduction

The differences between private and public educational institutions are becoming more difficult to articulate due to the enactment of affirmative social legislation such as Title VII and Title IX and the resultant increased attention by the courts. It is useful to set forth some history, analysis and specific examples of this phenomenon as it relates to the campus student disciplinary process.

Background

There is a basic legal premise founded in constitutional law that public institutions are subject to the authority of the government that created them and private institutions are protected from governmental control. For instance, a private institution may obtain its own perpetual charter of incorporation which the government is prohibited from impairing (*Trustees of Dartmouth College v. Woodward*, 1819). Private schools justify their existence in the marketplace of education by being able to cater to interests (smaller class size, religious education, etc.) which their public counterparts cannot address due to legal or political constraints.

Public institutions and their officers are subject to the federal and state constitutions in the performance of their duties whereas private colleges and universities and their officers are not,[9] simply because they are not agents of government. This distinction is due to the basic American concept that the Constitution was designed to limit the exercise of governmental power, not affect the rights of private citizens generally to control the use and enjoyment of their own property.

The Courts

The rights of Americans to keep the influence of government out of their private affairs, including their campuses, has traditionally been protected by the federal courts. For instance, in order for a court to apply Section 1983 and Section 1985 civil rights protections as well as those grounded in the Constitution, a finding by the court of "state action" is required. The process of making this finding is essentially a matter of distinguishing the public institution from the private institution, or the public portion of an institution from the private portion. The judicial trend since the early 1970s has been to make it less likely that state action will be found in any particular case. Moreover, although government funding is often a central consideration in the state action determination, it is not the dispositive factor (*Rendell-Baker v. Kohn*, 1982).

Essentially, three approaches to the state action doctrine have appeared in the courts. First is the delegated power theory, whereby the

The Administration of Campus Discipline . . .

private entity acts as a governmental agent in performing government-ally delegated tasks. Second, there is the public function theory, where the private university or college performs a function that is generally considered a governmental responsibility. Finally there is the government contacts theory, under which the independent institution receives prestige, encouragement, and resources from its connection with government.

The first theory, delegated power, was relied on in *Powe v. Miles* (1968). In that case the court determined that New York State had delegated authority to Alfred University to operate a state ceramics school on campus, thus students attending the ceramics school were entitled to due process protections while students attending other schools within the university were not. The same theory failed to produce a similar result in *Wahba v. New York University* (1974). In that case, a research professor had been fired from a governmentally funded research project on a private college campus without being afforded even an informal hearing as due process would mandate. The court held that state action was not present because the government did not exercise even the slightest bit of managerial control over the project, and thus the professor was not entitled to due process.

The second theory, public function, has been used infrequently in the education context because courts have consistently recognized that education has substantial roots in the private sector and cannot be considered solely a public function (*Rendell-Baker v. Kohn*, 1982).

The third theory, the government contacts theory, is the most utilized of the three. This theory focuses not on the general state involvement with private institutions, but rather on state involvement in the particular activity giving rise to the lawsuit (*Jackson v. Metropolitan Edison Co.*, 1974). In *Benner v. Oswald* (1979), students at Pennsylvania State University challenged the process by which members of the university's board of trustees were chosen. In applying the government contacts theory, and noting the numerous contacts between the university and the state, the court held that state action was present.

Research institutions should note that government agreements are obviously also government contacts and most public funding documents specifically incorporate intrusive legislation as a condition of receipt of public money. Often, the contractually imposed mandates extend far beyond the department actually receiving the funds and permeate much of the institution's internal structure such as its personnel policies and purchasing procedures.

Courts are more likely to find state action in age, sex or racial discrimination cases no matter which theory is being applied. In *Williams v. Howard University* (1976) the plaintiff raised two claims against Howard University, one asserting racial discrimination, the other asserting a deprivation of due process. The court, distinguishing between the two claims, held that although the university was the recipient of substantial federal funding, this was not a sufficient basis for a finding of state action as to the due process claim; however the federal funding was sufficient to demonstrate state action as to the racial discrimination claim.

The Congress

The Constitution does not offer the same protections afforded faculty, staff and students at public universities to those involved in the private academic community. This does not mean that members of the private community have no recourse for a real or perceived deprivation of their rights; while the courts have been reticent to expand state action, Congress hasn't shared that hesitation. Certainly since the sixties, Americans have been given a plethora of non-constitutional legislative protections, which are available to members of the community at private as well as public universities.

Discipline Cases

With all of that background in mind, the due process clause of the Fourteenth Amendment mandates that before students at a public institution are sanctioned for misconduct they are entitled to notice of the charges against them and a hearing opportunity (*Goss v. Lopez,* 1975)[10]. At such a hearing the student is entitled to present a defense, produce explanatory testimony, and examine the hearing report. *Dixon v. Alabama State Board of Education* (1961) has become the basic case for beginning the discussion of due process in the public campus disciplinary system.

Proceeding from there, additional concepts have from time to time been discussed by the courts. Some of these are:

1. Right to limit the scope of regulations so as not to impinge upon free speech. A code must demonstrate a material and substantial connection with discipline (dress codes; demonstrations; hate speech) (*Healy v. James,* 1972)[11]. A disciplinary proceeding at a public institution that gives rise to a defense based on the First Amendment is always problematical. Regulations should be carefully drafted with an attorney and should be thoroughly challenged before they are published. Since these caveats apply only to agents of the state, private institutions may choose to prohibit some assemblies and inhibit some forms of speech on their private property—as indeed may any landowner within the general boundaries of each state's laws. Great care should be taken however to not deviate so far from public reality that not only is the educational value of the challenged code a fiction, but its attempted enforcement may stimulate some local state judge into creating new law simply on the basis of "public policy."

The Administration of Campus Discipline . . .

2. Right to substantial evidence as basis of decision (*Esteban v. Central Missouri State College*, 1967). Substantial evidence may be viewed as such evidence that a reasonable mind might accept as adequate to support a conclusion. Administrators should deliberately avoid imposing a heavy burden of proof on the system. Criminal systems require unanimity, administrative systems do not.

3. Right to refuse to testify if testimony might incriminate the student in a criminal proceeding (even a subsequent criminal proceeding—remember, there is no double jeopardy) (*Furutani v. Ewigleben*, 1969).

4. Limited right to confront and cross-examine witnesses (appears to be implicit in the concept of a hearing, but was specifically not guaranteed in *Dixon*) (*Esteban v. Central Missouri State College*, 1967).

5. Limited right to have counsel present only if case is presented on behalf of the college by counsel (or experienced law student) (*Osteen v. Henley*, 1993).[12] or if the student is facing related criminal charges in a municipal court (*Gabrilowitz v. Newman*, 1978). Counsel does not have the right to cross examine witnesses or even participate in the process of the hearing. It is important to note here that no campus proceeding should be delayed pending the outcome of a municipal case unless, of course, campus codes require a criminal conviction as the basis for jurisdiction for the campus system. Administrators should take great care to avoid the nexus of a municipal conviction as the only means of establishing a violation of the student code and should draft their codes accordingly, focusing on conduct rather than a conviction.

6. Limited right to appeal. Nevertheless, there should always be an appellate process. It should be efficient, expeditious and confined to a review of the proceedings from which there is an appeal. It should not of itself constitute a new hearing, but may direct a new hearing as an appropriate resolution for an error previously committed.

7. No right to a transcript; but if there is an appeal process, the process becomes tainted, if not unworkable, without a transcript.

8. No right to an explanation of a board's decision.

9. No right to a public hearing (in fact it would appear that the Family Educational Rights and Privacy Act of 1974 [FERPA] would discourage it)

Academic Integrity Cases

The due process protections granted to public university students during hearings based solely upon academic infractions are less stringent than those granted during misconduct hearings (*Militana v. Univeristy of Miami*, 1970).[13] Students are currently entitled only to notice from school authorities that they are deficient in meeting minimum academic performance (*Gaspar v. Burton*, 1975). The courts have seemed to reason that they are less qualified to make academic evaluations than are school officials. While many campuses define academic dishonesty as a disciplinary matter, some offer an entirely different internal process for adjudication of these issues. The courts may look at these processes differently, but will always at least hold the campus to the protections theoretically afforded its students by its own published procedures.

The Contract Theory

Students and employees of private institutions still have little procedural protections in disciplinary proceedings. They are not entitled to the hearings or administrative reviews that are guaranteed in the public sector. The protections afforded are contractual in nature arising from the institution's policies and the agreements to attend or work at the institution and abide by its published policies.[14] The governing rules, therefore, are the published policies as set forth in the college catalogue, student handbook, employee manual, tenure agreement, etc., and should provide for written notice of the infraction to be heard, a hearing with the ability to confront witnesses and review the material being presented, assistance by an advisor, and an appeal.

The courts have traditionally protected students from actions which are clearly arbitrary although still within the private institution's stated policy (*Slaughter v. Brigham Young University*, 1975). Individuals are held only to a standard of conduct which reasonably sets forth the expectations of the institution. In addressing construction of the contract between the students and university, the court in *Cloud v. Trustees of Boston University* (1983) stated that the applicable standard was that of "reasonable expectations—what meaning that party making the manifestation, the university, should reasonably expect the other party to give it." Private universities are required to act in the exercise of honest discretion based on facts within the school's knowledge (*Carr v. St. John's University*, 1962).

Search and Seizure

Students at a private university, unlike their counterparts at public institutions, also do not enjoy constitutional search and seizure protections. While some public institutions have retained the rights for some health and safety inspections, generally their students enjoy full constitutional protection from searches without warrants. As long as government law enforcement officials are not directly or indirectly involved in the search or seizure, and university security officers have not been given public arrest or search powers, the private university is constrained only by its (contract) policy statement and so may have its own rules (or lack of rules) regarding searches (*U.S. v. Clegg*, 1975; *People v. Zelinski*, 1979). Private college students and employees also are not ensured of any First Amendment freedoms except as are agreed upon in the contract (hate speech codes, rules of assembly, use of bulletin boards, publication of campus newspapers, etc.) (*Frisby v. Schultz*, 1988).

CONCLUSIONS

All campuses can avoid unnecessary confusion and litigation by effecting some simple procedures:

A. Promulgate clear and concise catalogues and handbooks which:
   1. clearly enunciate what conduct the college expects and what rights it gives;
   2. are consistent with each other [catalogue, handbook(s), resident life agreement, work-study document, off-campus tutorials, cooperative programs, etc.];
   3. avoid the use of the phrases "due process" and "double jeopardy" and other constitutionally precise legal terms unless the college must or chooses to extend such rights and commits to possess and fund the expertise to do so;
B. Develop and use published disciplinary codes which:
   1. are fair (notice, hearing, advisor, transcript, appeal) or are more than fair;
   2. are reviewed regularly so as to be current with the flexible concepts of fair play;
   3. protect the rights of victims as well as perpetrators (present at hearing, right to advisor);
   4. will not, if adjudicated, give rise to "bad law" that affects the entire world of academia.

Acknowledgments

Part of this material was written for and presented at the 1993 Law and Higher Education Conference presented by Stetson University College of Law. Stetson College of Law has granted approval for its use. The author also wishes to acknowledge the encouragement and assistance of Professor Robert Bickel of the Stetson University College of Law, Mickki L. Harrington, Esq., Patricia Melita and Diane Santspree, all of the law firm of Pattison, Sampson, Ginsberg & Griffin, P.C., and Ronald D'Allessandro, Jr., a student at the Albany Law School of Union University.

Endnotes

1. *Esteban v. Central Missouri State College*, 277 F. Supp. 649 (W.D. Mo. 1967). Although campus judicial proceedings are not bound by the Federal Rules of Evidence, the student is entitled to: the opportunity for advance inspection of any affidavits or exhibits the college intends to submit at the hearing; the opportunity

to present their own version of the facts, by personal statements as well as affidavits and witnesses; the right to hear evidence against them and question (personally, not through counsel) adverse witnesses, etc.

2. "It rests with that evidence which, when fairly considered produces the stronger impression, and has the greater weight, and is more convincing as to its truth when weighed against the evidence in opposition thereto." *Black's Law Dictionary* 1344 (4th Ed. 1968).

3. *Gideon v. Wainwright*, 372 U.S. 335, 344-345 (1963), "reason and reflection require us to recognize that in our adversary system of criminal justice, any person haled into court who is too poor to hire a lawyer cannot be assured a fair trial unless counsel is provided for him." And citing *Powell v. Alabama*, 287 U.S. 45, 68-69 (1932) "The right to be heard would be in many cases, of little avail if it did not comprehend the right to be heard by counsel."

4. U.S. Constitution, 5th amendment. "No person shall be held to answer for a capital or otherwise infamous crime, unless on a presentment or indictment of a Grand Jury."

5. U.S. Constitution, 6th amendment. "In all criminal prosecutions, the accused shall enjoy the right to a speedy and public trial, by an impartial jury of the state and district wherein the crime shall have been committed." This clause is applicable to the states through the Fourteenth Amendment. See also: *Duncan v. Louisiana*, 391 U.S. 145, 149 (1968): "the Fourteenth Amendment guarantees a right of jury trial in all criminal cases which—were they to be tried in a federal court—would come within the Sixth Amendment guarantee."

6. *Benton v. Maryland*, 395 U.S. 784 (1969). The Double Jeopardy clause of the Fifth Amendment ("[N] or shall any person be subject for the same offense to be twice put in jeopardy of life or limb") is applicable to the state through the Fourteenth Amendment.

7. U.S. Constitution, 6th amendment ". . . and to be informed of the nature and cause of the accusation; to be confronted with the witnesses against him." *Pointer v. Texas*, 380 U.S. 400, 403 (1965): "The Sixth Amendment's right of an accused to confront witnesses against him is a fundamental right and is made obligatory on the states by the Fourteenth Amendment." And citing *Alford v. United States*, 282 U.S. 687, 692 (1931) the right of cross-examination is "one of the safeguards essential to a fair trial."

8. *Griffin v. Illinois*, 351 U.S. 12, 19 (1956). "There can be no equal justice where the kind of trial a man gets depends on the amount of money he has. Destitute defendants must be afforded as adequate an appellate review as defendants who have money enough to buy transcripts." See also: *Douglas v. California*, 372 U.S. 353 (1963).

9. *In re Civil Rights Cases*, 109 U.S. 3 (1883), conduct that is exclusively private is not violative of the Fourteenth Amendment.

10. *Goss v. Lopez*, 419 U.S. 565, 574 (1975), "the State is constrained to recognize a student's legitimate entitlement to a public education as a property interest which is protected by the Due Process clause and which may not be taken away for misconduct without adherence to the minimum procedures required by that clause.

11. *Healy v. James*, 408 U.S. 169, 187-188 (1972). "The college, acting here as the instrumentality of the state, may not restrict speech or association simply because it finds the views expressed by any group to be abhorrent."

12. *Osteen v. Henley*, 13 F.3d 221, 225 (7th Cir. 1993). Even if a student has a constitutional right to consult counsel . . . we do not think he is entitled to be rep-

resented in the sense of having a lawyer who is permitted to examine or cross-examine witnesses, to submit and object to documents, to address the tribunal, and otherwise to perform the traditional functions of a trial lawyer.

13. *Militana v. University of Miami*, 236 So. 2d 162 (Fla 3rd DCA 1970). Notice of charges and an opportunity to be heard are certainly essential to due process and required when a student is dropped from school for disciplinary reasons; however, such is not required when the dismissal is for academic failure.

14. The best discussion I've seen on the subject of the rights of the private college and its students regarding discipline is in: Stoner, E. N. II & Cerminara, K. L. (1990), Harnessing the Spirit of Insubordination—A Model Student Disciplinary Code, *Journal of College and University Law*, 17 (2), 89-121.

_____

References

Benner v. Oswald, 592 F.2d 174 (3rd. Cir. 1979)

Benton v. Maryland, 395 U.S. 784 (1969).

Black, H.C. (1990). *Black's law dictionary*. St. Paul, MN: West Publishing.

Carr v. St. John's University, New York 17 A.D. 2d 632 (2d Dept. 1962).

Cloud v. Trustees of Boston University, 720 F.2d 721 (1st Cir. 1983).

Dixon v. Alabama State Board of Education, 294 F.2d 150 (5th Cir. 1961).

Esteban v. Central Missouri State College, 277 F. Supp. 649 (W.D. Mo. 1967)

Family Educational Rights and Privacy Act, 20 U.S.C. §1232g, 1974.

Federal Rules of Evidence. 801(c).

Fisher v. United States, 425 U.S. 391 (1976).

Frisby v. Schultz, 487 U.S. 474 (1988).

Furutani v. Ewigleben, 297 F. Supp. 1163 (N.D. Cal. 1969).

Gabrilowitz v. Newman, 582 F.2d 100 (1st Cir. 1978).

Gaspar v. Bruton, 513 F.2d 843 (10th Cir. 1975).

Gideon v. Wainwright, 372 U.S. 335, 344-345 (1963)

Goss v. Lopez, 419 U.S. 565, 574 (1975).

Griffin v. Illinois, 351 U.S. 12, 19 (1956).

Healy v. James, 408 U.S. 169, 187-188 (1972).

Jackson v. Metropolitan Edison Co., 419 U.S. 345 (1974).

Militana v. University of Miami, 236 So. 2d 162 (Fla 3rd DCA 1970).

Osteen v. Henley, 13 F.3d 221, 225 (7th Cir. 1993).

People v. Zelinski, 24 Cal 3d 357 (1979).

Powell v. Miles, 407 F.2d 73 (2d Cir. 1968).

Rendell-Baker v. Kohn, 457 U.S. 830 (1982).

Slaughter v. Brigham Young University, 514 F.2d 622 (10th Cir. 1975), cert. denied, 423 U.S. 898 (1975).

Title VII, 42 U.S.C. §2000e—2(a).

Title IX, 20 U.S.C. §1681.

Trustees of Dartmouth College v. Woodward, 17 U.S. 518 (1819).

U.S. v. Clegg, 509 F.2d 605 (5th Cir. 1975).

Wahba v. New York University, 492 F.2d 96 (2d Cir. 1974).

Williams v. Howard University, 528 F.2d 658 (D.C. Cir. 1976).

In re Winship. 397 US 358 (1970).

Chapter III

Student Judicial Records, Privacy and the Press's Right to Know

Dennis E. Gregory

INTRODUCTION

Since the early 1960s significant changes have occurred in the way students are disciplined at colleges and universities in the United States. Public institutions, in particular have undergone a series of changes which have provided students with many additional rights and have caused administrators of student judicial affairs at institutions to constantly seek to upgrade their knowledge on both student development and legal issues.

The theory of *in loco parentis* yielded to a strict constitutional approach to student conduct. The constitutional approach then yielded to a contractual approach, more reflective of the direction taken at private institutions. Student consumerism and specific state and federal legislation which addressed issues of race, gender, campus safety, and many other issues have also impacted the approaches used by institutions to address student behavior.

At this point, most enlightened institutions have relaxed the rigid legalistic systems of adjudication developed in the 60s or 70s and are moving toward systems that maintain Constitutional and legislative protections while offering options and making their systems more administratively based. Many institutions have begun to include mediation and alternative dispute resolution as part of their system.

Since the basic due process rights for students were established in the 1960s and 1970s, perhaps no areas of student conduct professional practice has engendered more questions than those related to how institutional officials deal with student conduct records. This is true, despite the fact that the Family Educational Rights and Privacy Act (1974), commonly known as FERPA, has been on the federal books now for over two decades. Often raised questions include: how much

55

can, or should, a judicial official tell a parent about a child's conduct record?; How long, and in what manner, should conduct records be kept by an institution?; What if a police officer arrests a student and the student faces both criminal and student conduct charges?; Are either the police or student conduct records public or protected?

Student judicial affairs professionals are taught that the student conduct system is part of the student development program of the institution, and should be used to provide developmental opportunities and growth for students who violate institutional policies. In many cases, however, parents, the press, and society as a whole, may view judicial processes and records privacy as methods that institutions use to hide crime on campus. These constituencies may also believe that institutions hide treatment of college students which is more lenient than treatment of the general population.

While FERPA has addressed many of the issues related to student records, a great number of issues are not addressed by the act. The following section of this chapter seeks to provide answers to questions about many of those issues. A later section of this chapter will deal with recent changes to FERPA, the state of the law, as well as questions and challenges which are being raised by the press and others in the U.S. today regarding the impact of FERPA.

Also in question is the act's future effectiveness in light of state open records, freedom of information and open meetings laws. Suggestions that FERPA does not really prohibit release due to its status as a precondition for Federal funding, suggestions by some courts that Section 1983 of the U.S. Code may be used as a way to challenge FERPA decisions, and a call for amendment to the law by the Secretary of Education will undoubtedly have impact for some time to come.

STUDENT CONDUCT RECORD KEEPING

How Long Should Records be Kept

There appears to be no direction on the part of FERPA with regard to what records should be maintained by an institution. In fact, newly posted regulations, described below, specifically describe the flexibility of the act in this regard. The only specific guidance that is provided is that after 1974, when the act was passed, no record may be destroyed after a request has been made for access to that record. In other words, there is a prohibition against institutional staff destroying material that may be part of the student's record in order to keep the student from gaining access to the records.

Anecdotal information indicates that prior to the passage of FERPA in 1974, some deans of students and other officials may have kept lists of perceived problem students or have made notations in student's records which were prejudicial or which violated due process rights.

It is important for a detailed record keeping system to be developed and maintained by judicial offices. Many institutions have developed sophisticated computer databases for this purpose and others still maintain index cards and file folders on each student whose case is dealt with by the office. Much of how record keeping is accomplished by a particular institution depends on the case volume, available computer and other resources, and the number and sophistication of the staff available to work with the system. In any case, being able to find student records quickly and the ability to accurately determine past violations are critical to an efficiently run judicial affairs office.

Accurate and efficient record keeping is also necessary in order for the institution to keep appropriate statistics on the number and type of violations which occur. Several commercially available databases have been developed specifically for such record keeping and other general-purpose databases may be adapted for this purpose. Some institutions have had proprietary systems developed by their own internal administrative computing programs to meet the specific needs of their institutional systems.

Generally, the judicial records on a particular student should be maintained until the student has left the institution for the final time due to graduation, transfer, or permanent academic dismissal. Upon completion of final matriculation, records related to serious violations, defined as those violations that result in removal from the institution for some period of time, should be maintained for some specified period of time.

Anecdotal information would indicate that five years after matriculation is common for many institutions. After this time a summary of the serious violations and the related penalties may be kept in order to facilitate reference checks for jobs, graduate school, security clearances, and the like. It would appear inappropriate to keep records of minor violations, defined as those for which a penalty of less than removal from the institution, which would have little or no impact on future requests for information.

Many institutions destroy all records of disciplinary violations and penalties after some set period since it is felt that youthful indiscretions should not be kept to haunt adults many years later. This practice would also seem appropriate in light of the allegedly "educational" purpose of student conduct systems, which are intended to allow students to develop and mature as citizens during their college years, and at most are intended to separate violators from the educational institution which has higher standards of behavior than society at large. The view of some student judicial affairs administrators and others is that most records should be destroyed immediately upon graduation if all sanctions have been fulfilled since the judicial process is meant to be an internal educational effort and should have no impact on post-college life.

There is some debate as to whether a record should be kept, while still in school or thereafter, for those persons who are charged with an offense and are subsequently found not responsible for any violations. While such a record would not be a violation of due process or other ethical standards, it appears that to maintain such records would violate the spirit of the purpose for judicial systems.

Exceptions to the Rule

Exceptions to the general policy on records maintenance would include records of those students who are expelled or permanently dismissed from an institution, records of persons who are indefinitely suspended from an institution and must complete some tasks before possible reinstatement, and those who leave the institution prior to adjudication of serious charges or with uncompleted disciplinary sanctions. In these cases it would appear appropriate to maintain the entire student record permanently.

What Records Should Be Kept?

A student disciplinary record should, at a minimum, include the following for all serious charges:

1. A copy of the letter which notifies the student of the charges and the proposed hearing;
2. Copies of any evidence that was used as part of the hearing process as well as an audiotape and/or a transcript of the hearing;
3. A notice of the finding of the person or body who hears the charges (If a decision of responsibility for one or more violations is found. This should include the sanction that is imposed.);
4. Any material related to appeals which result from the case and changes which may result related to the finding or the sanction; and
5. A notice that the student has completed any assigned sanction, or has left the institution before sanction completion.

Items that should not be a part of the disciplinary record include the following:

1. Notes made by the investigator of the incident which are not part of the record of the hearing;
2. Any notes made by the board or hearing officer during the hearing process or deliberations.
3. Any material which is not relevant to the charges which are dealt with in the hearing or appeal process (i.e. notes from others regard-

ing their opinions about the case, material about other students who are not directly related to the case); and

4. Any material that is relevant to the student but not his or her judicial history (i.e. class schedules, academic material from courses, etc).

As described above, the proper development and maintenance of student conduct records is essential to the appropriate operation of a judicial programs office. It is also essential so that students and others seeking access to these records will not be provided with irrelevant and potentially illegal information. FERPA provides mechanisms by which these records can be accessed by students and parents and it is essential that only those records that are relevant are included among those provided. In the material to follow, the development and appropriate implementation of the law are described.

THE FAMILY EDUCATIONAL RIGHTS AND PRIVACY ACT

The Family Educational Rights and Privacy Act was ratified by Congress in 1974 after introduction by Senator James Buckley of New York and Senator Claiborne Pell of Rhode Island, as part of the Higher Education Amendments of 1974. This legislation was not passed in the normal manner for such laws (i.e. through the committee process), but was instead introduced on the floor of the Senate in August of 1974. It became clear almost immediately that there were problems with the law and amendments were introduced by Senator Buckley in December of 1974. (Lowery, 1995) The two primary purposes for the law are:

1. To guarantee parents of students under the age of 18 who are enrolled in elementary or secondary schools access to student education records, and to provide similar access to any student enrolled in institutions of post secondary education, and;

2. To limit access by others to these records without the consent of the student and/or parent (Congressional Record, 1974).

In the original version of the law, a "laundry list" of records that were to be covered by the act were included. Among that list were "... verified reports of serious and recurrent behavior patterns." (1974 U.S. Code Cong. and Admin. News, 2133). This indicates Congressional intent to include disciplinary records as protected by the law. In the amendments to the law passed in December 1974, Congress substituted the term "education records" for the list previously identified " (6794).

It appears that the primary impetus for passage of the law was to assure that parents of elementary and secondary students had access to test scores and other material sometimes entered into records by teachers and school administrators, and then denied to parents of these students. Limitations of access and the inclusion of post secondary education became part of the law's focus during debate on the floor of the Senate.

Upon passage of the act in 1974, higher education officials raised an outcry. Complaints of unnecessary federal intrusion were often heard during that period. Twenty years of experience with the law, however, has now shown that the impact of the law has been benign at worst and in most cases positive. The Family Policy Compliance Office of the Department of Education, and its director LeRoy Rooker, have made FERPA a model for the proper implementation of federal law.

Amendments to FERPA

FERPA has been amended several times since its original passage in 1974. Most relevant of those amendments are the following:

Higher Education Amendments of 1992. In the Higher Education Amendments of 1992 (1992) the law was changed to accommodate court decisions rendered in the cases *Bauer v. Kincaid* (1991) and *Student Press Law Center v. Alexander* (1991) which dealt with the questions of whether campus police records were protected by FERPA. According to the Amendment, "(ii) records maintained by a law enforcement unit of the educational agency or institution that were created by that law enforcement unit for the purpose of law enforcement" are not protected by the act.

This change was prompted by the work of the Student Press Law Center and other groups of journalists and came as a result of increased fear that institutional officials were hiding campus crime. This change has provided salutary results and has been supported by higher education professional associations including the Association for Student Judicial Affairs (Bennett, 1995).

The Student Right to Know and Campus Security Act. The Student Right to Know and Campus Security Act was passed by Congress in 1990. This law was also a result of concern that campus crime was on the increase and that victims of crimes of violence and of sexual assault, in particular, were not being adequately supported and kept informed, and that campus officials were using student conduct systems to hide these crimes. (Bennett, 1995)

According to regulations published to implement the amendment of FERPA:

> Nothing in this section shall be construed to prohibit an institution of post-secondary education from disclosing, to an alleged victim of any crime of violence (as that term is defined in Section 16 of Title 18), the results of any disciplinary proceeding conducted by such institution against the alleged perpetrator of such crime (20 U.S.C. Section 1232g.(b) (6) 1993).

In addition, The Student Assistance General Provisions indicate:

Both the accuser and the accused shall be informed of the outcome of any institutional disciplinary proceeding brought alleging a sex offense. Compliance with this subsection does not constitute a violation of the Family Education Rights and Privacy Act (20 U.S.C. 1232g). For the purposes of this paragraph, the outcome of a disciplinary proceeding means only the institution's final determination with respect to the alleged sex offense and any sanction that is imposed against the accused (30 CFR Section 668.47(a)(12)(vi), 1993).

This means that an institution may notify the victim of a crime of violence of the results of a disciplinary proceeding and must notify the victim of a sex offense of the results of a disciplinary hearing against the alleged perpetrator. Such notifications will not be a violation of FERPA (Bennett, 1995).

COURT CHALLENGES TO FERPA

In addition to the changes to FERPA which have resulted from various amendments, there have been several court cases over the years which have impacted the enforcement of FERPA in post-secondary education and student judicial affairs. Each of these cases, except one, raise issues related to state open meetings laws and FERPA. Two cases raise the issue of whether FERPA actually prohibits the release of records. The most specific to the issues described above are those that have challenged the act's restriction on the release of judicial records. These latter cases have occurred in Georgia, Louisiana, and Oklahoma.

Student Bar Association Board of Governors, etc. v. Byrd

In *Student Bar Association Board of Directors, etc. v. Byrd* (1977) the student bar association of the University of North Carolina School of Law challenged the right of the faculty of the school to close its meetings. Upon appeal, the Supreme Court of North Carolina indicated that the faculty of the school was not a body covered by the North Carolina Open Meetings Law, and thus, could close its meetings. One argument raised by the state in defense of meeting closings was that student records might be discussed there, and that such records were protected from release by FERPA. The court dismissed this particular claim by noting:

The Buckley Amendment does not forbid such disclosure of information concerning a student and, therefore, does not forbid opening to the public a faculty meeting at which such matters are discussed. The Buckley Amendment simply cuts off Federal funds, otherwise available to an educational institution that has the policy or practice of permitting the release of such information. (p. 419)

The court went on, however to indicate:

Of course, a violation of the Buckley Amendment could well result, not only in termination of any otherwise available federal financial aid to the School of Law but also in the termination of any such aid to the entire University ... the possibility that all further Federal financial aid to the entire University of North Carolina, including its component institutions, may be jeopardized by an interpretation of the Open Meetings Law making it applicable to meetings of the faculty of the School of Law is an additional reason for care in so construing the Open Meetings Law. (p. 420)

Subsequent to this ruling the institutions of the University of North Carolina system did continue to interpret the Open Meetings Law to allow faculty meetings and other functions such as student judicial hearings to be closed as exceptions to the law. This implies that while a strict interpretation of FERPA does not state a prohibition of release, the impending loss of federal funds would so damage the institution that enlightened public policy would prohibit such release as part of an open meetings law.

Red and Black Publishing Co. v. Board of Regents

In *Red and Black Publishing Company v. Board of Regents* (1993) the student newspaper at the University of Georgia sued the university to gain access to the results of a judicial hearing against a fraternity accused of hazing. The Supreme Court of Georgia eventually ruled, among other things, that FERPA did not cover judicial records, and that both judicial hearings and judicial records should be open to the public as a result of the Georgia open records and open meetings laws.

In a related development which came later in the pursuit of open meetings at the University of Georgia, an attorney general's opinion (1989) was cited by Peter D. Brown (personal communication, May 8, 1996), associate director of judicial affairs, as being the impetus which has opened the deliberations of hearing boards at Georgia to public scrutiny. According to Brown, "The Legal Affairs Office consulted the Attorney General's Office and was told that deliberations must be open as no applicable exemptions are listed in the Open Meetings Act. The AG's Office referenced an Attorney General's Opinion that dealt with the State Ethics Commission closing meetings after hearing evidence (89-6)" (1).

The "Red and Black" case appeared to be the opening salvo by the Student Press Law Center and other media organizations in an attempt to open judicial records at institutions across the country. The decision of the court and the subsequent decision by the Attorney General of Georgia appear to be in direct opposition to decisions elsewhere in the country.

Shreveport Professional Chapter of the Society of Professional Journalists v. Louisiana State University in Shreveport

In *SPJ v. LSU Shreveport* (1994) the editor of the LSU student newspaper, supported by the local chapter of the Society of Professional

Journalists, sued the university to gain access to judicial records in a case in which student government officials were charged with misappropriating funds from a textbook sale. Judge Scott Crichton ruled, in the District Court of Caddo Parish, that while the Louisiana open records law did cover these records, that both the Louisiana Constitution's right to privacy and FERPA required that the university keep the records private. Judge Crichton indicated that the loss of federal funds which may result from the release of student conduct records was indeed a restriction against release under FERPA. SPJ filed an appeal in this case but withdrew their appeal prior to its hearing on the merits of the case. This decision would appear to echo the decision in North Carolina.

The decision in this case appears to have been quite a surprise to many commentators who believed that the journalists would roll through state courts gutting the protections put in place by FERPA. As of this writing, no further suits have been filed by media organizations since the decision in this case.

Stephen Selkirk v. University of Oklahoma et. al.

In *Selkirk v. University of Oklahoma* (1994) a group of students desecrated a teepee which had been erected to celebrate Native American Awareness Week. One of the students in the teepee during the process sued to gain access to the results of a disciplinary hearing held against students who committed the damage. Selkirk alleged that he was a victim of a crime of violence and should, thus, have access to the decision. The district court ruled that Selkirk was not a victim of a crime of violence and that as a result, FERPA prohibited the release of these records.

Eastern Connecticut State University v. Freedom of Information Commission

The most recent case dealing with FERPA and student judicial hearings occurred in Connecticut. In *Eastern Connecticut State University v. Freedom of Information Commission* (1996) a faculty member who had brought charges against a student which were heard in an open hearing sought to acquire a copy of the tape recordings of the hearing. He was refused a copy of the tape and filed a complaint with the Freedom of Information Commission. The commission ruled in his favor and the university appealed to the circuit court in Hartford.

The court ruled that the recordings should be produced since FERPA restrictions were "merely a precondition for federal funds" (1174) and not a prohibition of release, and that the Connecticut Freedom of Information Law covered student judicial hearings. The court cited the North Carolina case described above without reference to the public policy implications.

This case clearly confirms the legal maxims that bad cases make bad law. The facts that the student judicial case was heard in an open hearing and that the faculty member in question should have been defined as having a legitimate educational interest, should have prohibited this case from ever leaving the campus. It is anticipated that the Connecticut Freedom of Information Law may be amended to exclude student judicial hearings as a result of this case and the public policy implications of this decision.

The federal courts have not yet dealt with the issues raised above. How these courts would deal with the issues of state versus federal law and the limitations placed upon FERPA as "merely a precondition for federal funds" (1174) is unknown. It is this author's opinion, however, that the state court decisions that limit the application of FERPA would be overturned.

THE DEPARTMENT OF EDUCATION AND FERPA

1996 Final Regulations for FERPA Implementation

On March 14, 1996 the Department of Education issued a Notice of Proposed Rulemaking (1996) which solicited comments on proposed changes to FERPA. These proposed changes encompassed a variety of issues including, but not limited to: the broadening of the definition of "records" to include "computer media"; changes in the manner by which institutions must notify parents and students of their rights under the act; disclosure of records to juvenile justice systems; and disclosure of records pursuant to court orders and subpoenas.

The items of most direct importance to student judicial officers were clarifications about release of disciplinary records to those with a "legitimate educational interest in the behavior of the student" (p. 10665) and release of record information to officials in other institutions which may be necessary to protect a "safe school environment" (p. 10665).

Final Regulations regarding these issues were released by the Department of Education on November 21, 1996 (1996). The regulations made explicit reference to the fact that institutions had the right to maintain, and disclose under certain restrictions, disciplinary records of students. In response to questions regarding whether there was a legal obligation under FERPA to release information regarding a student who might pose a "significant risk," the regulations indicate that there is no legal obligation to do so. As a result, no liability would attach to institutional officials who fail to do so. The regulations also chose not to define a single standard as to what a "significant risk" would be, but to allow individual institutional officials to do so.

The Administration of Campus Discipline . . .

1995 Final Regulation for FERPA Implementation

In August of 1993 The Department of Education issued a Notice of Proposed Rulemaking (1993) which solicited comment on potential changes in FERPA regulations. In order to collect further comments the Department issued a "Second Notice of Proposed Rulemaking" (1993) in December of 1993. After collecting comments from a wide variety of journalists, professional associations, educational institutions, and others the Department issued its "Final Regulations" (1995) regarding FERPA on January 17, 1995.

In these regulations the Department of Education clarified a number of issues related to "law enforcement records," clarified how a "law enforcement unit" is defined at an institution of post-secondary education, and reiterated that student conduct records are, in fact, protected under FERPA.

The Secretary of Education's Letters to Congress

At the time of the issuance of these regulations, Secretary of Education Riley wrote a letter to the ranking majority members of the Senate Committee on Labor and Human Resources and the House of Representatives Committee on Economic and Educational Opportunities (1995) in which he indicated:

> In contrast to law enforcement unit records, the Department has been legally constrained to treat the records of a disciplinary action or proceeding as "education records" under FERPA, that is, subject to inspection and review by parents and eligible students and protected against non-consensual disclosure except in statutorily specified circumstances, ... (Riley, 1995, p. 2)

The Secretary goes on to say:

> Although we think it is clear that the definition of "education records" includes student disciplinary records, it is also the case that crime on our nation's college campuses and in our elementary and secondary schools has escalated since 1974 when FERPA was enacted. In light of this development and the ongoing public and media attention to the issue, we believe that the various competing interests need to be identified and balanced in the legislative forum. The Congress may find that public access to disciplinary records concerning criminal and other nonacademic misconduct is an appropriate response to the problem of maintaining safe college campuses. (p. 2)

The Secretary concludes:

> In any case, I would like to propose that the Department work with Congress to help resolve these disputes, including assisting Congress in drafting an appropriate FERPA amendment to address the issue of nonconsensual disclosure of student disciplinary records. (p. 3)

Thus, it is clear that Secretary Riley posits a desire for Congress to readdress the issue of FERPA's application to student disciplinary records. As of this writing neither the House or the Senate have addressed this issue.

Model FERPA Implementation Materials by the Department of Education

In April 1995 the Department of Education issued a revised set of documents intended to assist institutions to develop and or revise policies and procedures for implementing FERPA. These documents include:

1. **Student Records Policies and Procedures for State University** which is "a model for colleges and universities to use in meeting the requirements of Section 99.6 of the regulations implementing the Family Educational Rights and Privacy Act of 1974" (1995). This document is a detailed guide to the requirements of the regulations and the ways in which institutions may develop policies correctly.

2. **FERPA Model** which is "a guide for the person, office, or task force making plans to develop an institutional compliance model" (1995). This is a planning outline that provides a step-by-step process for model development.

3. **Model Notification of Rights Under FERPA,** which is a one-page form letter which may be used by institutions to notify students of their FERPA rights (1995).

These documents and other information related to FERPA may be obtained by contacting:
Ellen Campbell, Family Policy Compliance Office
Office of Management, U.S. Department of Education
600 Independence Avenue, S.W.
Washington, D.C. 20202-4605
Telephone: (202) 260-3887 • TDD Service 1-800-877-8339 • FERPA@ed.gov

POINTS AND ISSUES TO REMEMBER ABOUT FERPA

1. There is no right to private action under FERPA—This means that a student whose rights have allegedly been violated under FERPA may not sue based upon the law itself. The method of remedy developed by the Department of Education has been to file a complaint with the Department after which an investigation would potentially ensue. A decision as to whether a breach has occurred would be made, a search for a means to resolve any problems would be attempted, and the government, if appropriate, would impose a penalty. The primary penalty that is described in the Act is the loss of federal funds by the offending institution.

While this is true, several Federal courts (*Lewin,* 1996; *Doe,* 1996; *Belanger,* 1994; *Brown,* 1994; *Obersteller,* 1994; *Umstead,* 1994) have, in the last three years, allowed impacted parents and students to sue under a section of the Civil Rights Act of 1871 (42 U.S.C. §1983) in order to dispute alleged violations of FERPA. Section 1983 provides:

> Every person who, under color of any statute ... of any State ... subjects, or causes to be subjected, any citizen of the United States or other person within the jurisdiction thereof to the deprivation of any rights, privileges, or immunities secured by the Constitution and laws, shall be liable to the party injured in an action at law, suit in equity, or other proper proceeding for redress.

Thus, officials at public institutions must be aware of this potential threat of suits where none existed prior to 1994. An excellent discussion of the four 1994 cases noted above is included in the Winter 1996 issue of *The Journal of College and University Law*. A discussion of the application of Section 1983 as it applies to FERPA, a description of the other cases noted, as well as a detailed description of issues related to hearing rights under FERPA are included in an article by Baker (1997) in the *Education Law Reporter*.

2. Students at colleges and universities gain standing for FERPA protection, rather than their parents, even if they are under 18 years of age.

3. Parents may gain access to student records, if institutional regulations permit it, as long as they can certify that the student is "dependent" as defined by IRS regulations. A copy of the parent's income tax form for the most recent year showing the student as a dependent is appropriate proof.

4. If a student is listed as a "dependent" of one parent in a family of divorce, then both parents may have access to student records.

5. The Student Right to Know and Campus Security Act has amended FERPA to allow the institution to make the victim of a crime of violence aware of the judicial action taken against a perpetrator and requires an institution to make the victim of a sexual assault aware of the judicial action taken against a perpetrator.

6. If an institution wishes to do so, they may notify students each semester, at registration, of their opportunity to prove that they are independent students. If students fail to do so, the institution may assume that they are dependent for parental notification purposes. The opposite is also true. The institution may assume that all students are independent unless the students say that they are not, or the parents provide tax forms.

7. The institution may determine that anyone from the president to resident advisors have a "legitimate educational interest" to access student " education records." Care should be taken, however, to assure that such decisions are not made in arbitrary or capricious ways.

8. Institutional "law enforcement" records are not protected by FERPA. "Education Records" are protected by FERPA and investigations con-

ducted by police for purely educational (read student conduct) reasons are defined as education records.

9. Only institutional officials may violate FERPA. Student newspapers, unless they are acting as an agent of the institution, cannot violate FERPA, although they may face libel and other potential charges for release of records, etc.

10. Independent institutions as well as public institutions are covered by FERPA. In most states independent institutions are not covered by state open meeting, open record and freedom of information laws.

11. Some states' open records laws, etc. specifically exempt "education records," while others do not.

12. For the purposes of FERPA and legal challenge, cases of cheating, plagiarism and other forms of academic dishonesty are "behavior" issues rather than "academic" issues. This is true despite media organizations attempts to separate the two for notification purposes, presumably in order not to raise "academic freedom" issues among faculty.

13. The institution, whenever possible, should reach an agreement with local law enforcement officials about what types of cases the local officials wish to be referred to the prosecutor for action. They should also agree about which cases should be dealt with on campus through student conduct hearings alone. This is not intended to hide crime, but merely to keep minor cases from clogging up the courts. This may also be used to deal with violations of institutional policy that may also be potential violations of the law but which, due to different standards of proof, etc. may be more effectively dealt with on campus. No criminal activity that occurs on campus and/or is committed by college students should be withheld from local law enforcement officials. Hiding such cases creates unacceptable institutional liability and is ethically questionable at best.

CONCLUSION

Recently issued federal regulations and statements from the Secretary of Education reinforce the interpretation that FERPA prohibits institutions of higher education from releasing the records of student judicial actions, except in limited circumstances, without the permission of the student. Two of four recently decided court cases have also upheld this interpretation of the law while two have indicated that FERPA does not restrict release of records but is merely a funding precondition. Thus for the moment, except in Georgia and Connecticut, the interpretation that student judicial records are protected from release by FERPA is the law of the land.

The Secretary of Education's challenge to Congress; and the student and professional media's desire to have access to student judicial records; do indicate that while the battle may have been won, the war may not be over. It would appear that FERPA, as a federal law, would take precedence over state open records and open meetings laws, thus, this author would posit that should such a challenge reach the federal courts, these state laws will have little future impact on the interpretation of whether records should be released or hearings opened.

Of further concern, however, is whether media organizations will begin to pressure Congress to change FERPA to remove the current restrictions on release of student judicial records, and whether Congress may see this as both a means to reduce campus crime and a media benefit. While the media have not yet begun their assault on Congress, and Congress has not dealt with this issue as a result of other priorities, the higher education community in general and the student affairs profession in particular, must be attentive to efforts to begin this process.

Of additional concern to judicial affairs professionals is the potentially increased use of "Section 1983" as a route to bring suit for alleged FERPA violations, when no such right to action was originally provided under the act. Two of the six cases noted above involved colleges (*Lewin*, 1996 and *Brown*, 1994). To this point the cases have resulted in findings against institutions or school districts only on very limited bases and with benign results. Such judicious handling of cases by the courts is, however, not guaranteed in the future.

Student judicial programs should be used as part of the educational program of a college or university in order to assist students to become better citizens and to live up to higher standards of conduct than those expected of the general population. Release of student judicial records to the media may have a perceived societal benefit in the short term, but the negative impact which such action would have on the climate of the campus would chill reporting of crime and other violations of institutional policy rather than decrease its occurrence. Students will not be willing to face a potentially poorly prepared student press nor a tabloid type professional journalist seeking to sensationalize an unfortunate injury to a fellow student or other violation of institutional policy.

As noted elsewhere in this monograph, student judicial affairs is an administrative activity which has as its primary purposes the enforcement of institutional rules and policies and the educational development of the institution's students. FERPA serves as recognition of that fact in its requirements that such records, like other educational records, may not be released. This is as it should be.

EPILOGUE

There is no greater testimony to the importance of the Family Educational Rights and Privacy Act (1974) than what has occurred with regard to the act since this chapter was begun. Despite several additions and updates which have been included in the body of the chapter above, change continues. Thus, described below, are recent activities in the Congress, the courts and the Department of Education related to the act.

Congress

On February 12, 1997, Congressman John J. Duncan, Jr. and Congressman Charles E. Schumer introduced H.R. 715, known as the Accuracy in Campus Crime Reporting Act of 1997 (hereafter ACCRA) which had been developed by a collection of journalists organizations and "victims rights" groups with the reported intent, "to close loopholes in campus crime reporting laws (1997, 1). The bill is currently pending in the Postsecondary Education, Training and Lifelong Learning Subcommittee of the Education and Work Force Committee of the House. The subcommitte heard testimony on the bill in July 1997 and there has been intense lobbying, debate and discussion on both sides of the issues as to the value of the bill and some of its provisions.

Major provisions of the bill include the following:

1. Adds to the list of those persons who must report crime statistics for use within the annual report required by the Campus Security Act (1990). Also requires that crime statistic categories agree with the Uniform Crime Reporting standards used by the FBI. Requires each school to submit these statistics to the Department of Education for inclusion in a national annual report.

2. Requires every federally funded institution to maintain a log of all alleged crimes which occur on campus and to make this log public within twenty-four (24) hours. Requires that the names and addresses of all persons charged be included and allows the inclusion of the names and addresses of witnesses, etc.

3. Requires that all campus disciplinary proceedings and records which involve alleged violations of the law be open.

4. Indicates specifically that records of "criminal misconduct" dealt with by campus judicial processes are not protected "education records" as described in FERPA.

5. Lays out a minimum sanction of loss of one percent (1%) of federal funding for each act of non-compliance with the law.

As noted above, there has been intense debate regarding this bill. Of particular concern to judicial officers is the provision opening hearings and records, as well as the inclusion of some categories of individuals in the reporting mechanism.

Several amendments to ACCRA have been proposed by those opposed to portions or all of the bill. Recent speculation is that Congressman Schumer will propose a substitute bill which may be more acceptable to higher education officials.

The Courts

In January 1997, the editor of the student newspaper at Miami University in Ohio filed suit before the Supreme Court of Ohio asking for the release of records of the Miami University Disciplinary Board (1997). *The Miami Student* argued that the university, by failing to release the requested records, violated the Ohio Public Records Act (1997). The university, on the other hand, argued that such a release violated FERPA. On July 9, 1997, the Supreme Court of Ohio, citing the *Red and Black* case from the University of Georgia, decided in favor of the plaintiff newspaper and ordered the release of the records.

Subsequently, the Attorney General's Office in Ohio, in response to the decision by the Ohio Supreme Court, filed a *writ of certiorari* before the Supreme Court of the United States. In a summary disposition memo on December 8, 1997 the Court denied the *petition for certiorari* (1997) thus leaving the Ohio decision in force.

The Department of Education

After the decision by the Supreme Court of Ohio, requiring Miami University to release the records of judicial hearings to the student newspaper, Mr. LeRoy Rooker, Director of the Family Compliance Office of the Department of Education, wrote a letter to James C. Garland, president of Miami. In his letter (1997), Rooker informed President Garland that by releasing these records with information which might identify individual students, the university may be violating FERPA and thereby risk losing its federal funds. This, of course, put the university in the position of violating either the federal law or the decision of the state supreme court, no matter which way they chose to proceed. This resulted in the *petition for certiorari* to the United States Supreme Court described above.

On January 23, 1998, the deadline by which Miami University was required to release the student disciplinary records to the student newspaper, the Department of Education filed a complaint in the U.S. District Court in Columbus, Ohio (1998). This complaint asked the court to enjoin Miami from releasing these records since to do so would allegedly violate FERPA and would cause "irreparable harm to the students who legitimately expect privacy and confidentiality in their school's on-campus disciplinary process" (1998).

This saga is by no means ended. While the court issued a temporary injunction to avoid the release of records, a hearing on the complaint has not, as of this writing taken place. Thus, it appears that there will be no respite or final decision regarding a piece of legislation passed in 1974 in the foreseeable future.

References

Accuracy in Campus Crime Reporting Act, HR 715, 105th Congress, First Session, February 11, 1997.

Accuracy in Campus Crime Reporting Act Summary, Security On Campus, Inc., www@soconline.org/ACCRA/Summary.html, 1997, 1.

Baker, T.R. (In press). Inaccurate and misleading: Student hearing rights under FERPA. *Education Law Reporter.*

Bennett, B.B. (1995). Open Records Law and Student Disciplinary Records: Expanded Media Access to Student Records. *Stetson University College of Law Conference on Law and Higher Education Issues in 1995.*

42 U.S.C.A. §1983, (West 1981).

Family Educational Rights and Privacy Act, 20 U.S.C. §1232g (1974).

Family Educational Rights and Privacy Act of 1974, 1974 Congressional Record 39858-39864 (December 13, 1974).

Family Educational Rights and Privacy; Notice of Proposed Rulemaking. *58 Federal Register,* 42836-42837 (August 11, 1993).

Family Educational Rights and Privacy; Second Notice of Proposed Rulemaking. *58 Federal Register,* 68298-68300 (December 14, 1993).

Family Educational Rights and Privacy; Final Regulations. *60 Federal Register,* 3464-3469 (January 17, 1995).

Family Educational Rights and Privacy; Notice of Proposed Rulemaking. *61 Federal Register,* 10663-10670 (March 14, 1996).

Family Educational Rights and Privacy; Final Regulations. *61 Federal Register,* 59291-59299 (November 21, 1996).

FERPA Model. Department of Education, Family Policy Compliance Office (April 1995).

Georgia Attorney General Opinion 89-6 (1989) (West 1995).

Government Seeks Injunction Against Disclosure of Student Records, News Release, United States Department of Education, January 23, 1998.

Higher Education Amendments of 1992, 106 Stat. 448 (1992)

Lowery, J.W. (1995). Open Records Law and Student Disciplinary Records: Expanded Media Access to Student Records. *Stetson University College of Law Conference on Law and Higher Education Issues in 1995.*

Model Notification of Rights Under FERPA. Department of Education, Family Policy Compliance Office (April 1995).

Ohio Public Records Act, R.C. 149.43, 1997 edition.

Riley, Richard W. (January 10, 1995). Letters to the ranking majority members of the Senate Committee on Labor and Human Resources and the House of Representatives Committee on Economic and Educational Opportunities.

Robinson, J.H. & Pieronek, C. (1996). The Law of Higher Education and the Courts: 1994 in Review. *The Journal of College and University Law,* 22, 367-893.

Rooker, LeRoy S. Letter to Dr. James C. Garland, President Miami University, August 7, 1997.

Student Assistance General Provisions, 30 CFR 668 (1994).

Student Records Policies and Procedures for State University. (April 1995) Department of Education, Family Policy Compliance Office.

Student Right to Know and Campus Security Act, 20 U.S.C. §1092 (1990)
U.S. Code Cong. and Admin. News, 1974

Cases

Bauer v. Kincaid, 759 F. Supp 575 (W.D. Mo. 1991).

Belanger v. Nashua, New Hampshire School District, 856 F. Supp. 40 (NH. 1994).

Brown v. City of Oneonta, 858 F. Supp. 340 (N.D.N.Y. 1994).

Doe by and Through Doe v. Knox County Board of Education, 918 F. Supp. 181 (E.D. Ky. 1996).

Eastern Connecticut State University v. Freedom of Information Commission, 2 Conn. Ops. 1173 (Hartford, November 4, 1996).

Lewin v. Medical College of Hampton Roads, 910 F. Supp. 1161 (E.D. Va. 1996); 931 F. Supp. 443 (E.D. Va. 1996).

*Miami University v. Miami Student (97-606), Certiorari—*Summary Disposition, 522 U.S., Monday, December 8, 1997.

Obersteller v. Flour Bluff Independent School District, 874 F. Supp. 146 (S.D. Tex. 1994).

Red and Black Publishing Company v. Board of Regents, 427 S.E. 2d 257 (Ga. 1993).

Shreveport Professional Chapter of the Society of Professional Journalists and Michelle Millhollon v. Louisiana State University et al., Unpublished (La. Dist. Ct., Caddo Parish, March 4, 1994).

State ex rel. The Miami Student et al. v. Miami University, __Ohio St. 3d__ (Oh. 1997).

Stephen Selkirk v. University of Oklahoma et al., Case No. CJ 94-1514 BH, Unpublished minute op. (Okla. Dist Ct., Cleveland Cty. November 7, 1994).

Student Bar Association Board of Governors, Etc. v. Byrd. 239 S.E. 2d 415 (Supreme Court of North Carolina 1977).

Student Press Law Center v. Alexander, 778 F. Supp.1227 (D.D.C. 1991).

Umstead v. Town of Webb Union Free School District Board of Education, 1994 WL 396194 (N.D.N.Y. July 13, 1994).

United States of America v. The Miami University and Ohio State University, Case number C298-0097 (S.D. Oh., January 23, 1998).

Part Two

Student Conduct Issues

Chapter IV

Adjudicating
Campus Sexual Assault Cases

Patricia S. Terrell

In recent years, most college judicial proceedings involving the adjudication of sexual assault cases have been vilified in the popular press. Depending on the writer's and the reader's perspective, the proceedings appear to be flawed and biased toward either the survivor/victim or the accused. Comments from members of the legal profession, notably district attorneys, focus on the inadequacy of college judicial proceedings to adjudicate such cases citing the lack of legal training of judicial officers, the absence of judicial safeguards for the accused routinely available in the courts, and the limited role of attorneys in campus judicial cases, just to mention a few.

However, even though few survivors/victims choose to file charges through the campus judicial system, even fewer choose to file charges in the criminal courts. And in no way should adjudication of a campus sexual assault prevent or discourage the victim/survivor from pursuing concurrent charges in the criminal and/or civil courts. The student judicial system is not a substitute for the criminal and civil courts but an additional alternative for survivors/victims when the accused is a college student.

All of the criticisms notwithstanding, sexual assaults and acquaintance rape are violations of law and student codes of conduct. Universities cannot ignore their responsibility to provide a safe environment where all students are free to pursue their educational goals. Although research reports vary on the magnitude of the problem of sexual assault on college campuses, it is widely assumed that sexual assault is the most underreported crime on campus and violation of student codes of conduct. Colleges must provide a means of holding students accountable for violations of their own student codes. Although some cases adjudicated by campus judicial systems involve male students as survivors/victims, the overwhelming majority of survivors/victims are female. When a student is sexually assaulted, whether by a stranger or an acquaintance, the student has several options. The student may choose to: (a) file criminal charges through the legal system; (b) file civil charges through the legal system; (c) file charges through the campus judicial system; (d) file concurrent charges through all three; and (e) mediation. For those survivors/victims who do not choose to file charges through the judiciary, mediation provides "benefits that hearings based on legal models cannot" (Sisson and Todd, 1995, p. 263).

Mediation can provide "the survivor/victim an opportunity to confront the accused in a safe environment and to regain a feeling of control in her life. At the same time, it allows the accused a chance to examine his behavior with less need to be defensive" (Sisson and Todd, 1995, p. 264). (For a discussion on the procedures and conditions for mediation in sexual assault cases and its use on a specific campus, see Sisson and Todd, 1995.) Of course, survivors/victims may also choose to do nothing.

Although campus sexual assault cases continue to be the most underreported crime occurring on college campuses, the *Chronicle of Higher Education* reported that forcible sex offenses increased 3.1% at 796 campuses which responded to a 1995 survey (February 3, 1995). Authorities are unsure whether the actual number of sexual assaults has increased or whether more survivors/victims are coming forward to report them as a result of heightened media attention and better educational programming at the secondary and collegiate levels. Regardless of the reason, an increase in reported sexual assaults may effect an increase in adjudication through the campus judicial system.

Adjudicating sexual assault cases, regardless of the venue in which the charges are heard and whether the accused is a stranger or an acquaintance of the survivor/victim, is especially problematic for a variety of reasons: (a) usually there is no physical evidence of the sexual assault, e.g., a rape kit test; (b) the assault may be reported weeks or months afterward, thwarting the timely collection of testimony and evidence; (c) there are often no witnesses to the actual incident; (d) witness statements on the behavior and actions of the survivor/victim and accused prior to and following the incident may be contradictory; (e) one or both parties may have been drinking alcohol thus affecting their memory and perceptions of the incident; and (f) the survivor/victim may have "frozen" in fear preventing her from physically or verbally expressing her non-consent while the accused may not have verbally asked for consent and interpreted the survivor/victim's silence and inaction as consent.

Burling (1993) notes that in some states, the "lack of objection by a woman is not evidence of consent" (p.14) while in other states, if a woman is responsive and doesn't communicate her objections, it is not a sexual assault. As a result, it is usually difficult to ascertain the facts from the evidence and testimony in these cases. The resulting decision is often based on who is the more credible and believable, the survivor/complainant or the accused.

In recent years, Congress and many state governments have attempted to ensure that survivors/victims and the accused, to a lesser extent, are afforded essential rights in the adjudication of their campus sexual assault cases. The Crime Awareness and Campus Security Act of 1990 requires collection and reporting of sex offenses, including forcible and non-forcible rape and sexual assault. The Higher Education Amendments of 1992 (Public Law 102-325) outline general requirements for adjudicating sexual assault cases, including: (a) the development of a sexual assault policy; (b) procedures for reporting a sexual offense; (c) educational programs to heighten awareness; (d) identification of possible sanctions assessed against a student found guilty or responsible of a sexual offense; (e) procedures for a campus judicial hearing; (f) making sure the complainant is aware of their right to notify law enforcement personnel; (g) availability of counseling services for survivors/victims; and (h) offering options in having the complainant's class and housing assignments changed if they are reasonably available (Quinn, 1994). Of course, any state legislation regarding the adjudication of campus sexual assault cases should also be a part of any policies, procedures, or educational efforts offered by the institution.

The courts have continued to affirm the right of educational institutions to discipline their students through their own judicial process. [Goss v. Lopez (1975)]. The NASPA (1993) *Statement Concerning Campus Disciplinary Procedures and the Criminal Law in Sexual Assault Cases* noted that "Universities conduct disciplinary hearings in order to promote and preserve a harmonious academic community conducive to learning"(p. 2). The *Statement* also noted "The college has a strong interest in disciplining students or others who disrupt the academic community whether or not the same conduct has been or could be punished under the criminal law. The university has the power to discipline a student for sexual assault even though the same student was also tried in the criminal courts" (NASPA, 1993, p. 2).

This decision was more recently affirmed in *Ahlum v. Tulane University* (1993), in which a student brought suit against Tulane University after he was found guilty of sexual assault in a campus judicial hearing. The Court found that although "the student was not permitted to be represented by legal counsel, the assistant director of residence life presented the university's version of the facts, there was some conflicting testimony whether the act was consensual, and the tape recorder malfunctioned," Tulane's disciplinary procedures "go well beyond that required of public schools" (Gehring, 1993, p. 6). Although the student was not afforded legal counsel, the Court noted that Tulane was not represented by legal counsel. Since the procedures were designed to be nonadversarial, having a university staff member present the university's version of the facts was "not offensive" (Gehring, 1993, p. 6). Even though the tape recorder malfunctioned, there was over 100 pages of testimony and investigative reports available to the appeals committee for their review. And lastly, even though there was conflicting testimony regarding whether the intercourse was consensual, the court found that "Clearly, the board had before it ample evidence to suggest that Ahlum's conduct was a breach of Tulane's standards of conduct" (Gehring, 1993, p. 6).

It is important to note that Tulane University is a private institution. Many state institutions have decided to allow the accused student the right to consult legal counsel when criminal charges against the student are pending. Most universities still do not permit the accused student to be represented by legal counsel at a campus judicial hearing, even when criminal charges are pending. In *Osteen v. Henley* (1993), the United States Court of Appeals for the Seventh Circuit, said:

The most interesting question is whether there is a right to counsel, somehow derived from the due process clause of the Fourteenth Amendment, in student disciplinary proceedings. An old case (by the standards of constitutional law) says yes (*Black Coalition v. Portland State District No. 1*, 1973), but the newer cases say no. At most the student has a right to get the advice of a lawyer; the lawyer need not be allowed to participate in the proceeding in the usual way of trial counsel, as by examining and cross-examining witnesses and addressing the tribunal.

Especially when the student faces potential criminal charges, it is at least arguable that the due process clause entitles him to *consult* [emphasis added] a lawyer, who might for example advise him to take the Fifth Amendment. The court went on to say that it was reluctant to further bureaucratize university judicial proceedings, and that universities had the right to operate "free of heavy-handed governmental, including judicial, interference" (*Osteen v. Henley*, 1993).

Generally, the prior sexual history of the complainant and the accused is irrelevant to the charges at hand. Some campuses exclude the prior sexual history of the complainant and the accused from the presentation of evidence. Many states have "rape shield laws" which prevent the presentation of such evidence in a criminal proceeding. Some universities have included a rule in their judicial procedures that the prior sexual history of the complainant may only be presented when the accused is asserting consent as a defense. Others, such as the University of North Carolina at Chapel Hill, have included a rule that "the complainant's prior sexual history can only be introduced into evidence when it pertained to 'the past history of the victim and the accused'" (*Synfax*, March 29, 1993, pp. 69-70). Judicial officers are encouraged to consult with their legal counsel for advice on the appropriate procedure to be followed on their own campus.

Although there is no right to remain silent in a campus judicial proceeding, some campuses have afforded this right to the accused, especially if there is pending criminal litigation (see *Picozzi v. Sandalow*, 1986).

THE ROLE OF UNIVERSITY LEGAL COUNSEL

Due to the egregiousness of the violation and the possibility of concurrent criminal and civil action, the judicial officer's best resource and advisor is the university legal counsel. It is suggested that the judicial officer meet with university legal counsel as soon thereafter as the incident is reported to campus authorities and schedule a regular meeting time to discuss progress and developments in the case. University legal counsel will probably have helpful suggestions on conducting the investigation, gathering evidence, and identifying any problems in the adjudication process unique to the case.

It is further recommended that all written communications with the involved students, their parents, or legal counsel, be cleared through university legal counsel. Legal counsel for the involved students generally should be directed to communicate with university legal counsel rather than the judicial officer. If the judicial officer chooses to meet with legal counsel for the involved students, the officer should consider having university legal counsel present as well. A written record of telephone conversations with the involved students, their parents, and their legal counsel, which includes the date and time of the telephone call and the issues discussed should be made immediately following the call. Of course, these records should also be shared with university legal counsel.

Lastly, it's generally a good idea to discuss any deviation from the written procedures with university legal counsel. Although any deviation from the written procedures should be discouraged, there may be an occasion that such a deviation is reasonable and is agreed to by both parties. For example, if one party requests a reasonable delay in the scheduling of the hearing, e.g., the complainant's father is out of the country and will not return for two weeks, it's a good idea to consult with university legal counsel.

REVIEW OF SEXUAL ASSAULT POLICIES AND PROCEDURES

The student code of conduct should include definitions of sexual assault and sexual misconduct. For an example of a broadly defined sexual misconduct offense, see Stoner, E. and Cerminara, K. (1994).

The definition of consent and what constitutes consent is still being debated on many campuses. "For example, it's not uncommon on a college campus for students to misunderstand each other about the issue of 'consent,' especially when both may be impaired by alcohol. A women may report to college officials that a male companion 'went too far,' while conceding she sent mixed signals" (*Synfax,* 1996, p. 482). Since it is common on college campuses for one or both parties to have drunk alcohol, universities should consider the issue of intoxication with regard to consent. Some student codes explicitly state that an intoxicated person is incapable of giving consent.

One of the most contentious issues regarding sexual assault cases, is the process of identifying hearing board members or hearing officers and what type of training hearing board members or officers should receive. Depending on the perspective of the complaining party, either the hearing board is insensitive to the survivor/victim due to lack of training or the hearing board is biased against the accused due to training that stresses sensitivity to the survivor/victim's issues. A good way to mediate these differences is to ensure that a male/female training team discusses the issues from a balanced perspective. Training should include such issues as values clarification, victimization, sexual assault and acquaintance rape education, questioning and investigative techniques, weighing the evidence, and standard of proof. Psychology faculty, counseling center staff, and rape crisis centers are good resources for identifying trainers.

The best time to ensure that procedures for adjudicating sexual assault cases are adequate and complete is before a case is reported. All too often universities decide to revise their procedures following adjudication of sexual assault cases due to the "inadequacy of the procedures." For purposes of this article, "procedures" is defined as a three-step process. The first step involves providing assistance and support to the survivor/victim and accused as soon as notice is brought of the incident which could occur prior to the filing of formal charges. The second step involves the filing of charges and the actual judicial hearing. The third step involves the appeal, if filed, and appropriate follow-up.

The Complaint

It is helpful to have a two-step process that provides the survivor/victim with the option of filing an informal complaint or a formal complaint. An informal complaint becomes a formal complaint when the survivor/victim decides to pursue the complaint through the judicial process as a complainant. When filing an informal complaint the survivor/victim gives a complete statement of the facts of the incident, is offered an opportunity to have their housing assignment changed, is offered counseling and/or the name of a support person on campus, and is offered an opportunity to have their classes changed, assuming the survivor/victim has a class with the alleged assailant and a class change is feasible. Also, it is generally a good idea to provide a written checklist of the legal and judicial options available to the survivor/victim. At this point, the alleged assailant may not be contacted, depending on the wishes of the survivor/victim. If, after considering the options available, the survivor/victim decides to pursue a formal charge through the judicial system, the judicial officer should then interview the accused and provide, at the minimum, a referral to counseling and/or the name of a support person, and discuss the judicial process thoroughly.

Step I. Informal Complaint

Survivor/Victim:

May provide a written statement of the incident to judicial officer;

Referred to counseling/rape crisis center;

Offered a housing reassignment and/or class reassignment, if the latter is feasible;

Given the name of an advocate/support/advisor on campus;

Provided with a checklist of options, including criminal, civil, student judicial; and mediation, if available;

Provided information on student judicial system and process;

Encouraged to seek legal counsel.

Alleged Assailant:

No contact unless requested to do so by survivor/victim.

Step II. Formal Complaint

Survivor/Victim, Now Complainant:

Expresses intention to pursue complaint;

Provides written statement on the incident;

Given information in writing on judicial system including investigation, hearing, time line, standard of proof, appeals process;

Advised against any contact with the accused and accused's friends/family;

Advised to report harassment by accused to judicial officer;

Notified of outcome of investigation;

Charges filed/charges not filed;

Hearing held;

Notified of outcome of hearing.

Alleged Assailant, Now Accused:

Contacted and informed of formal charge by complainant;

Referred to counseling;

Given the name of an advocate/supporter/advisor;

Encouraged to seek legal counsel;

Advised against any contact with the complainant and complainant's friends/family;

Advised that the complainant may file criminal and civil charges in addition to current student judicial charges;

Provided with information on student judicial system and process— including investigation, filing notice of charges, time line, standard of proof, and appeal process.;

Notified of outcome of investigation;

Charges filed/charges not filed;

Hearing held;

Notified of outcome of hearing and if found responsible, given information on appeals process.

Step III. Follow-up

Survivor/Victim, Now Complainant:

Notified in writing of outcome of appeal;

Provided on-going counseling assistance;

Alleged Assailant, Now Accused;

Notified in writing of outcome of appeal;

Provided on-going counseling assistance, if remains enrolled as a student.

The Investigation of the Allegations

Some universities do not investigate formal charges by a complainant and just proceed with the hearing with the burden of proving the case placed on the complainant. Others investigate the charges, determine whether it is likely that a violation has occurred and place the responsibility for proving the case against the accused on the judicial officer.

Once a formal charge is filed, an investigation usually follows. The investigation may be conducted by the judicial officer, a committee appointed by the judicial officer, and/or the campus police. Campus police will use their own standard protocols for investigation of an alleged criminal offense. However, if the investigation is being conducted by a judicial officer or committee of the university, the following protocols are recommended. Witnesses interviewed should be advised of confidentiality. The complainant and/or the accused should be interviewed separately and should be allowed to be accompanied to the interviews by either their parents, friends, or university assigned advisor. They may request that they be accompanied during the interview by their legal counsel.

If university policy permits the presence of legal counsel, the judicial officer/investigating committee should also be accompanied by university legal counsel. This is suggested as a safeguard for the judicial officer/investigating committee and ensures a level playing field. Each interview should be documented in writing by the interviewer. Once all available evidence is gathered and weighed and all appropriate witnesses interviewed, if it is likely that a violation of the student code of conduct has occurred, then the university proceeds to schedule a hearing.

The Hearing

Timely, written notice of the hearing should be sent to both the accused and the complainant and should include the date, time, and location of the hearing, whether the hearing is closed or open, the names, identities, and a brief summary of all witnesses' testimony, and copies of all documents to be presented. The accused should be notified of the exact violation, including the page number from the appropriate student publication, the accused is alleged to have committed. A separate pre-hearing briefing is recommended for both the accused and the complainant to discuss the impending hearing.

A check-list of issues would include the following: confidentiality issues; ordering of the testimony and witnesses; standard of proof; role of legal counsel or other advisor, if permitted to attend; role of parents and/or support person; and appellate review procedures (see *Appendix A*). Who can appeal and the grounds for appeal should also be discussed during the pre-hearing briefing. It is important to establish reasonable expectations of the process for both the complainant and the accused.

The hearing board members or hearing officer should be selected based on a rotational system, if possible, with sensitivity to selecting a board based on a balanced gender and ethnic distribution representative of the campus community. The hearing board members should have no obvious biases, e.g., president of men against rape student organization, sorority sister of the complainant. At the beginning of the hearing, the process should include an opportunity for either party to challenge any hearing board member or officer whom they believe to be biased. Other issues to be covered at the beginning of the hearing include confidentiality issues, decorum of participants and witnesses, any scheduled breaks, and the ordering of the testimony and witnesses, among others.

Usually the complainant presents her case first followed by the accused. Some universities allow both the complainant and the accused to make brief opening statements, followed by the presentation of the complainant's case against the accused including calling any witnesses for the complainant; and then the accused's case, including calling any witnesses for the accused; with closing statements made first by the complainant and then the accused. The burden of proof is on the accuser or the complainant.

The standard of proof used in student judicial cases varies from "preponderance of the evidence," a lower standard, to "clear and convincing," a higher standard. It is not recommended that universities use the legal standard of "beyond a reasonable doubt." However, the same standard of proof used for other violations of the student code of conduct should be used for sexual assault cases. Creating a double standard whereby different standards of proof are used based on the violation that has allegedly occurred, is sure to be suspect and open to criticism on the basis of political correctness. Pavela (1992) recommends that, at the minimum, a preponderance of the evidence should be the standard of proof used for a finding of guilt or responsibility.

At the end of the hearing and before the hearing board or hearing officer recesses to begin deliberations, the chair of the hearing board or the hearing officer should ask that any questions regarding policies or procedures be directed to a third party, e.g., the judicial officer or dean of students. Parents, friends, and witnesses for the accused and the complainant should be advised against making any comments to, or having any conversations with, any member of the hearing board following the hearing.

Recently, at one university, a hearing board member reported to the dean of students that he had been approached by a member of the accused's family as he was leaving the building where the hearing was held (and prior to deliberations). The hearing board member did not allow the family member's comments to affect his decision but was uncomfortable and was unsure how the complainant and the complainant's family would view such comments, if they had observed them. Fortunately, the judicial notebook and training procedures for hearing board members at this university required that they report any such contact to the dean of students. As a result, this admonition was added at the end of each hearing.

Most universities maintain a record of the hearing by audiotape. If an audio taping system is used, the system should be set up by professional media staff with microphones placed strategically to record all comments with a back-up recorder left in the hearing room if the system fails. Many an appellate board has met to hear the audiotape of a hearing only to learn that the batteries didn't work or the microphone was of such poor quality that words were indistinguishable! Video taping the hearing is not recommended since it can provide a chilling atmosphere for both parties as well as judicial board members.

Once the hearing board or officer has determined whether the accused is guilty or responsible (some campuses use the term "responsible" or "not responsible" rather than guilty or innocent to distinguish the procedures from a criminal case) for the specified charges, a written copy of their decision should be sent to both the accused and the complainant, with information to the accused on how to file an appeal, or schedule an appointment to discuss how to file an appeal, if appropriate. It is also recommended that the accused, if found guilty or responsible, "should be given a short statement of reasons for the judgment" (Pavela, 1992, p.278). It's also a good idea to review the written decision with university legal counsel before it's mailed (*Synfax*, May 9, 1994). Following the appeal, the accused and complainant should be notified in writing of the appellate decision.

Common Complaints About Adjudicating Campus Sexual Assault Cases

Campus groups, especially special interest groups, often report feeling that administrators, judicial officers, and judicial board members are insensitive to either the complainant or the accused. It's important to not revictimize the survivor/victim in the judicial process and to remember that the accused is not responsible until proven responsible. Counseling support for both is important to provide a fair and objective system.

Oftentimes, the complainant or the accused has unrealistic expectations about the process and the outcome, the standard of proof, the timetable, etc. Clear, detailed communication between the judicial officer, counseling staff, and advocate/supporter and the participants is essential.

The definition of sexual assault, sexual misconduct, and sexual offense may be criticized for being too broad or overly vague. Some definitions read exactly like the criminal statues and others define sexual assault as only "sexual intercourse against the will of the individual." Both extremes should be avoided. Consultation with university legal counsel, faculty, administrators, and students is key in developing a definition that is workable and understandable.

A few years ago several university students complained publicly in the national press that they had not been advised of their right, and in fact, had been discouraged from filing concurrent criminal and civil charges. In another case, an accused student reported that university officials told him he did not need a lawyer. A checklist of rights and options for both complainants and accused ensures that all parties are advised and encouraged to investigate all options. Also, referral of the complainant to a sexual assault counselor/advisor and the accused to a counselor/advisor provides another safeguard to ensure that both are adequately advised of their rights and options by a neutral third party.

Murphy's Law also applies to student judicial hearings. One judicial officer spent weeks investigating a sexual assault case only to learn during the hearing that another student, who had since left the university, was an inadvertent witness to the assault. The hearing board decided to recess and grant an extension of time to allow the judicial officer an opportunity to contact and interview the witness. Of course, the accused objected to the delay but the decision of the hearing board prevailed. Procedures for handling judicial cases should include how additional evidence, which becomes available after the hearing has commenced, will be considered. Also, illnesses of hearing board members, particularly if the hearing is protracted, should also be covered in the judicial procedures.

It is important to caution the accused against having any contact with the complainant and channeling all communication through the judicial officer. The accused should also be advised that the accused's friends should not have any contact with the complainant. Such contact, however well intentioned, could easily be interpreted as harassment or intimidation.

Although every attempt is made to maintain confidentiality of the charges and the proceedings, it is not unusual for a friend of a friend of the accused or the complainant to blab to the news media or others on campus. The judicial officer should explain to both the accused and the complainant what precautions the judicial office takes to ensure confidentiality but that if friends of either party discuss the case with others, there's no realistic way to ensure that the process stays confidential. Both parties should be advised against discussing the case with the media while the case is in process. While this may appear that the university has something to hide, it prevents the case from being tried in the media, who may be one step ahead of the campus judiciary, and two steps behind in having all of the available information.

One of the most common complaints about student judicial proceedings is the perceived lack of training of the judicial officer and the hearing board and/or hearing officer. The job description for the student judicial officer should include the education, knowledge, and experience required to successfully fulfill the role of adjudicating campus judicial cases. Even if the job required an attorney by training, there is no basis for concluding that legal training will ensure a fair and effective process. And, of course, members of juries have no training on sexual assault or victimization, yet are selected to sit on juries that hear these cases.

Legal counsel for the complainant and the accused will probably argue that the university jeopardizes the rights of the accused if the university hears student judicial charges against the accused before criminal and or civil charges. Criminal and civil charges can take months or years to wind their way through the justice system. In the meantime, an accused student is going to class, perhaps living in the residence halls, and participating in out-of-class activities. The university has an obligation to its own community to ensure students' safety. It is usually in the university's best interest to adjudicate student judicial charges as expeditiously as possible.

One of the great fallacies of sexual assault cases is the perception that the university or university administrators have a vested interest in the outcome. Although this may be the perception, especially when student athletes or other high profile students are accused, it is important that the judicial officer follow the same written process and procedures used for all sexual assault allegations. It should be noted that once the press obtains information about an alleged sexual assault and perhaps even the identity of the complainant and the accused, the judicial officer has the same responsibility to uphold issues of confidentiality as defined by the Family Educational Rights and Privacy Act.

Role of the Media

Although the majority of sexual assault cases on a college campus are handled outside the glare of media attention, the media may become aware of and interested in the case if it comes to their attention either through the filing of concurrent criminal or civil charges or when notified by either the complainant or accused. When the media inquires about a sexual assault case, the media should be referred to a university spokesperson. This person may be the student judicial officer or another student affairs or public relations staff person. Public relations and university legal counsel should approve any press releases to the media. It's always acceptable to say to a reporter, "I don't know, I'll have to call you back" or "I can't answer that because there's a federal law called the Family Educational Rights and Privacy Act which protects the confidentiality of student records and restricts the release of student judicial information."

Before giving an interview to the media, it's a good idea to list objectives you want to accomplish in your interview. For example, you may want to convey the importance of allowing a complainant the opportunity to file concurrent charges in the campus judicial system as well as in the criminal and civil courts. Usually reporters will be satisfied with information about the student judicial system and the process and respect the university's right to confidentiality about a specific case. Send copies of any news releases to both the complainant and the accused and keep them appraised of media inquiries. Neither should be surprised by something in the newspaper.

While the case is still in process, brainstorm outcomes with university legal counsel and public relations staff. Discuss how the institution will respond and what it will say in each of the different scenarios. For example, what will be the university's response if the accused is found not guilty/not responsible by the campus judiciary but guilty in the criminal courts, or vice versa. Educating the public and the media about the differences between the two systems and why there could be different outcomes is an important role.

Follow-up

Counseling support should continue to be offered to the complainant for as long as the complainant desires (consistent with university policy). Counseling support for the accused should continue through the appellate stage and as long as the accused is enrolled. Of course, if the accused's enrollment is terminated, counseling support would no longer be available.

SUMMARY

Regardless of how conscientiously the judicial officer has followed every procedure, afforded every viable fundamental fairness to both parties, and has worked with the highest standards of professionalism, integrity, and sensitivity—criticism of the way the case was adjudicated is likely to occur. As stated at the beginning of this article, sexual assault cases are, by their very nature, contentious and divisive. Don't take the resulting criticism personally. Short of mediation, it's impossible to find a win-win solution for both parties.

The professional goals of the student judicial officer should be threefold: (1) continue to enhance the officer's own professional development in related issues; (2) continue to seek ways to improve the adjudication of sexual assault cases; and (3) continue to educate the larger community on sexual assault issues and campus judicial systems.

Lastly, although the officer may know the code, the process, and the procedures by heart and know the legal foundations from front to back, there is no substitute for a caring, compassionate administrator!

Appendix A

Sample Student Judicial Pre-Hearing Briefing Checklist for Accused and Complainant

❑ Provided a copy of the student code of conduct and student judicial procedures

❑ Reviewed the hearing format on pages . . .

❑ Submitted a list of witnesses whose testimony will be presented, in person, and all documents and evidence that will be presented, in writing, at the hearing. These should be provided to the judicial office by (deadline date and time). Each party will receive a copy of the other party's list and copies of all evidence that will be submitted at the hearing __ hours before the commencement of the hearing

❑ Rights provided to the accused and the complainant include: (1) to be present throughout the hearing; (2) to question and cross examine all witnesses; (3) to be informed, in writing, of the outcome of the hearing; and (4) not to have the sexual history of either party discussed during the hearing. However, evidence of a recent consensual sexual relationship between the accused and the complainant may be considered if the accused asserts consent as a defense.

(*Note:* Consult university counsel regarding the language here to ensure its compliance with state rape shield laws.)

❑ Hearing will take place even if the accused does not attend. The university may choose to drop the charges against the accused if the complainant does not attend.

(*Note:* While some universities may choose to drop charges if the complainant does not attend the hearing since the university's case is based in large part on the eyewitness testimony of the complainant. In these cases, it is unlikely that a hearing board would find the accused student responsible for sexual assault without the first person testimony of the complainant. However, the university may decide to hold the hearing without the complainant if there is sufficient evidence, e.g., witnesses to the assault, to proceed. A statement similar to the above which offers the option to the university is recommended.)

❑ The hearing officer is a (faculty/staff/student/retired judge). *OR* The hearing board is composed of (composition, e.g., 3 students, 1 faculty and 1 staff member).

❑ Hearings are closed/open

❑ One support person from the university community (faculty, staff, or student) may attend. *OR* The judicial advisor chosen by the accused/assigned to the accused may attend.

This person may not participate in the hearing and cannot speak or write notes to the accused. *OR* This person may only advise the accused but not participate in the hearing through questioning, speaking, etc. *OR* This person may speak on behalf of the accused and participate fully in the hearing.

(*Note:* It is a good idea to clarify the role of an advisor for the accused and complainant before the hearing.)

❑ Parents may also attend as support persons and observers. However, they may not speak or write notes to the accused or the complainant or otherwise participate in the hearing. Parents that are disruptive may be asked to leave the hearing.

❑ Neither the accused nor the complainant may be represented by legal counsel.

❑ The standard of proof for student judicial cases is preponderance of the evidence *OR* clear and convincing.

❑ The hearing will/will not be audio/video taped. A copy of the tape/transciption of the tape is available to the accused or the complainant at their expense.

❑ The decision of the hearing board will be sent by mail to the accused and the complainant as soon as it is available. If found responsible, the accused will be provided information on the appellate process. Only the accused may appeal. The appeal will be reviewed by the (appellate body) which is composed of (composition). The decision of the appellate body is final. *OR* In addition, the accused may appeal the decision of the appellate body to the president whose decision is final.

(*Note:* A university may decide to allow either party to appeal the decision. It's important to be consistent and treat sexual assault cases the same as other judicial cases).

❑ Demeanor, attitude, and decorum are important and the board may take them into consideration. Questions about the process or procedures should be addressed to the hearing officer/hearing board chairperson. The chairperson may remove any individual who is disruptive or fails to follow guidelines set by the chairperson.

Student's Signature: _____ Date: _____

I understand that my signature acknowledges review of the above information regarding the hearing and appellate process.

References

Burling, P. (1993). *Acquaintance rape on campus: A model for institutional response.* Washington, DC: National Association of College and University Attorneys.

Gehring, D. (1993, October). Abreast of the law. *NASPA Forum,* p. 6

Lederman, D. (1995). Colleges Report Rise in Violent Crime. *Chronicle of Higher Education.* XLI (21). pp. A31, A42.

National Association of Student Personnel Administrators (1993). Statement concerning campus disciplinary procedures and the criminal law in sexual assault cases. Washington, DC: author, p. 2.

Pavela, G. (1992). Should colleges resolve sexual assault cases. *Synthesis: Law and Policy in Higher Education,* 4 (2), 276-278.

Pavela, G. (Ed.) (1993). More on sexual assault policies. *Synfax,* March 29, 1993, (93.71), pp. 69-70.

Pavela, G. (Ed.) (1994). Resolving sexual misconduct complaints in the 1990s. *Synfax,* May 9, 1994, (94.42), pp. 226-230.

Quinn, E. (1994). *Everything you wanted to know about the campus security act.* Outline of address presented at the NACUA Conference, October 6-8, 1994, Salt Lake City, UT (author).

Sisson, V. & Todd, S. (1995). Using mediation in response to sexual assault on college and university campuses. *NASPA Journal,* 32 (4), 262-269.

Stoner, E. & Cerminara, K. (1994). Harnessing the "spirit of insubordination": A model student disciplinary code. *Journal of College and University Law,* 17 (2), 89-121

Cases

Ahlum v. Tulane University. 617 So.2d 96 (La. App. 4th Cir. 1993).

Goss v. Lopez, 419 U.S. 565, 580 (1975).

Osteen v. Henley, 13 F.3d 221 (1993 U.S. App.).

Piccozzi v. Sandalow, 623 F. Supp. 1571, D.C. Mich., 1986.

Chapter V

Addressing Relationship Violence

Carolyn J. Palmer

Most violence occurs at home, at school, at work, and in other environments that are familiar to the people involved, and the people involved are generally familiar with each other. For example, Grayson (1993) emphasized that "relatives attack relatives and neighbors attack neighbors more often than one stranger attacks another stranger from a different part of town" (pp. 140-141). Similarly, violence on campus is more likely to involve students and employees who know each other than to be perpetrated by strangers who are "outsiders" to the institution.

College and university employees have not been immune from the increased frequency and severity of violence that threatens the campus as a workplace (Willits, 1994). In fact, some of the more alarming incidents reported in recent news headlines have involved faculty, administrators, residence hall staff, and other employees who were killed or seriously injured as a result of workplace violence. Although such incidents may be adjudicated in criminal courts, colleges and universities, through student judicial affairs, commonly address violence committed by students against other students, faculty, and administrators on campus. This chapter will focus primarily on what various studies conducted by the Campus Violence Prevention Center (Sherrill & Siegel, 1989) have identified as the most common form of violence on campus: student-to-student violence.

In its broadest sense, relationship violence encompasses all violence involving persons who have biological, marital, dating, working, academic, and any number of other types of relationships with each other. For example, conflicts between family members, neighbors, roommates, classmates, acquaintances, and even friends may result in acts of physical violence. However, the term "relationship violence" has come to be defined more narrowly as violence involving individuals who are married, partnered, living together, dating each other, or otherwise engaged in romantic or potentially romantic relationships. Many associate the term "domestic violence" with husbands and wives and, to a lesser extent, non-married partners who live together. An equivalent term that applies to many traditional-age, single college students is "courtship violence." Generally included as common forms of courtship violence are not only assault and battery, but also "date rape" and other types of sexual violence.

Although violence undoubtedly occurs between partners in some same-sex couples, most of the relationship violence that comes to the attention of college officials involves heterosexual couples: spouses (particularly if on-campus housing is provided for married students) and, to a much greater extent, dating partners, boyfriends and girlfriends, or ex-boyfriends and ex-girlfriends.

Common Factors Associated with Relationship Violence

Regardless of the exact nature of the relationship in question, incidents of relationship violence on campus tend to have several elements in common:

1. Disproportionate numbers of incidents, particularly the more serious ones, involve men's violence against women.
2. Incidents are commonly associated with the use or abuse of alcohol or other drugs by the perpetrators and/or victims.
3. Relationship violence generally occurs in a private location and is considered a private act that is "nobody else's business."
4. On-the-scene confrontation and intervention represent major challenges to police and "front line" staff.
5. Victims seldom officially report incidents or pursue disciplinary or criminal charges.
6. Cases that are reported and pursued within the institution's discipline system or the criminal justice system are very difficult to adjudicate.

Each of these common factors, along with their relationships to each other, will be addressed in the following sections of this chapter.

Men and Women as Perpetrators and Victims

Many, perhaps most, college judicial officers have dealt with incidents of violence that were committed by women students. In fact, in their book entitled *Campus Violence: Kinds, Causes, and Cures*, Whitaker and Pollard (1993) noted that women are increasingly becoming involved in the perpetration of violence. Nevertheless, they emphasized that female students are currently "the principal victims of campus violence" (p. xi) and that male students are "the most frequent immediate perpetrators of campus violence" (p. xiii).

Similar conclusions regarding the relationship of gender to campus violence resulted from a study involving 374 resident assistants (RAs) at twelve institutions (Palmer, 1995, 1996). Of the violent incidents that RAs described as the "most serious" incidents they had encountered (and where the genders of victims and perpetrators were identified), 90% involved male perpetrators, whereas 75% involved female victims. Only 7% of the violence against men (none of it sexual violence) was committed by women, all of whom were identified as "girlfriends." In contrast, 88% of the violence against women was committed by men.

More specifically, the "most serious" violent incidents victimizing women included rape or sexual assault (38%), assault and battery committed by men identified as "boyfriends" or "ex-boyfriends" (22%), violence by men whose relationships to victims were unspecified in the incident descriptions provided by the RAs (28%), and violence perpetrated by other women (12%).

In addition, this study found that men's violence against women was more injurious than women's violence against men. For example, the most injurious violence against a man by a woman involved being "slapped across the face by his girlfriend." Reports of men's violence against women also included slapping, though always in terms of "slapping [a woman] around." More commonly, men's violence was described as "punching," "kicking," or "beating up" women; "throwing" women across rooms, down stairs, or up against walls; or otherwise "attacking" or "assaulting" women in such a way as to break bones (particularly noses, jaws, and ribs), knock out teeth, and create other injuries requiring stitches or other forms of medical treatment (Palmer, 1995).

It is assumed that most college administrators, particularly judicial officers, are familiar with sex role socialization processes and other socio-cultural realities that foster aggression in men and submission in women. Further, it is assumed that they have a working knowledge of the rape trauma syndrome, the battered woman syndrome, and other psycho-social consequences of victimization that make it particularly difficult for women to report that the "significant other" men in their lives have physically harmed them and to seek justice in terms of ensuring that such men are held accountable for their actions. Thus, these and other issues linking gender to violence and victimization will not be fully examined in this chapter. However, readers may wish to note that Whitaker and Pollard (1993) devoted several chapters and chapter segments to these issues.

The Roles of Alcohol and Other Drugs

Many college administrators have recently been alerted to the dangers of Rohypnol ("rope," "roofies") and Gamma Hydroxybutyrate

(GHB), described as "the date rape drugs" (George Mason University, 1996, p. 1). Clearly, the potential impact of these powerful sedatives and other illicit drugs on our campuses should not be minimized or ignored. However, it is emphasized that "the" date rape drug of choice among college students is alcohol. Alcohol has long been used as a weapon against women's reluctance to engage in various sexual activities. Most students are undoubtedly familiar with the message reflected in a poster found on many campuses. This poster, described by Ellison, O'Shaughnessey, and Palmer (1991), shows a bikini-clad young woman holding a beer and has a caption reading, "If at first you don't succeed, give her another drink." If such advice is followed until individuals are rendered incapable of giving consent to sexual activities that occur, then alcohol may be considered a weapon for committing sexual offenses.

A national survey of over 17,000 students on 140 campuses (Wechsler, 1996) found that 19% of all students frequently "binged" (defined as having consumed five or more drinks in a row for men, and four or more drinks in a row for women). Of these students, 41% reported that they had engaged in unplanned sexual activity (compared to 8% of the students who drank, but did not binge). Wechsler emphasized that "when women abuse alcohol, they increase their risk of becoming victimized by unwanted or unprotected sex" (p. 23) and that women are especially at risk for experiencing "secondhand" effects, defined as problems resulting from someone else's drinking. Such problems may include unwanted sexual advances and various forms of violence.

One study conducted at a large university found that 62% of the non-sexual batteries associated with courtship violence were committed by men who had been drinking and that, when sexual assaults occurred, 71% of the women and 81% of the men had been drinking (Ellison et al., 1991). Although exact percentages generally vary from 50% to 95%, depending on a number of factors associated with specific studies, researchers tend to agree that alcohol is involved in the majority of violent crimes on campus.

Alcohol abuse contributes to the underreporting of sexual and other relationship violence. For example, consider the following reasons women students gave for not reporting rape:

1. I was so blitzed I couldn't even remember it. I just woke up half-naked on this guy's bed. At first I tried to deny that the worst had happened while I was passed out . . . but then I found out I was pregnant.

2. I begged and pleaded with him not to, but he did it anyway. Still, there was a part of me that kept wondering if it was my own fault for drinking so much I got myself into the situation in the first place.

The Administration of Campus Discipline . . .

3. Who would believe me? People usually think the woman asked for it. I know I didn't, but I also know I was so drunk I never saw it coming and couldn't stop it.

4. It was the first time I had sex, and I felt completely stripped of my dignity. I kept telling him to let go of me, but he wasn't listening. I'd had too much to drink and didn't have the strength to keep pushing him off me. I felt so dirty and so ashamed. How could I have let this happen?

5. What good would it have done? So a guy got a girl drunk and took advantage of her. What else is new? This has happened to almost every girl I know. (Ellison et al., 1991, p. 4)

Relationship Violence as a Private Act

Privacy issues contribute to the facts that sexual violence on campus has been referred to as a "hidden epidemic" (Ellison et al., 1991, p. 1) and victims of courtship violence have been referred to as "hidden victims" (Bogal-Allbritten & Allbritten, 1989, p. 201). . For example, this violence seldom occurs in public or quasi-public places where witnesses may be present. Instead, it most often occurs "behind closed doors," in part because it is considered a private matter of concern only to the individuals directly involved. Others who become aware of the violence and express concern or offer assistance are usually told that they should mind their own business, that they are imagining things (i.e., the violence is denied), or that the perpetrator didn't mean it (e.g., "was just drunk and out of control") and/or is sorry and promises never to do it again.

Possible exceptions, for which a few may even claim bragging rights within some segments of the student subculture, may involve sexual conquests or other violence that perpetrators feel justified in committing on the grounds that victims start it, deserve it, ask for it, or mean "yes" even though they keep saying "no." However, most relationship violence remains a secret or is excused, minimized, or denied by the perpetrators and/or victims.

Because intervention is often confused with "meddling" in the personal affairs of others, even those who do witness or obtain information about incidents may not want to "get involved" or to report what they know to college officials. Privacy issues also discourage victims from reporting relationship violence. For example, consider the following reasons for not reporting incidents:

1. Nobody else saw him smacking me around, so it would just be my word against his. He'd be innocent unless proven guilty, and I had no proof. It's as simple as that.

2. I was an ignorant freshman. I didn't know what to do, and I was too scared to do anything. I figured it would be easier to go through

it alone than go through the trauma of telling people. Besides, I knew the police couldn't do anything, since I didn't have any witnesses. (Ellison et al., 1991, p. 5)

The Challenges of On-Scene Confrontations and Interventions

Many perpetrators and even some victims strongly believe that others have no right to interfere with the very personal and private act of relationship violence. Because attempts to intervene may be greeted by verbal threats and/or physical assaults, even police officers who have been well-trained and are armed or otherwise capable of defending themselves may experience varying degrees of anxiety when called to the scene of domestic or courtship violence. Thus, it is understandable that staff and witnesses who are not as well prepared to deal with such violence may be afraid to confront it and/or to report it.

What happens, for example, when courtship violence occurring in residence halls comes to the attention of a staff member? Most live-in staff, including resident assistants (RAs), have been trained to call police immediately in cases of violence. However, it may be very difficult for a caring person (particularly a man) to stand by and watch someone (particularly a woman) continue to be battered while waiting for police to arrive. As a result, even though perhaps with fear and trepidation, some residence hall staff may attempt to intervene. Consider the following incidents described by RAs in Palmer's (1995, 1996) study:

1. Someone's boyfriend was drunk and became violent toward her. When I confronted him he turned that violence toward me.

2. The other RA went to call the police while I followed them. I kept telling him to stop, but he dragged her by the hair down the stairs and continued to beat her out in the courtyard. It took two police officers and three staff members to subdue him. One officer was bitten and required medical attention.

3. An ex-boyfriend assaulted his ex-girlfriend on my floor ... When I tried to get him to leave, he threatened to kill both me and the resident.

4. A guy on my floor was slapping his girlfriend around, and when I tried to break it up, he threatened to beat my ___. Truthfully, it scared the ___ out of me.

The Under-Reporting of Relationship Violence

One reason that the magnitude of the problem of relationship violence on campus remains "hidden" is that only a fraction of the incidents that occur are reported to police or college officials. Among the primary reasons that victims do not report relationship violence are:

1. Fear of retaliation by perpetrators who have already demonstrated their ability and willingness to harm them and/or threatened further harm if incidents are reported;
2. Lack of faith in "the system," referring to both the institutional judicial system and the criminal justice system, to respond appropriately; and
3. A wide variety of other cognitive, affective, and behavioral responses to victimization.

The first two reasons overlap or interact in the sense that many victims and witnesses alike do not believe that "the system" can adequately ensure their safety. The following incidents described by RAs serve as examples:

1. One of my students was raped. Friends took her to the hospital, but she didn't want police involved. She knew that even if the rapist was arrested, he'd be out on bail until his case went to court, and she was afraid of what he would do to her if she talked to the police.
2. A male visitor beat up his ex-girlfriend, who lives on my floor. I called my supervisor and my supervisor called the police, but the woman refused to press charges because she was scared for her safety. The police officer assured her that they could get a protection order for her, but she still refused. (Palmer, 1996, p. 274)

Depending on the extent to which the system is "disrespectful, disbelieving, or unduly cumbersome," reporting an incident or pursuing charges against the perpetrator "may lead to emotional and cognitive outcomes which are as difficult to manage as were the original effects of the violence" (Roark, 1993, p. 21). Some of the effects discussed by Roark include somatic stress symptoms (e.g., headaches or stomach problems) and disturbances in eating, sleeping, memory, and concentration.

Some victims of relationship violence believe they "deserved" to be physically assaulted; for example, "It was my own fault; I never should have argued with him and made him mad." Roark (1993) suggested that self-blame is associated with feelings of guilt or shame, a loss of self-esteem, and a loss of faith in one's own judgment. Other symptoms of victimization include shock, fear, loss of trust in others, loss of a sense of justice and fairness in life, depression, helplessness, and despair (Roark, 1993). Initial reactions to violence also involve feeling numb, confused, and disoriented (Cerio, 1989). Perhaps as a result of any or all of the above reactions, some victims may, at least temporarily, be incapable of making decisions or taking actions that persons who have not experienced violence might consider to be rational, appropriate, or necessary. But regardless of the reasons, it seems clear that most incidents of relationship violence remain unreported.

Problems in the Adjudication of Cases of Relationship Violence

Although there may be many more unreported incidents of relationship violence that occurred than there are reported cases that did not occur, false reports do exist. And clearly all due process and other rights must be afforded to those who have been accused, as well as to those who have accused them. Regardless of how bizarre an allegation may seem or how meager the evidence may be, campus judicial officers must follow all procedures outlined by law and by institutional policy in thoroughly investigating and fairly adjudicating each and every reported incident.

The procedures in question are, of course, more difficult to implement when victims, witnesses, and others who may have knowledge of reported incidents do not cooperate with the disciplinary process. Unfortunately, for many of the reasons cited in the previous section in reference to non-reporting, it is not uncommon for those who initially report sexual or other relationship violence subsequently to withdraw their allegations and/or refuse to testify at judicial hearings. These cases may leave judicial officers and others feeling frustrated and helpless, particularly if they are left with insufficient evidence to remove from the campus individuals they have reason to believe may be rapists, batterers, or other violent criminals who may jeopardize the safety and security of the original victims or others within the campus community.

Even when all who have information about an incident provide such information to investigators and student judicial affairs officers, it may be very difficult to decipher what actually occurred. As noted earlier in this chapter, witnesses are seldom present when relationship violence occurs, so many cases involve weighing one person's word against another's. One or both could lie, but even if both tell the truth as they perceive it to be, their perceptions of what happened may differ considerably, even if both were completely sober at the time. And if one or both had been drinking, as is commonly the case, recollections of the incident may be clouded by the alcohol that had been consumed.

As a result, many who hear cases involving allegations of sexual offenses or relationship violence may lose sleep wondering whose description of the incident to believe. All that can reasonably be expected is that they hear all of the evidence and use their best judgment in determining whether or not the evidence indicates that the accused is responsible for the alleged violation.

Resistance vs. Commitment to Addressing Relationship Violence

One of the more disheartening concepts we may encounter in our quest to solve the problem of relationship violence, or at least minimize its occurrence, is expressed in the second portion of the chapter title "Cures for Campus Violence, If We Want Them" (Pollard & Whitaker, 1993). Sad to say, the authors of this chapter may be correct in suggesting that there is considerable resistance to campus violence reduction. Normally, one of the first steps in the problem-solving process is acknowledging that the problem exists. Yet some administrators continue to distort or deny the extent and seriousness of violence on their campuses. Indeed, some may believe that drunken revelry is a normal and acceptable part of the student experience, that "boys will be boys," that aggression cannot be restrained, that violence is inevitable, and that the personal freedoms of students should not be restricted, even when the behavioral manifestations of such freedoms hurt other people.

Pollard and Whitaker (1993) also noted the irony related to the observation that *in loco parentis* faded into history because students wanted to be treated as adults, whereas the resulting climate on some campuses allows students to avoid some of the responsibilities of adulthood. In fact, they suggested that some schools may not hold students accountable for their actions because they fear that enrollments of traditional age students may decline "if prospective students can not count on four years of suspended consequences for their behavior" (p. 288).

Even within institutional cultures that are generally supportive of standards for student conduct, judicial officers may encounter administrators, trustees, parents, or others who wish to trivialize disciplinary incidents, criticize disciplinary processes, and minimize disciplinary sanctions. Thus, professionals in student judicial affairs must be prepared to address conflicts based on a wide range of opinions regarding institutional responses to disciplinary incidents.

Many college presidents and other senior administrators have taken reasonable measures to address problems related to campus violence. However, it appears that some institutional officials, instead of claiming that they do not know what to do, should simply admit that they do not want to do what they know needs to be done to "cure" the epidemic of rape and other violence against women on their campuses. For example, some may not be motivated to provide educational programs that challenge male peer groups whose beliefs and attitudes support the superiority, dominance, and aggression of men and foster the objectification, exploitation, and victimization of women.

Some may not want to hire more security personnel or schedule more professional staff to work on campus at night and on weekends, when violence is most likely to occur. Some may not wish to vigorously enforce policies regarding underage drinking or effectively address problems related to alcohol abuse, perhaps in part due to fear that some students may pack their bags and move out of campus residence halls or even transfer to other schools where they believe they can drink more freely. And some may not be willing to "spoil students' fun" by providing appropriate supervision for fraternities and their parties or for other student groups and their activities, even when they are known or suspected to represent high risks for alcohol abuse and/or sexual violence.

Clearly, resistance to various endeavors designed to reduce the incidence of relationship violence takes many forms, including benign neglect of various problems and "doing nothing" in hopes that the problems will miraculously solve themselves. Degrees and types of resistance vary tremendously from one campus to another, depending largely on the visions, values, and commitments of institutional leaders. Among these leaders are student judicial officers, whose role in addressing relationship violence is enormous. Judicial officers should inform, enlighten, and influence others throughout the campus community and coordinate various endeavors designed to address the problems associated with sexual and other forms of relationship violence.

RECOMMENDATIONS FOR JUDICIAL OFFICERS
Make Prevention a Priority

Many of the duties of judicial officers are reactive in nature, as they are expected to investigate and adjudicate disciplinary incidents that have already occurred. However, becoming more proactive by devoting time and expertise to policy development and communication, student programming, staff training, and other prevention efforts may yield great benefits to students and others in the campus community, as well as to judicial officers themselves.

The old saying that "an ounce of prevention is worth a pound of cure" may sound trite, but it may also be an understatement when applied to relationship violence. Consequences of such violence include not only broken bones and other acute injuries that may soon heal, but long-term or permanent physical, mental, emotional, social, economic, and other injuries, some of them debilitating. And since there is no known cure for death resulting from homicide or suicide, prevention may indeed be worth life itself (i.e., priceless).

Identify High-Risk Groups and Target Prevention Efforts

Historically, campus rape awareness and other violence prevention efforts have focused on potential victims, whereas comparatively little attention has been devoted to the very persons whose violence was to be prevented. However, it is my personal belief that, just as persons of color cannot (do not have the power to and should not be expected to) solve the problem of racism, women cannot (do not have the power to and should not be expected to) solve the problem of men's violence against women. To be sure, it is important to continue to inform women of issues related to relationship violence, high-risk behaviors associated with the probability of rape, and strategies for maximizing their personal safety. However, men must contribute to the effort to stop other men from raping and assaulting women.

Fortunately, in the recent past, increased attention has been given to developing rape education programs specifically for college men. In fact, many institutions provide training sessions for male peer educators who volunteer to present rape awareness programs on men's floors in residence halls, in fraternity houses, and to other groups of male students. These and similar programs that may be successful in deconstructing male myths regarding rape, informing men of the potential consequences of rape, and positively influencing men's attitudes and behaviors with respect to women should certainly be supported and perhaps expanded.

Some subgroups of students are apparently more likely than others to use various means to perpetrate sexual assault and other violence. For example, the journal *Violence Against Women* recently devoted an entire special issue (June, 1996) to the topic of "Fraternities, Athletes, and Violence Against Women on Campus." Its lead article summarized Boeringer's (1996) study of 477 male undergraduates, which found that, compared to non-athletes, athletes reported a higher likelihood that they would (if they could be guaranteed of no reporting or punishment) use force to make a woman engage in sexual activities when she did not want to. This study also found that, compared to other men, fraternity members were significantly more likely to report actually having used alcohol and verbal coercion to gain sexual access to women who, for example, "didn't really want to have sex."

In their commentary on Boeringer's research and other studies reported in this special issue, Koss and Cleveland (1996) emphasized that the male student culture in general provides considerable peer group support for rape and other victimization of women. Thus, fraternity members and athletes are certainly not alone in perpetrating violence against women on campus. These authors hypothesized that other subgroups of male students (not fraternity members and not athletes) may simply use other sexual access strategies (not the ones included in this study) to achieve the same ends with sexually-reluctant women.

Peer group norms undoubtedly differ not only from one campus to another, but from one sub-group of students to another on the same campus. Thus, it is incumbent on judicial officers to gather information regarding which groups are likely to experience which problems in order to target specific groups with appropriate programs. For example, it appears that even those who rape have their standards. That is, they perceive the same outcome to be acceptable if they use some strategies, but unacceptable or "wrong" if they use other strategies. So, if a given fraternity on your campus supports attitudes and behaviors related to the "give her another drink" method, but condemns the use of physical force, then rape programs should focus on issues pertaining to the alcohol method of committing acquaintance rape.

This example was used because one of the greatest risk factors associated with relationship violence (for both perpetrators and victims) is alcohol. In fact, alcohol is one of the best predictors of all types of violence on campus. Not surprisingly, several housing officers participating in Palmer's (1993) study of violence in residence halls predicted that there will be little progress in solving the campus violence problem unless or until serious efforts are made to address the campus alcohol problem. Consequently, all judicial officers are urged to take the alcohol problem seriously and to urge others to do the same.

Continue to Educate Yourself and Others

If you are reading this sentence (and hopefully this entire book), you are obviously committed to your own continuing education. Indeed, if you read extensively, review audiovisual materials, participate in listservs, make use of the Internet and Web, attend professional conferences, and so forth, you may occasionally suffer from information overload. But the more you learn, the more you can teach others.

Your knowledge, experiences, and insights may be invaluable to many people who want or need to gain better understanding of students, student conduct, and any number of other topics. For example, judicial officers generally know much more about the legal duties of institutional employees than do perhaps 99% of such employees. Indeed, it appears that too many people get their legal information (or misinformation) from television. For example, during interviews of two resident assistants, it became obvious that they completely misunderstood a legal concept. When I asked where they had gotten their information, they responded, "they had a case just like this on L. A. Law" and "I heard it on Geraldo."

Be sure to include faculty in your educational efforts. Faculty need, and often want, a better understanding of what occurs in their students' lives when they are not in the classroom. Women faculty, in particular, are often the first campus employees to recognize the symptoms of relationship violence in their students, particularly commuters. I am aware of rapes that were reported to at least four faculty, two of whom contacted me for advice because they did not know how to assist victims, where to refer victims for assistance, or what to do with the information they had about the incident.

The Administration of Campus Discipline . . .

Serve as a Link Among Individuals, Departments, or Programs

Judicial officers can not and need not be directly involved in all programs, committees, or task forces that address issues related to relationship violence. However, they can often identify those in different units who share common interests or can help to meet each other's needs and serve as a link in bringing them together to discuss possible cooperative endeavors. Extension of this link to persons off-campus may yield many positive outcomes.

For example, professionals employed by a community agency called "The Link" have been actively involved in Bowling Green State University's Coalition Against Sexual Offenses (CASO). By working collaboratively with CASO members representing health, wellness, prevention, counseling, judicial, police, housing, athletic, academic and other services on campus, they have made many valuable contributions, including the development of educational materials, presentation of campus programs, and provision of counseling and advocacy services to many students who have been raped or otherwise victimized.

It is particularly important that judicial officers develop and maintain positive working relationships with representatives of law enforcement and criminal court systems in the off-campus community (Palmer, 1993). It may also be wise to communicate and cooperate with local government officials, hospital administrators, emergency response personnel, news reporters, and appropriate others in the broader community, where many students may live, and where some students may become involved in relationship violence.

Hope for the Best, but Prepare for the Worst

Judicial officers may be in unique positions to contribute to institutional preparation and planning for major incidents that everyone hopes will never occur. One role they may play involves the identification of useful resources that allow those on one campus to learn from the experiences (both positive and negative) of those on other campuses. One such resource is Siegel's (1994) book, *Campuses Respond to Violent Tragedies*, which provides intensive case studies of relationship violence (including multiple rapes, assault and battery, and murder-suicide), along with arson, hostage-taking, serial murders and other violent tragedies. After-the-fact reflections by administrators who responded to the incidents include discussions of things they're glad they did (e.g., had a comprehensive and well-known crisis management plan in place before catastrophe struck), mistakes they made or things they wish they had done differently, and follow-up actions they have taken on their campuses to prevent or more effectively address similar tragedies in the future. Siegel also provides a very useful summary, set of suggestions from others, and crisis preparation checklist.

Protect, Respect, and Help the Accusers and the Accused

In his recent article entitled "Campus Adjudication of Rape Cases," Sandeen (1996) emphasized that absolute confidentiality must be maintained when rapes are reported. "Despite our best efforts, it is still very difficult for most victims to report rape ... [They] are already traumatized; if they cannot trust the confidential nature of the process once they report the assault, their personal condition will only get worse" (p. 2).

Because the reporting of relationship violence is commonly inhibited by fear of retaliation and psychological symptoms of victimization, it is essential that victims who do come forward to report incidents are assured that every effort will be made to protect their physical safety and emotional well-being, as well as their privacy (Palmer, 1996).

In a 1992 personal communication, Rhoten (as cited in Stevens, 1993) reported that "according to directors of student conduct offices, the number of reported rapes and other sexual violating behavior complaints against college men has increased approximately 50% during the last five years" (pp. 239-240). It is not very likely that the number of sexually offending men or the actual number of sexual offenses increased by 50% during this period of time. Rather, Koss and Dinero (as cited in Stevens, 1993) explained that the increase in reporting may be related to "friendlier, more accessible judiciary reporting and review procedures on college campuses" (p. 241).

Even though we appear to know much more about the victims than the perpetrators of relationship violence, it seems reasonable to suggest that confidentiality, sensitivity to emotional reactions, fair and respectful treatment, accessibility to judicial information, and other considerations are similarly important to those who have been accused of sexual or other acts of violence. In addition, both individuals may need referrals to counseling, legal, academic, or other services.

Roark (1993) noted that some perpetrators experience guilt and other emotional reactions to their violent actions, depending on whether they have sense of responsibility for such actions. However, some truly believe their use of violence, particularly violence against women, was justified; acceptable; or the fault of the victims, the alcohol that may have been involved, frustrating life circumstances, and other phenomena external to themselves. Because of the great diversity of opinions regarding the efficacy of counseling that is coerced or mandated after allegations of violence have been made, it is strongly recommended that judicial officers consult with counseling professionals before referring perpetrators to them.

Provide Effective Training for Judicial Board Members

Most students, faculty, and staff who serve on judicial committees are required to attend one or more training sessions. At the very least, these sessions outline campus-specific policies and procedures related to the disciplinary process. Hopefully, one session will focus on issues related to relationship violence, particularly sexual violence. One of the more outstanding resources for training judicial board members is a videotape entitled *Effective Approaches to Adjudicating Cases of Campus Sexual Assault.*

Produced by the Association for Student Judicial Affairs (ASJA, 1995), this videotape includes several scenes in which actors play the parts of individuals involved in the occurrence, reporting, and adjudication of an incident of sexual misconduct. In the initial scene, a male and female student who met in a class have their first date, during which they consume two pitchers of beer, and then return to the woman's room where sexual intercourse occurs without the woman's consent. Subsequent scenes include the woman's reporting of the incident to her RA, the woman's discussion with a police officer, separate pre-hearing meetings of both students with the judicial officer, the actual hearing conducted by a student judicial board, and the board's deliberations regarding responsibility for the alleged violation and determination of the disciplinary sanction.

Although the entire tape is only 32 minutes long, the training session would last for perhaps 90 minutes or more. This is because after each scene a facilitator briefly identifies the major points and asks viewers to stop the tape to discuss specific questions or issues. These involve definitions of "consent," the role of alcohol, confidentiality, making referrals to other resources, informing students of the charges and their rights and assurances, outlining disciplinary procedures, serving as an adviser to a judicial board, and many other important topics that would be relevant to those involved in the disciplinary process on any campus.

CONCLUSIONS

Most campus violence is student-to-student violence. Victims and perpetrators generally know each other as a result of current or previous associations with each other in social, academic, living, working, and other environments. However, the term "relationship violence" normally refers to violence involving dating, romantic, sexual, or marital partners. On most campuses where traditional age, single students predominate, heterosexual dating or "boyfriend-girlfriend" couples account for much of the relationship violence that comes to the attention of college officials. In the vast majority of the cases, men will be the alleged perpetrators and women will be self-identified or reported by others to be the victims.

Because incidents of relationship violence are considered to be personal and private, generally occur in locations where witnesses are not present, and often involve the use or abuse of alcohol, they are particularly difficult for police and staff to confront, for victims to report, and for judicial officers to adjudicate. Nevertheless, professionals in student judicial affairs may be uniquely capable of addressing these problems by educating themselves and others and by providing vision and leadership for campus-wide efforts to prevent or minimize the occurrence of relationship violence and to provide medical, counseling, legal, and other services to those involved if it does occur.

It should perhaps be noted that this chapter has emphasized "addressing" (as opposed to "solving") the problem of relationship violence on campus. In all honestly, I do not know the ultimate solution, but I suspect that it will require major shifts in societal paradigms concerning gender socialization, male-female relationships, sexuality, alcohol, violence, and other related topics. To be sure, specific individuals and incidents require the immediate attention of judicial officers. By helping their students and their colleagues today, they will undoubtedly be contributing to the longer-term solution to one of the major social problems of our times.

References

Association for Student Judicial Affairs (1995). *Effective approaches to adjudicating cases of campus sexual assault* (videotape). Charlotte, NC: University of North Carolina–Charlotte, Media Services.

Boeringer, S. B. (1996). Influences of fraternity membership, athletics, and male living arrangements on sexual aggression. *Violence Against Women,* 2 (2), 134-147.

Bogal-Allbritten, R. B., & Allbritten, W. L. (1989). The hidden victims: Courtship violence among college students. *Journal of College Student Personnel,* 26 (3), 201-204.

Cerio, N. G. (1989). Counseling victims and perpetrators of campus violence. In J. M. Sherrill & D. G. Siegel (Eds.), *Responding to violence on campus* (New Directions for Student Services, No. 47, pp. 53-63). San Francisco: Jossey-Bass.

Ellison, H. Y., O'Shaughnessey, M. E., & Palmer, C. J. (1991). *Sexual and other violence on campus: Developing an institutional response.* Paper presented at the annual conference of the National Association of Student Personnel Administrators, Washington, DC, April.

George Mason University, Health Promotion & Risk Reduction Services. (1996). *This mickey is no mouse . . . The dangers of rohypnol and GHB: "The Date Rape Drugs."* Brochure. Fairfax, VA: Author.

Grayson, P. (1993). Keeping their antennas up: Violence and the urban college student. In L. C. Whitaker & J. W. Pollard (Eds.), *Campus violence: Kinds, causes, and cures* (pp. 139-150). Binghamton, NY: Haworth Press.

Koss, M. P., & Cleveland, H. H. III. (1996). Athletic participation, fraternity membership, and date rape. *Violence Against Women, 2* (2), 180-190.

Palmer, C. J. (1993). *Violent crimes and other forms of victimization in residence halls.* Asheville, NC: College Administration Publications.

Palmer, C. J. (1995). *Focus on Courtship Violence.* Unpublished tape recorded research data. Bowling Green, OH: Bowling Green State University, Department of Higher Education and Student Affairs.

Palmer, C. J. (1996). Violence and other forms of victimization in residence halls: Perspectives of resident assistants. *Journal of College Student Development, 37* (3) 268-278.

Pollard, J. W., & Whitaker, L.C. (1993). Cures for campus violence, if we want them. In L. C. Whitaker & J. W. Pollard (Eds.), *Campus violence: Kinds, causes, and cures* (pp. 285-295). Binghamton, NY: Haworth Press.

Roark, M. L. (1993). Conceptualizing campus violence: Definitions, underlying factors, and effects. In L. C. Whitaker & J. W. Pollard (Eds.), *Campus violence: Kinds, causes, and cures* (pp. 1-27). Binghamton, NY: Haworth Press.

Sandeen, A. C. (1996). Campus adjudication of rape cases. *About Campus, 1* (5), 2-3.

Sherrill, J. M., & Siegel, D. G. (1989). *Responding to violence on campus* (New Directions for Student Services, No. 47). San Francisco: Jossey-Bass.

Siegel, D. (1994). *Campuses respond to violent tragedy.* Phoenix, AZ: Oryx Press.

Stevens, M. A. (1993). College men and sexual violation: Counseling process and programing considerations. In L. C. Whitaker & J. W. Pollard (Eds.), *Campus violence: Kinds, causes, and cures* (pp. 239-258). Binghamton, NY: Haworth Press.

Wechsler, H. (1996, July/August). Alcohol and the American college campus: A report from the Harvard School of Public Health. *Change,* pp. 20-25, 60.

Whitaker, L. C., & Pollard, J. W. (1993). *Campus violence: Kinds, causes, and cures.* Binghamton, NY: Haworth Press.

Willits, B. (1994). When violence threatens the campus workplace. *College and University Personnel Association* (CUPA) Journal, Winter, 17-23.

Chapter VI

Expression, Harassment and Hate Speech: Free Speech or Conduct Code Violation

Brent G. Paterson

*Congress shall make no law respecting an establishment of religion, or pro-
hibiting the free exercise there of; or abridging the freedom of speech, or
of the press; or the right of the people peacefully to assemble, and to petition
the Government for a redress of grievances.*
—first amendment to the U.S. Constitution

One cannot discuss harassment and hate speech without focusing on freedom of expression. Freedom of expression as dictated by
the First Amendment is often a misunderstood concept. It seems that
some students and student groups believe that harassing and hateful
behavior is actually free speech. Students advocate that they can say
whatever they want, to whomever they want, whenever they want
regardless of how others may receive that information. As we know,
the First Amendment is not as broad as some would like to interpret.

Why is freedom of expression so important? To our forefathers
who wrote the U.S. Constitution, individuals needed to be free from
the type of religious persecution that our founders faced from England.
They sought a country where speech should not be restricted simply
because the ideas expressed may be offensive to some. As Justice Hugo
Black wrote, "freedoms of speech, press, petition and assembly guaranteed by the First Amendment must be accorded to the ideas we hate
or sooner or later they will be denied to the ideas we cherish" (*Communist Party v. SACB*, 1961).

The courts have carefully protected the right of free speech. In
Bridges v. California (1941), the U.S. Supreme Court defined protected
speech by stating that the "substantive evil must be extremely high,
before the utterances can be punished." The U.S. Supreme Court established the standard for free speech in public schools in *Tinker v.
Des Moines Independent School District* (1969) by ruling that forbidden
conduct must "materially and substantially interfere with the school's

normal operations." In a more recent case, *U.S. v. Eichman* (1990), The U.S. Supreme Court recognized that desecration of the flag may be as offensive to many individuals as ethnic and religious epithets. However, the Court went on to state, "If there is a bedrock principle underlying the First Amendment, it is that the government may not prohibit the expression of an idea simply because society finds the idea offensive or disagreeable" (*U.S. v. Eichman*, 1990).

REGULATING SPEECH

Free speech activities can be regulated if college and university policies are narrowly tailored and allow for ample means of communication. Wright (1969) presented three principles for regulating free speech that have been supported by court decisions.

1. Expression cannot be prohibited because of a disagreement with or dislike for its content

2. Expression is subject to reasonable regulation of time, place and manner.

3. Expression can be prohibited if it becomes action that materially and substantially interferes with the normal activities of the institution or invades the rights of others. (see Buchanan, 1988, p. 57).

The type of forum for an activity affects the extent to which speech can be regulated. The U.S. Supreme Court in *Perry Educational Association v. Perry Local Educational Association* (1983) defined three types of public forums—traditional, limited public, and nonpublic. The traditional public forum includes such areas as city or campus streets and parks. Regulations governing free speech in a traditional forum must be content neutral and narrowly tailored to serve a significant government interest, but provide for ample alternative channels of communication. However, you may regulate time, place, and manner. For example, you might restrict a group from marching down the main street of campus an hour before the homecoming football game because of the effects on traffic flow. You might, however, allow the march earlier in the day or at a location not likely to affect traffic flow.

The limited public forum includes those areas of campus that the college or university chooses to open to the public although not required to do so. Such areas include conference and meeting facilities, arenas, stadiums, museums, galleries and other such facilities. A few years ago, the president of the United States came to speak on our campus. The speech was held in our coliseum and free tickets were available to the campus community and public. Originally, it appeared that the tickets were simply to limit the number of persons attempting to enter the facility. However, the tickets were for another purpose.

During the president's speech, a small group of individuals dressed in military fatigues and holding a banner began to shout their objections to the government's handling of MIAs from the Vietnam War. Quickly, the Secret Service surrounded these individuals and escorted them out of the facility. The tickets to the event had established it as a limited public forum. All individuals attending the speech were invited guests and therefore expected to behave with certain decorum. Individuals who failed to meet the expectations were invited to leave.

By contrast, a U.S. senator recently announced his candidacy for president on the steps of the administration building on our campus. The public stood on the lawn outside the building while listening to the speeches. Some protesters were present with banners and shouting slogans. This event was held in a public forum so the protesters were not asked to leave nor told to stop their chants.

The third type of forum is the non-public forum. These forums are not required to be open to the public and are usually governed by institutional regulations. Typically we think of non-public forums as being classrooms and residence halls. For example, your college catalog or student handbook probably has information about needing to be registered and have paid fees for a class in order to attend the class. You may allow others to audit or visit a class with permission of the instructor. Likewise, most residence halls today are locked 24 hours a day and only guests of the residents are permitted to enter the halls during certain hours.

Many institutions have established designated free speech areas where one can demonstrate and proselytize on virtually any subject. Activities in such designated free speech areas are permitted so long as the activity does not cause an immediate threat of destruction of institutional property, injury to human life on the campus or imminent threat of willful disruption of the orderly operation of the institution.

Besides regulating the forum (place) and manner, institutions can regulate time. Institutions can establish an advance reservation policy for free speech areas and set the length of time for an event as well as the time at which it can occur. In *Bayliss v. Martine* (1970), Southwest Texas State University suspended students for violating a university policy regulating the time and place of demonstrations and requiring a 48-hour advance registration for use of the demonstration area. The Fifth Circuit Court ruled that "regulation is a valid exercise of the university's right to adopt and enforce reasonable nondiscriminatory regulations as to time, place and manner of student expressions and demonstrations." It is reasonable to limit activities that, because of the location and time, might disrupt classes, sleep for residence hall students, or other university activities.

In regards to manner, free speech activities are not an excuse to violate the law or university regulations. For example, book burning as a protest may be viewed by the organizers as a free speech activity. However, it may be a violation of institutional polices on open flames and city fire ordinances. A troubling situation for administrators today is the resurgence of fasts for a certain cause. While the student may be entitled to refuse to eat as a protest, if the fast is continued for a long period of time it becomes a health issue. It is difficult to know when the institution should intervene for the health and safety of the fasting students. Medical personnel should aid administrators in determining when is the right time to intervene.

In regulating First Amendment activity it is vital that decisions are made content-neutral. Administrators can find this decision to be a challenging one. As student judicial affairs officers, we often are requested to act on a situation where another administrator, a faculty member, or a student finds the speech of another member of the university community offensive. It is especially troublesome when the speech of others seems to violate the civil standards of the university community. For example, most of us would agree that the members of Sigma Chi fraternity at George Mason University might have acted with insensitivity when they staged an "ugly woman contest" in which one participant appeared in black face with a black curly wig and curlers and used pillows to accent his chest and posterior.

Some of us also may have felt compelled to take action against the fraternity like George Mason University did. Following an outcry from women and ethnic minority students, the university placed the fraternity on probation for two years. The fraternity sought relief from the university sanctions in federal court, claiming that their First Amendment rights had been violated. The federal court ruled that the University imposed sanctions against the fraternity not because of a conduct violation but because several student groups perceived the skit as offensive. The court agreed with the fraternity stating, "One of the most persistent and insidious threats to the First Amendment rights has been that posed by the 'heckler's veto,' imposed by successful importuning of government to curtail 'offensive' speech at peril of suffering disruptions of public order" (*Iota Xi Chapter of Sigma Chi Fraternity v. George Mason University*, 1991). In hindsight, the action of the federal court could have been predicted since the action by the university was based on content.

Speech can be regulated based on the content when a compelling governmental interest in limiting the speech exists. The courts have established that the following categories meet the standard of compelling governmental interest—incitement to lawless action, fighting words, obscenity, defamatory speech, and commercial speech (Youngblood, 1995). Even when restricting speech because of these categories, one must be careful.

SPEECH CODES

Today, colleges and universities still struggle with how to employ the use of civil communications without infringing upon an individual's right to freely express their views. Of much debate is how to address hate speech—speech vilifying expression that serves only to denigrate and injure minorities, religious groups, women, and other identified groups. We can learn from the court decisions that have virtually put an end to hate speech codes. From the author's point of view, the intent of the speech codes at the University of Wisconsin, the University of Michigan, and Stanford University were to create an environment that fostered civil communications and discouraged harassing speech and conduct. However, what all of these codes failed to do, according to court decisions, is to clearly differentiate between communication that may be offensive and communication that clearly violates the First Amendment.

The University of Michigan had the unfavorable distinction of being the first institution to be directly challenged in court for a campus hate speech code. Following prompting from the Michigan House of Representatives and the United Coalition Against Racism to establish a set of rules governing hostile speech on campus, the university developed the Policy on Discrimination and Discriminatory Harassment of Students in the University Environment (Kelly, 1995). The policy subjected students to discipline for "any behavior, verbal or physical, that stigmatizes an individual on the basis of race, ethnicity, religion, sex, sexual orientation, creed, national origin, ancestry, age, marital status, handicap, or Vietnam era veteran status" (*Doe v. University of Michigan*, 1989).

According to the court, the university sought to prohibit certain speech by means of an anti-discrimination policy because the university disagreed with the ideas or messages being conveyed or because people found such speech offensive. However, the court ruled that if the university established reasonable and nondiscriminatory time, place and manner restrictions narrowly tailored and provided for ample means of alternative communication, it could regulate speech and conduct (Paterson, 1994).

The second major court challenge to a campus speech code involved the University of Wisconsin. The Wisconsin rule prohibited racist or discriminatory comments, epithets, or other expressive behavior directed at an individual with the intention to demean or create a hostile environment. Upon challenge in federal district court, the university argued that speech regulated by the rule were "fighting words" as defined in *Chaplinsky v. New Hampshire* (1942), a U.S. Supreme Court decision. The court found that the rule was overly broad as a content-based rule and did not meet the criteria of "fighting words" as currently interpreted. "It is unlikely," the court indicated, "that all or nearly all demeaning, discriminatory comments, epithets, or other expressive behavior which creates an intimidating environment tends to provoke a violent response . . . The problems of bigotry and discrimination sought to be addressed here are real and truly corrosive to the educational environment. But freedom of speech is almost absolute in our land" (*UWM Post v. Board of Regents of the University of Wisconsin*, 1991).

In the aftermath of the demise of the Wisconsin rule, the associate dean of students at the University of Wisconsin was reported in a March 28, 1993 *Los Angeles Times Magazine* article to have said that "he was dismayed to find 'that [p]eople were perfectly willing to restrict speech when it served their agendas'" (Pavela, 1993, p. 80). Examples of complaints filed with the dean of students office included a complaint from one student because a painting of the Pope was displayed with a condom affixed to it; another complaint of age discrimination involved a student upset that he had been called a "primitive dinosaur," and a white student called a "redneck" wanted action against a black woman who made the statement.

To many, the decision of a California superior court judge finding the speech code at Stanford University unconstitutional came as a surprise. The speech code prohibited harassment which included "discriminatory intimidation by threats of violence and also includes personal vilification of students on the basis of their sex, race, color, handicap, religion, sexual orientation, or national or ethnic origin" (*Robert J. Corry, et al., v. The Leland Stanford Junior University*, et al, 1995.).

Personal vilification is further defined to include speech or other expression "intended to insult or stigmatize an individual or a small number of individuals on the basis of the characteristics listed previously, addressed directly to the individual or individuals whom it insults or stigmatizes, and makes use of insulting or "fighting" words or nonverbal symbols." The decision of the court included a review of *Chaplinsky v. New Hampshire* (1942), *UWM Post v. Board of Regents of University of Wisconsin* (1991), *R.A.V. v. City of St. Paul* (1992) and *Wisconsin v. Mitchell* (1993) and discussion on the implications of these cases for the Stanford Speech Code. The court ruled that the university "cannot proscribe speech that merely hurts the feelings of those who hear it."

In discussing the implications of the *R.A.V.* case, the court indicated that the university had other means available to prevent the type of harassment they seek to regulate. The court suggested that the university could "continually press upon their students ... the need to be respectful of each other" (*Corry v. Stanford University*, 1995). It cited educational programs and publications as means to accomplish this goal. The court did agree that a penalty enhancement scheme tailored along the lines of *Wisconsin v. Mitchell* might also be a means for addressing racism and hate on campus.

Does the First Amendment apply to private institutions? Typically, the answer is no. However, there may be state laws that change the situation. In California, a law was adopted in 1992 (the "Leonard Law") providing that private colleges not "make or enforce any rule subjecting any student to disciplinary sanctions solely on the basis of conduct that is speech or other communication that, when engaged in outside the campus or facility of a private postsecondary institution, is protected from governmental restriction by the First Amendment ..." (Pavela, 1995).

RACIALLY HOSTILE ENVIRONMENT

In March 1994 the Office of Civil Rights (O.C.R.) in the Department of Education issued a Notice of Investigative Guidance that establishes guidelines for investigations by O.C.R. of incidents of racial harassment against students. These guidelines rely heavily on standards developed for a hostile environment existing in a sexual harassment case (see *Meritor Savings Bank v. Vinson*, 1986). O.C.R. defined a racially hostile environment as:

> ... harassing conduct (e.g., physical, verbal, graphic, or written) that is sufficiently severe, pervasive or persistent so as to interfere with or limit the ability of an individual to participate in or benefit from the services, activities or privileges provided by a recipient. A recipient has subjected an individual to different treatment on the basis of race if it has effectively caused, encouraged, accepted, tolerated or failed to correct a racially hostile environment of which it has actual or constructive notice. (Office of Civil Rights Notice of Investigative Guidance, p. 11449)

Further, O.C.R. indicated that it will evaluate the hostile environment based upon how a reasonable person of the same age and race as the victim, under similar circumstances, would feel their educational experience had been affected. According to the guidelines, in most cases harassment will consist of more than a casual or isolated incident except cases that are sufficiently severe to include injury to persons or property or conduct threatening injury to persons or property.

Acts creating a hostile environment may be directed at anyone and need not be targeted at the complainant (Office of Civil Rights Notice of Investigative Guidance, pp. 11449-11450).

WHAT CAN COLLEGES AND UNIVERSITIES DO TO ADDRESS HATE BEHAVIOR?

A fine line exists between the educational interests of an institution of higher education and denying freedom of expression. It appears that speech codes or any attempt to develop similar language in a code of conduct will be found unconstitutional. However, colleges and universities are not without recourse in addressing hate behavior. The following are suggested means for addressing such behavior:

1. A top-level administrator can publicly reaffirm the need for freedom of expression on campus while indicating dislike for the content and showing how the action affects the university community.

2. Conduct toward others in a hostile or discriminatory manner is still likely a violation of the code of conduct. Destruction of property, threatening the safety of others, repeated harassment of an individual are all examples of actions that can be dealt with as violations in typical codes of conduct.

3. Reasonable time, place and manner restrictions on the use of university facilities can curb the effect of hate speech.

4. Penalties for violations of the code of conduct can be enhanced when the violation is motivated by prejudice or hate.

5. Avoid phrases in the code of conduct which reference certain groups or classifications and the language "because of" or "on the basis of" specific factors (Youngblood, 1995).

SEXUAL HARASSMENT

Originally, sexual harassment was viewed as a workplace issue that required an element of power over another. Today, college and university campuses are dealing with sexual harassment claims against professors and an ever-increasing number of complaints from students about sexual harassment by fellow students and complaints from faculty about sexual harassment from students. In this chapter, discussion will be limited to situations where a student is the harasser.

Student harassment is covered under Title IX of the Education Amendments of 1972. The generally accepted definition of sexual harassment, which follows, was developed by the Equal Employment Opportunity Commission in its 1984 guidelines and modified to reflect the inclusion of students under Title IX.

Unwelcome sexual advances, requests for sexual favors, and other verbal or physical conduct of a sexual nature constitute sexual harassment when:

1. Submission to such conduct is made either explicitly or implicitly a term or condition of a person's employment or *academic advancement;*

2. Submission to, or rejection of, such conduct by an individual is used as the basis for decisions affecting an individual's employment or *academic standing;*
3. Such conduct has the purpose or effect of unreasonably interfering with a person's work or *academic performance* or creating an intimidating, hostile or offensive work, *learning or social environment* (EEOC Guidelines on Discrimination Because of Sex, 1984). Wording in italics was added to reflect coverage of students under Title IX (Sandler, 1994)

Courts refer to the first two conditions as *quid pro quo* harassment which basically means something given or withheld in exchange for something else. Such cases in higher education typically involve a supervisor making demands that might affect a subordinate's status as an employee or a faculty member suggesting methods (sexual demands) for improving a grade.

Quid pro quo harassment complaints are most often handled through a human resources department or affirmative action officer, if the alleged harasser is a staff member of the university, and by the provost or academic dean, if the harasser is a faculty member. Student judicial affairs administrators may become involved when a student in a position of power harasses another student, i.e. a resident advisor in a coed hall suggesting that he will not report a violation in exchange for a sexual favor or a student worker who supervises other student workers making unwanted sexual advances and suggesting that he/she might affect the other student's work status. *Quid pro quo* cases are often the most flagrant cases (Sandler, 1994).

The more difficult cases involve hostile environment sexual harassment. The concept of a hostile environment as a form of sexual harassment was determined by the U.S. Supreme Court in *Meritor Savings Bank v. Vinson* (1986). In this case, the court determined that an environment can be so hostile that it interferes with a person's ability to work. Hostile environment sexual harassment is very common on college and university campuses and most often involves peer harassment. In the not too distant past, such behavior might have been discounted as "boys will be boys."

Hostile environments can be created by offensive sexual bantering and joking, offensive pictures and graphics, using sexual or vulgar language in conversation, sexual graffiti, and sexual innuendos (Sandler, 1994). Today, hostile environment cases involving the use of computers are common (see chapter on Computer Misuse).

The Region IX director for O.C.R. wrote the following to college officials in California in order to define sexual harassment under Title IX:

... As to students, sexual harassment under Title IX may be defined as unwelcomed sexual advances, requests for sexual favors, or other physical or verbal conduct of a sexual nature, imposed on the basis of sex, that could: (a) deny, limit, or provide different aids, benefits, services or opportunities; (b) condition the provision of aids, benefits, services, or opportunities; or (c) otherwise limit a student's enjoyment of any right, privilege, advantage, or opportunity protected by Title IX.

Sexual harassment occurs when: (1) submission to such conduct is explicitly or implicitly made a term or condition of the individual's education or is used as the basis for educational decisions affecting that individual (quid pro quo harassment); or (2) the conduct has the purpose or effect of unreasonably interfering with the individual's educational performance, or otherwise limiting the ability of that individual to benefit from services, opportunities or privileges, by creating an intimidating, hostile or offensive education environment. (Santa Cruz Violation Letter, pp. 2-3)

Exhibiting offensive materials in the workplace has been held to create a hostile environment. In *Robinson v. Jacksonville Shipyards, Inc.* (1991) a female employee filed sexual harassment claims because there were pictures of nude and semi-clothed women throughout the workplace in magazines, clippings, calendars and plaques on the walls. The shipyards admitted that these pictures existed and that no employees had been disciplined for reading or displaying the pictures.

In determining if a hostile environment existed, the court imposed a five-element test. The court determined that: (a) the complainant belonged to a protected category; (b) the complainant was subjected to unwelcome sexual harassment; (c) the harassment was based on sex; (d) the harassment affected a term, condition or privilege of employment; and (e) the shipyards management knew or should have known of the harassment and failed to take, prompt, effective remedial action (Sandler, 1994). Specifically, the court stated, "A reasonable woman would find that the working environment at the shipyard was abusive. This conclusion reaches the totality of the circumstances including the sexual remarks, the sexual jokes, the sexual oriented pictures of women . . ." (*Robinson v. Jacksonville Shipyards, Inc.*, 1991).

A more recent court decision seems to cloud the issue of what constitutes a hostile environment. A female officer of the El Paso Police Department filed suit on the basis of comments published in the police association newsletter. The Fifth Circuit Court determined that the few offensive comments in the newsletter were insufficient, by themselves, to create a hostile environment. The court recognized the conflict with the First Amendment in such cases. It stated, "Where pure expression is involved, Title VII steers into the territory of the First Amendment. It is of no use to deny or minimize the problem because, when Title VII is applied to sexual harassment claims founded solely on verbal insults, pictorial or literary matter, the statue imposes content-based, viewpoint-discriminatory restrictions on speech" (*DeAngelis v. El Paso Municipal Police Officers Association*, 1995).

These cases show the lack of clarity in defining a hostile environment. As with other forms of harassment, because verbal, written or electronic communication or visual displays may be offensive to an individual does not mean it is harassment. The frequency with which such communication or displays occur, the vulgarity of the communication or display, and the effects of the communication or visual display upon the individual's employment or academic performance or learning or social environment are important issues to determine in sexual harassment claims at colleges and universities.

In handling sexual harassment cases the process is extremely important. Every college or university should have a clearly articulated sexual harassment policy that is written in easily understood language, not "legalese." It needs to demonstrate the college's or university's commitment to prevent and address sexual harassment and encourage potential victims to file complaints. Most importantly, the policy should be readily available to everyone in the campus community. Continual education should be provided to faculty staff and students on sexual harassment. Common elements to include in a sexual harassment policy include:

1. Statement of commitment;
2. Statement describing sexual harassment as illegal and prohibition against such activity;
3. Definition of sexual harassment with examples;
4. Statement about confidentiality;
5. Statement about false charges and retaliation;
6. Statement about scope of coverage including off campus violations;
7. Statement about coverage of other forms of harassment, i.e. sexual orientation;
8. Description of the person(s) to contact if an individual is experiencing sexual harassment;
9. Statement about possible sanctions;
10. Description of informal complaint procedures and contact(s) to file an informal complaint;
11. Description of formal complaint procedures and contact(s) to file a formal complaint;
12. List of rights of the accused and the complainant.

Many students are not interested in filing formal complaints in sexual harassment cases. In such situations, the student may only want the accused to be informed of how his/her behavior is affecting students. In other situations, mediation might be used to resolve the dispute. Especially in peer harassment situations, the complainant may simply want the other person to know how he/she feels and establish conditions for any further contact, if any.

Using a mediator to facilitate this process can be highly effective. The process is confidential and no official records of the mediation session are kept by the university. Thus, the often-expressed concern from a complainant that, I do not want to get the accused in any trouble, is avoided. It is important to realize that mediation requires the voluntary cooperation of both parties and that at any time either party can stop the mediation process.

When students are alleged to have committed sexual harassment and the complainant wishes to pursue formal action then the normal university disciplinary procedures might be followed. It is suggested that if the institution normally uses a hearing officer to determine whether a violation occurred and determine possible sanctions, a judicial board or ad hoc hearing panel be used to hear sexual harassment cases. The judicial board or ad hoc panel should be trained in sexual harassment issues and procedures. Membership on the judicial board or panel should include faculty, staff and students. Appeals of decisions made by the judicial board or panel should follow the normal disciplinary appeal procedure.

As with many difficult cases that find their way to student judicial affairs administrators, sexual harassment cases need to be handled with sensitivity to the plight of both the complainant and the accused. Be certain to follow your procedures. Deviating from established procedures is an invitation for a lawsuit.

CONCLUSIONS

It seems that the federal government is not helping matters. Court decisions and Office of Civil Rights rulings appear to contradict each other. Institution's ability to establish its expectations for student behavior continues to be eroded by interference from the courts and Congress. The court decisions of the 1960s that in effect abolished *in loco parentis* have left their marks on higher education. The more recent consumerism from students and parents and support from the government continue to change the manner in which institutions must operate. While the intent is often good, i.e. the Cleary's push for release of statistics on campus crime, the result seems to be more bureaucracy without substance. Meanwhile, parents are saying I know what is right for my son or daughter so I expect the institution to treat him or her accordingly.

While the application of the First Amendment to the higher education setting is always open to debate, we can predict, with a high level of confidence, that there will continue to be challenges for colleges and universities in this area in the future. We need to be advocating the importance of free and open discussions in the academic environment. At the same time, we need to educate everyone in the university community that civil communication is an expectation. We need to go beyond tolerance and expect all members of the university community to treat others with respect.

We can safely say "hate speech codes" are dead. While some of the behavior exhibited by students may be offensive, we should avoid making decisions on content. Instead, we can look to our codes of conduct to determine if an offense occurred. For example, racist graffiti painted on someone's residence hall room door can be addressed as damage of university property. If it is determined through a hearing that a violation occurred, the sanction can be enhanced when the offense was motivated by prejudice toward a person because of factors such as race, religion, ethnicity, disability, national origin, age, gender, or sexual orientation. Other common violations may include direct threats to physically harm another, stalking, assault, telephone harassment, and violation of the computer use policy. Nothing should stop us from visiting with students about their actions even if it is not a violation of the discipline code.

References

Buchanan, E.T. III (1988). Constitutional issues: Protecting the rights and interests of campuses and students. In M.J. Barr (Ed.), *Student affairs and the law* (pp. 47-73). San Francisco: Jossey-Bass.

Kelly, S.A. (1995, October). *Recent developments in First Amendment jurisprudence.* Presentation at the Texas A&M University System Higher Education Law Symposium, College Station, TX.

Office of Civil Rights March 10 Notice of Investigative Guidance, Federal Register, vol 59, No. 47, pp. 11449-11450.

Paterson, B.G. (1994). Freedom of expression and campus dissent. NASPA Journal, 31(3), 186-194.

Pavela, G. (Ed.). (1993, April 26). The politics of the Wisconsin speech code. *Synfax Weekly Report*, 80-81.

Pavela, G. (Ed.). (1995, March 6). Stanford speech code unconstitutional. *Synfax Weekly Report*, 332-335.

Sandler, B.R. (1994). *Educator's guide to controlling sexual harassment.* Washington, D.C.: Thompson Publishing.

Santa Cruz violation letter (communication from Region IX Office of Civil Rights, April 29, 1994).

Wright, C.A. (1969). The constitution on the campus. *Vanderbilt Law Review, 22,* 1027-1088.

Youngblood, J.W. (1995, October). *First Amendment conflicts: Too much of a good thing or a good law gone bad?* Presentation at the Texas A&M University System Higher Education Law Symposium, College Station, TX.

Cases

Bayliss V. Martine, 430 F.2d 873 (5th Cir. 1970)

Bridges v. California, 314 U.S. 252 (1941).

Chaplinsky v. New Hampshire, 135 U.S. 568 (1942).

Communist Party v. SACB, 367 U.S. 1 (1961).

DeAngelis v. El Paso Municipal Police Officers Association, 51 F.3d 591 (5th Cir. 1995).

Doe v. University of Michigan, 721 F. Supp. 852 (E.D. Mi. 1989).

Iota Xi Chapter of Sigma Chi Fraternity v. George Mason University, 733 F. Supp. 792 (E.D. Va. 1991).

Meritor Savings Bank v. Vinson, 447 U.S. 57, 67 (1986).

Perry Educational Association v. Perry Local Educational Association, 460 U.S. 37 (1983).

R.A.V. v. City of St. Paul, 505 U.S. 377 (1992).

Robert J. Corry, et al. v. The Leland Stanford Junior University, et al., No. 740309, February 27, 1995).

Robinson v. Jacksonville Shipyards, Inc., 760 F. Supp. 1486 (M.D. Fla. 1991).

Tinker v. Des Moines Independent School District, 393 U.S. 503, 89 S. Ct. 733 (1969).

UWM Post v. Board of Regents of the University of Wisconsin, 774 F. Supp. 1163 (E.D. Wisc. 1991)

U.S. v. Eichman, 58 L.W. 4744, 4746 (U.S. Supreme Court 1990).

Wisconsin v. Mitchell, 113 S. Ct. 2194 (1993).

Part Three

Student Organization
Conduct Issues

Chapter VII

Disciplining Student Organizations

Glenn W. Maloney

Nearly every college has experienced student rebellions or riots, some more serious than others. In certain cases, they eventuated in broken windows or cracked furniture; in others, they resulted in deaths. All involved some kind of collective action, either of a class or of a whole student body. These outbursts could be found in all sections of the country. These rebellions posed perplexing problems for college authorities. Whatever their cause, the outbreaks were bound to damage the reputation of an institution ... They would occasion severe criticism ... by parents, trustees, and the public in general (Brubacher & Rudy, 1976. p. 53).

Does some of this sound at all familiar? Is it a description of the campus unrest of the sixties or administrative issues of the 1990s? No, Brubacher and Rudy are describing pre-Civil War college events and issues. Are colleges in the 1990s still experiencing disruptions from student groups? Do administrators worry how campus events are viewed by outside constituents? Most of us can probably agree that our student groups continue to challenge and question many of our requirements and restrictions.

This chapter will look at the ability of colleges and universities to establish reasonable rules to regulate how, when and where student organizations can use institutional facilities and the ability to discipline student organizations that fail to comply with these rules. Issues surrounding valid rules and due process are addressed and recommendations and guidelines for disciplining student organizations are offered. As stated in *Student Services and the Law* (Barr & Associates, 1988) each institution must adapt this information to be consistent with its "own mission, environment, location, and circumstances" (p. 284).

RECOGNITION

From higher education's earliest days students were forming groups. At first, students formed groups by traditional class breakdowns, shortly followed by literary societies. And with groups came problems. "As early as 1667 the Harvard Board of Overseers imposed penalties" on groups of students participating in forms of "predatory adolescent aggression" (Brubacher & Rudy, 1976, p. 46).

Literary societies, which were educational, political, professional and social organizations all in one, "commanded the kind of passionate student loyalty which was later accorded to fraternities and athletic teams" (Brubacher & Rudy, 1976, p. 47). Minutes of their meetings "indicate that horseplay and frivolity" occurred (Brubacher & Rudy, p. 47). Phi Beta Kappa, although started as a literary society in 1776, stood apart from other literary societies because of "its high degree of selectivity and its secrecy" (Brubacher & Rudy, p. 26). By the time Phi Beta Kappa dropped its secrecy requirements the fraternity movement was well established. Characteristics attributed to secret societies included elaborate initiations and abusing newcomers (Brubacher & Rudy).

In spite of some attempts by university officials, state lawmakers, and even the courts, the number of fraternities continued to grow. Besides the increase in fraternities, and other similar social clubs, the early nineteenth century saw the establishment of numerous other organizations including academic, religious, recreational and those formed around social issues. One of which was the Intercollegiate Socialist Society organized by Upton Sinclair (Brubacher & Rudy, 1976, p 131).

The Intercollegiate Socialist Society was the birthplace of the League for Industrial Democracy, which spurred an offshoot called the Student League for Industrial Democracy which later gave rise to the Students for a Democratic Society (Brubacher & Rudy, 1976). Students for a Democratic Society (SDS) was "the principle student organization that sparked the student resistance of the New Left" (Brubacher & Rudy, p. 350). The organization "had hundreds of campus chapters and at its peak some 75,000 members" (Brubacher & Rudy, p. 350).

When the SDS applied for a chapter at Central Connecticut State College, they were turned down. University officials stated that they did not approve of the student organization's relationship with the national SDS, and that the organization's philosophy of violence would cause campus disruption (Maloney, 1988, p. 285). The campus organization sued Central Connecticut State College and the case found its way to the Supreme Court.

In 1972 the Court ruled, in *Healy v. James* (1972), that denial of recognition to a local chapter of Students for a Democratic Society violated the individuals' First Amendment rights of association. The Court

The Administration of Campus Discipline . . .

opinion stated that Central Connecticut State could not deny the student organization recognition because the college disagreed with the group's philosophy or because of the student group's association with an unpopular organization (*Healy*, 1972; Maloney, 1988).

As a result of the *Healy* (1972) case, an organization cannot be denied recognition because it is unpopular, or advocates unpopular views. The decision in *Healy* has made it virtually impossible for public colleges and universities to prohibit the formation of student groups that are willing to comply with reasonable regulations (Maloney, 1988).

The Court did, however, give schools the right to deny recognition "to any group that reserves the right to violate any valid campus rules with which it disagrees" (*Healy*, 1972, p. 2352). The Court stated "activities need not be tolerated where they infringe reasonable campus rules, interrupt classes, or substantially interfere with the opportunity of other students to obtain an education" (*Healy*, p. 2350).

Private Schools

The application of *Healy* (1972) and other constitutional issues discussed throughout this chapter is different for public and private institutions. "Public institutions and their officers are fully subject to the constraints of the federal Constitution, whereas private institutions and their officers are not. Because the Constitution was designed to limit only the exercise of government power, it does not prohibit private individuals or corporations from imposing on such freedoms as free speech, equal protection and due process" (Correnti, 1988, quoting Kaplan, 1985, pp. 17-18).

"In general, the courts have ruled that private institutions are not constrained by the first amendment of the Constitution in their dealings with students, as long as they follow the policies and procedures outlined in official institutional publications" (Correnti, 1988, p. 29). Private schools can be held to standards and policies articulated in their publications. Although some courts have "expressed reservations regarding the strict applicability of the contact relationship" (Shur, 1988, p. 92), there are "a number of cases [that] illustrate the application of contract law to higher education [and] most of them have occurred in private institutions" (Correnti, p. 36).

Public institutions are required to grant students certain freedoms and due process protections, but Charles Alan Wright (1969) states that "Americans often become so obsessed with questions of constitutionality that they give insufficient attention to considerations of wise policy" (p. 1035). Wright contends that a wise institution might give its students more freedoms than the minimum required by the constitution. Surely a private institution of higher education would not want to give its students anything less.

REGULATION

As stated above, *Healy* (1972) did allow colleges and universities to enforce "reasonable campus rules" (p. 2350). Student organizations often seek recognition so that they may access certain university buildings and grounds. Most groups want to hold meetings, distribute literature, post signs, raise funds, and sponsor speakers. In order to accommodate these activities in an orderly fashion and without disruption to other functions of the institutions, officials promulgate rules and regulations. But whether some campus rules are reasonable or not has been the subject of litigation.

Unconstitutional Rules

The Fifth Circuit declared unconstitutional a regulation that stated: "All events sponsored by student organizations, groups, or individual students must be registered with the Director of Student Activities, who, in cooperation with the Vice President for Student Affairs, approves activities of a wholesome nature" (*Shamloo v. Mississippi State Board of Trustees*, 1980, p. 625). In this case students were disciplined for taking part in an unauthorized demonstration. *Shamloo* is important because it is a case where a campus rule contained some language ruled unconstitutional and therefore unenforceable. The Fifth Circuit Court held that a reasonable rule of time, place, and manner could not include a provision that only allowed "wholesome" activities.

Policies could restrict a group's ability to interfere with the flow of traffic, to disrupt classes, or use obscene materials. But policies may not regulate content. University administrators should not be in the position to decide what is "wholesome." "Limiting approval of activities only to those of a 'wholesome' nature is a regulation of content" (*Shamloo*, p. 523). Policies should not attempt to regulate what is said but instead they need to address when, where and how an activity is to be conducted.

In *Iota Xi Chapter of Sigma Chi Fraternity v. George Mason University* (1993) a fraternity was disciplined for sponsoring an "ugly woman contest" in the cafeteria of the student union. The contest included a Caucasian man dressed as a black women with exaggerated features. In his affidavit to the court, the dean said that the university:

> ... does not and cannot condone this type of on-campus behavior which perpetuated derogatory racial and sexual stereotypes, tends to isolate minority students, and creates a hostile and distracting learning environment. Such behavior is incompatible with, and destructive to, the University's mission of promoting diversity within its student body [and] sends a message to the student body, and the community that we ... are not serious about hurtful and offensive behavior on campus (p. 392).

However, the Fourth Circuit Court of Appeals said that the university could not "sanction Sigma Chi for the message conveyed by the 'ugly woman contest' because it ran counter to the views the University sought to communicate" (*Iota Xi Chapter of Sigma Chi Fraternity v. George Mason University*, 1993, p. 393). University discipline could have been imposed if Sigma Chi had used the facility without permission, damaged the facility, refused to pay costs incurred from using the facility, illegally possessed or sold alcohol at the event, violated university policies regarding fundraising activities or for any number of other legitimate reasons, but not because of the message, regardless of how abhorrent that message seems to others.

The Fourth Circuit's opinion was issued after the Supreme Court's decision in *R.A.V. v. City of St. Paul* (1992). In this Supreme Court case, the City of St. Paul passed an ordinance prohibiting "the display of a symbol which . . . arouses anger, alarm or resentment in others on the basis of race, color, creed, religion or gender" (p. 2540). There were several opinions written in the case concurring that the policy went too far in limiting First Amendment rights. In addition the Court saw the policy as trying to regulate content. The opinion stated that the First Amendment does not permit the government "to impose special prohibitions on those speakers who express views on disfavored subjects" (p. 2541).

An institution may wish to control the manner in which social fraternities rush or pledge new members. Many service, honorary and professional organizations also use probationary pledge periods. Unless the regulation pertains to all student organizations it would be considered an unconstitutional rule targeting some unfavored groups. (It should be pointed out that this does not preclude groups from voluntarily joining an organization like an interfraternity council which can have its own set of rules that may include rush and pledge guidelines. But the sanctions that could be imposed by such a group would involve limiting benefits or membership to the council.)

Another common example of rules targeting specific groups are those against homosexual groups. There is a long legal history of courts telling institutions of higher education that they cannot enforce regulations because of sexual orientation. Many campuses since the *Healy v. James* (1972) decision have tried to deny recognition to gay student organizations and have lost in court (Maloney, 1988).

Most recently, the Alabama legislature passed a law attempting to restrict the activities of gay and lesbian groups on college campuses in that state. The state law prohibited:

Any college or university from spending public funds or using facilities, directly or indirectly, to sanction, recognize or support any group that promotes a lifestyle or actions prohibited by the sodomy and sexual misconduct laws of the state" (*Healy*, 1996, p. A29).

A federal judge ruled the law unconstitutional. Relying heavily on the Supreme Court's decision in *Rosenberger*, the judge "declared that public colleges could not deny funds to campus groups based on the viewpoints of those groups" (*Healy*, 1996, A29).

It may be possible to discipline a group if they were actually found engaging in illegal activity (Some states still consider sodomy a crime). But you cannot deny a group of students access to university activities because you don't like what they advocate. An example—many campuses have chapters of NORML (National Organization for the Reform of Marijuana Laws) but no campuses would tolerate the possession or use of marijuana.

Campus administrators should not shy away, however, from promulgating and enforcing rules to maintain an orderly, educational environment. We can regulate groups but not merely because we don't like their purpose. The Supreme Court, while striking down a regulation that restricted only religious groups, stated that the holding did not prohibit the university from establishing reasonable time, place, and manner regulations (*Widmar v. Vincent*, 1981). In 1984 the Court ruled that restrictions on expression are valid provided that:

> ... they are justified without reference to the content of the regulated speech, that they are narrowly tailored to serve a significant governmental interest, and that they leave open ample alternative channels for communication of the information (*Clark v. Community for Creative Non-Violence*, 1984, p. 3069).

Religious Groups

The First Amendment contains the sentence "Congress shall make no law respecting an establishment of religion, or prohibiting the free exercise thereof." This is often plainly interpreted to mean the separation of church and state. But application of this to all levels of government and all of public education can create disagreement among reasonable people.

In trying to uphold the First Amendment, public institutions have attempted to impose restrictions on religious organizations. Regulations which have specifically targeted religious group activities have been overturned by the courts as regulations of content.

The University of Missouri at Kansas City's regulation that no group may use university facilities for religious worship or teaching was a typical university regulation meant to keep public institutions from violating the separation of church and state clause of the First Amendment. But the Supreme Court in *Widmar v. Vincent* (1981), and just recently in *Rosenberger v.*

Rector and Visitors of University of Virginia, (1995) has stated that it was not necessary to deny eligibility of campus groups to use campus facilities or apply for funding from a general fund, in order to avoid violation of the Constitution.

In *Widmar v. Vincent* (1981), Cornerstone, a student organization, was denied permission to use facilities for religious teaching or worship. The Court overturned this decision stating "the University seeks to enforce a content-based exclusion of religious speech" (at 278). In *Rosenberger v. Rector and Visitors of University of Virginia* (1995), a religious group, Wide Awake Productions, sought to have printing costs for its publication paid by the Student Activities Fund at the University of Virginia. The Student Activity fund was used by other groups for similar expenses. Wide Awake was denied the funds because the group's publication promoted a particular religious belief in violation of the university's guidelines for use of the fund. The Court overturned this exclusion stating the practice "required public officials to scan and interpret student publications to discern their underlying philosophic assumptions respecting religious theory and belief." This decision in not unlike the Fifth Circuit's decision in *Shamloo v. Mississippi State Board of Trustees* (1980), where administrators had to determine what was "wholesome."

University regulations should not be written with specific groups in mind. All registered or recognized student groups are alike in the eyes of the law. Groups may be categorized by officials for convenience of administration or for the ease of others to locate information about specific groups, but group type or purpose should not be used as a factor in promulgating regulations or imposing discipline.

Publications

It should be clear by now that campus administrators cannot control the content of programs sponsored by student groups and the same holds true for their publications. Institutions can regulate the distribution of campus publications. However, regulations about how, where, and when publications can be distributed should pass constitutional muster. But often the major campus publication is not merely the work of a student group but of an academic or auxiliary campus department.

The institution may provide space, equipment, vehicles, personnel, etc. for the orderly operation of these newspapers or magazines, and it would seem that more control could be exercised over them. But campus administrators should not be tempted to discipline campus publications without carefully reviewing the legal issues involved.

When university officials attempted to withdraw financial support, in order to shut down a campus paper that illegally discriminated in its staffing and advertising policies, the Fourth Circuit Court of Appeals said:

> Censorship of constitutionally protected expression cannot be imposed by suspending the editors, suppressing circulation, requiring imprimatur of controversial articles, excising repugnant material, withdrawing financial support, or asserting any other form of censorial oversight based on the institutions power of the purse (*Joyner v. Whiting*, 1973, p. 460).

In this case the Fourth Circuit said that "to comply with the First Amendment the remedy must be narrowly drawn to rectify only the discrimination in staffing and advertising" (*Joyner v. Whiting*, 1973, p. 463). In a similar case where a university attempted to restrict the distribution of a literary magazine that contained potentially offensive racist content, the Fifth Circuit ruled that "Speech cannot be stifled by the state merely because it would perhaps draw an adverse reaction from the majority of people, be they politician or ordinary citizens, and newspapers" (*Bazaar v. Fortune*, 1973, p. 572).

It was later agreed that the university could add a simple disclaimer to the publication (*Bazaar v. Fortune*, modified, 1973). The Supreme Court in *Papish v. University of Missouri Curators* (1973), in overturning the expulsion of a student editor, stated that the student "was expelled because of the disapproved content of the newspaper rather than the time, place, or manner of its distribution" (p. 670).

It should be clear that student organizations, disciplined because of the content of their activities are not considered wholesome, run contrary to the mission of the university, or upset others, will ultimately prevail in the courts. When establishing rules, campus administrators must be very careful to tailor them to be content-neutral and to regulate activities according to time, place and manner.

In attempting to maintain an educational environment free from disruption or harassment, university officials must often balance protecting students from unwarranted or inappropriate activities and defending the First Amendment—not always an easy choice. When drafting regulations, the First Amendment should always take priority. When crafting educational programs, one should consider strategies pertaining to tolerance, civility, and the appreciation of diversity.

Constitutional Regulations

University regulations have been upheld by the courts in cases where the rule is content-neutral and is simply restricting activities to a reasonable time and/or place, and merely asks students to conduct their activities in a reasonable manner. Indeed even in the landmark case of *Tinker v. Des Moines Independent School District* (1969), while the Court upheld the right of students to wear black armbands, it also stated that:

Conduct by the student, in class or out of it, which for any reason—whether it stems from time, place, or type of behavior—materially disrupts classwork or involves substantial disorder or invasion of the rights of others is, of course, not immunized by the constitutional guarantee of freedom of speech (p. 740).

Restrictions of Time, Place and Manner

In *Bayless v. Martine* (1970) a group of students challenged a campus rule requiring forty-eight hours notice for off-campus speakers and limiting demonstrations to specific locations and times. The Fifth Circuit held that the regulations were "a valid exercise of the University's right to adopt and enforce reasonable, nondiscriminatory regulations as to time, place and manner of student expression and demonstrations" (p. 878). In crafting such regulations always bear in mind that the regulations must pertain to all groups equally and must be content-neutral. A rule that prohibited the sponsorship of controversial speakers would not withstand a constitutional test. A rule that only permitted off-campus speakers that did not require security, although appearing to be neutral with regards to content, could be seen as favoring some speaker types over others.

The reason for the 48 hour rule in *Bayless v. Martine* (1970) was so that the campus could assess and accommodate security needs. A campus may also see the need to restrict events to a specific time of day in order not to interfere with the normal activities of the institution. For example, student organization events that are expecting large crowds may be limited to times of day where facilities such as auditoriums and parking lots are not being used by employees or students attending class. Events involving amplified sound can be restricted to locations and times to minimize disruption.

Campuses are not required to fund the cost of student organizations events and if costs are incurred for security, media equipment, room set-up, food, etc., the student group can be expected to cover those expenses. But if funding is available to one group it must be equally available to all groups.

Restrictions of Place

A coalition of student groups erected shanties outside the Rotunda, on the campus of the University of Virginia. The groups were attempting to influence the board of visitors to divest its holdings in corporations doing business in South Africa. When the university sought to enforce its regulation prohibiting structures "on the Lawn within 700 feet of the Rotunda" (*Students Against Apartheid Coalition v. O'Neil*, 1988, p. 736), the students sued. The Fourth Circuit upheld the regulation because it was content neutral, was narrowly drawn to meet a compelling state interest, and provided for alternative means of communication. The court stated "it is well established that aesthetic concerns alone constitute a permissible government intent" and that "the revised regulation is narrowly drawn to ensure maintenance of the architectural integrity of the upper lawn." (*Students Against Apartheid Coalition v. O'Neil,* p. 737,). The court also noted that structures were permitted in other areas throughout the campus.

Groups can be restricted to certain areas of the campus for activities of expression. But campuses, which can demonstrate a valid interest in restricting expressive speech, should not attempt to ban these activities altogether or try to create regulations that would only impact a specific type of organization.

Restrictions of Manner

Shortly after the *Tinker v. Des Moines Independent School District* (1969) decision the suspension of students charged with the distribution of false and inflammatory material was upheld by the Sixth Circuit (*Norton v. Discipline Committee of East Tennessee State University,* 1969). In using *Tinker* as a guide the court said that the students in the *Tinker* case "did not urge a riot, nor were they disrespectful to their teachers" (*Norton,* p. 194). The right to freedom of speech is not absolute. Student groups' right to distribute literature can be regulated. Rules prohibiting the distribution of materials that are obscene, libelous, or likely to incite immediate lawless action can be enforced.

In a similar ruling the Fifth Circuit upheld the suspension of students who organized and led a boycott that involved tables being overturned, bricks being thrown and a car vandalized (*Jenkins v. Louisiana State Board of Education,* 1975). In quoting from *Tinker,* the Fifth Circuit said this was not like the "silent, passive, expression of opinion, unaccompanied by any disorder or disturbance" (*Jenkins,* p. 1003).

In ruling on the Jenkins (1975) case the court said:

Although students certainly have the right to assemble peaceably and to urge a peaceful boycott, it is clear that their right to do so is not unbridled. Their First Amendment rights are not unlimited constitutional guarantees which may be exercised at any time, at any place, and in any circumstance (p. 1002).

Off-Campus Behavior

Whether or not any particular institution regulates the off-campus behavior of its student groups is dependent on a variety of factors including mission, size, location, history, politics, town-gown relationship, etc. Unless the group is officially representing the college or university this author strongly cautions against trying to regulate off-campus conduct. The same guidelines discussed regarding individual codes would hold true here.

A primary purpose of regulating student groups is to ensure the preservation of the academic environment of the campus. Only off-campus activities that have an impact on that academic environment should be of concern to campus administrators. Most instances of inappropriate conduct off the campus should be covered by some ordinance or law and should be left to the local or state law enforcement agencies.

Can you penalize a group for off-campus conduct? Yes, as long as you have a clear policy that can withstand the constitutional questions previously addressed. But don't just include fraternities or sports clubs in your off-campus jurisdiction. Enforcement needs to apply to all groups equally.

Group Discipline

The Supreme Court addressed the right to discipline organizations in *Healy v. James* (1972). Here the Court said:

> Associational activities need not be tolerated where they infringe reasonable campus rules, interrupt classes, or substantially interfere with the opportunity of other students to obtain an education (p. 189).

Assuming institutional rules will pass constitutional muster, how should officials go about disciplining a group that violates university policies?

Before pursuing disciplinary sanctions against a student organization the institution should have clearly defined guidelines on when an organization will be held accountable. An example of this type of policy would be:

An organization can be held responsible for breaking campus rules when:

1. One or more officers or authorized representatives, acting in the scope of their organizational capacities, commit the violation;

2. One or more of its members commit the violation after the action that constitutes the violation was approved by a vote of the organization or was part of a committee assignment of the organization;

3. The violation is committed at an activity funded by the organization;

4. The violation occurs as a result of an event sponsored by the organization;

5. One or more members of an organization or its officers permit, encourage, aid, or assist, in committing a violation;

6. One or more members of an organization fail to report to appropriate university authorities knowledge or information about a violation; or

7. When one or more members of an organization fail to satisfactorily complete the terms of any disciplinary penalty.

Who Imposes Discipline?

Which university office administers the discipline process for student organizations is up to each institution. In many cases the office which is responsible for registering groups, reserving facilities, and granting approval for organizational activity is also responsible for enforcement of regulations. But what about on campuses where these responsibilities are split, e.g. student government approves groups, the registrar's office and/or the campus union reserve facilities, and yet a different office is responsible for approving solicitation activities? In this case it may be best to let the same office which handles individual student conduct to also be responsible for group conduct.

Another scenario may involve the use of student panels similar to student hearing panels in individual cases. In the case of student groups, however, these peer panels may consist of students from similar organizations—a Greek board for fraternity and sororities; a club sports panel for recreational clubs; a college council for academic, honorary or professional organizations.

Again, one size does not fit all. Each institution must look at its own philosophy, organizational structure, traditions and problems to determine what will work best. Whatever method is chosen it should be clearly written, and provide for adequate due process.

Due Process

Regardless of which method of discipline is chosen the organization must be afforded certain measures of procedural fairness (*Joint Statement*, 1992). Anytime the university is imposing sanctions on student groups certain due process rights should be afforded, including: (Burke, 1995; Binder & Hauser, 1995).

1. Adequate notice of the charges;
2. The right to an impartial hearing, including sufficient notice for the group to prepare a defense;
3. The right to know the names of witnesses against them;
4. The right to know the results and findings of the hearing; and
5. The right to appeal.

Universities are not required to permit advisors or attorneys to participate in hearings. When students at State University of New York at Stony Brook were denied the right to legal representation they sued (Burke, 1995). In *Gruen v. Chase* (1995) the New York Court disagreed with the students stating:

> Due process requires that the petitioners [those being subject to discipline] be given the names of the witnesses against them, the opportunity to present a defense, and the results and findings of the hearing ... Here, the university complied with these requirements. In addition, the university informed the petitioners that they had

the right to an advisor and provided an advisor for them. Due process did not require the university to provide the petitioners with legal representation at the disciplinary hearing (Burke, p. 1; quoting from *Gruen v. Chase*, 1995, p. 262).

It may be important for student organization leaders to have advisors assist them with the organizational discipline process. Attorneys, on the other hand, who wish to actively participate will often view the process as the same as criminal court, which it is not. The developmental approach is to have student leaders actively involved in the organization's defense. It is the students who should ask and respond to questions, not their advisor or attorneys. The students should be permitted counsel but they do not need to actively participate. Participation in a discipline hearing can be just as educational to the students as learning how to run a meeting.

It is important that in any disciplinary proceeding that written procedures be followed. Courts consistently view failure to follow one's own rules as a violation of due process (Binder & Hauser, 1995; Burke, 1995; *Gruen v. Chase*, 1995). Finally, universities are not required to prove their case "beyond a reasonable doubt," but may choose to use a "preponderance of the evidence" standard in determining whether or not a violation occurred. University hearings are not the same as criminal proceedings. It is possible for a group of students to be found not guilty of a violation by the criminal authorities but to be found guilty by the university for the same set of facts.

Hearing

Most people think of a hearing as a formal process whereby a third individual or panel hears the case against a student group brought by the university. In the last seventeen years in working with student organizations and their compliance with university rules this author has only been involved in three such cases. In most cases the organization is given a chance to respond to a charge directly to the administrator responsible for student organizations. That is all that is required.

A hearing is simply an opportunity for the group representatives to respond to the alleged violation. It is generally up to this administrator, after reviewing the complaint and hearing the organization's defense, to assess the appropriate penalty. The organization should have the opportunity to appeal this initial decision.

In situations where a student panel is used, instead of an administrator, the panel would have the responsibility to review the complaint and listen to the group's side of the story before making a decision. Panels are more complicated because of the selection and training of panel members. But this can also be an educational experience and the option of student panels should not be rejected because it is not as simple as an administrative system. Using students in the discipline process can have other educational outcomes. Students have the opportunity to hone listening and questioning skills and apply their reasoning and analytical skills to real life problems. They are also confronted with making value and moral decisions and gain a better understanding of what is meant to be fair and consistent. Students participating on panels who gain a greater understanding of university regulation can become ambassadors, providing information to other student leaders before an infraction of the rules occur.

Appeal

The appeal process also does not necessarily mean a formal hearing. "The formality of any appellate procedures should be commensurate with the gravity of the offense" (*Joint Statement*, 1992). This author recommends that for minor penalties the student organization only be allowed to appeal to the next administrative level—usually a dean or vice president. For substantial penalties, such as a suspension of one year or longer, the student group should have the right to appeal to the highest administrative level, a university hearing officer or a student panel that has not yet heard the case.

Appeals can usually be avoided if the administrator and organization can agree that a violation has occurred and some sanction is warranted; the sanction is reasonable and consistent with similar cases in the past; and the sanction is not considered too harsh by the group.

Penalties

When assessing penalties through the disciplinary process it is important to review the *Joint Statement on Rights and Freedoms of Students* (1992). When the statement was originally written in 1967 it stated that discipline proceedings should "play a role substantially secondary to example, counseling, guidance, and admonition" (*Joint Statement*, 1992, p. 6). When the *Joint Statement* was revised 25 years later that statement was not changed, even though one could argue that the number of student groups has increased and the range of activities of groups has expanded drastically. Regardless of the actual policy violated by the group a good scolding with some follow up guidance, can sometimes be all that is needed to improve behavior.

In most cases when a student group has violated a university procedure, an appropriate meeting explaining the violation to the group, discussing why the university policy is present, discussing the university's interest in seeing the group avoid problems, and listening to the organization's perspective, can end in an agreement that the group will work to insure that the problem does not occur again. Many times student groups are encouraged to seek office advice before embarking on new activities so that proper guidance can be provided.

These methods can be much more rewarding than formal written disciplinary proceedings and usually just as effective.

Staff assisting organizations need to ask many probing questions throughout the planning process to fully understand what the group is trying to accomplish. If a complete understanding of the activity is gathered then all the appropriate information including specific policy issues can be brought to the group's attention before the event takes place. The better the information student groups receive on the front end of planning activities, the less likely they are to be involved in the discipline process after the activity. It is better to see a group several times during the planning process than just once for discipline.

But, in spite of our best advice, guidance, use of repeated warnings and second chances, groups will still need to be disciplined with more serious sanctions. It is incumbent upon the university to "state as specifically as possible the sanctions that may be imposed" (*Joint Statement*, 1992). It is most useful to have a wide range of penalties from minor to harsh, and to have the opportunity to combine penalties when appropriate. A list of penalties may include:

1. Written warning;
2. Probation for one or more semesters;
3. The requirement of restitution, community service, attendance at educational seminars, or other appropriate remedy;
4. Suspension of one or more specific privileges for one or more semesters (these privileges could include sign posting, literature distribution, facility reservations, fundraising, intramurals, eligibility for campus awards, etc.)
5. Long term cancellation of the group's recognition or registration.

There has been discussion on ACPA's Commission IV Listserv regarding the appropriateness of a permanent suspension. Individual penalty options almost always include a permanent expulsion for the most serious violations of the school's code. Permanent expulsion can be an appropriate penalty imposed upon a student who personally violated university standards. Student organizations, on the other hand, are very fluid. Members or officers of a group one semester may have no influence on the group in subsequent semesters.

A permanent suspension of a student group is not a penalty imposed upon the individual members or officers who committed the violation, but upon future members of the group. For example, a university spirit organization's whose purpose is to support the university's athletic teams through conspicuous attendance at events, receives a permanent suspension for organizing a hazing activity that resulted in one new member's death. Twelve years later, someone, who was only six years old at the time, wants to reform the group for its original purpose. Is it reasonable to respond that the group has been permanently suspended? In most cases, suspensions of six to ten years can serve the same punitive purpose.

It is important to include a statement similar to "or other appropriate penalty" in your list of penalties in order to allow for creative sanctions. An unusual sanction may make use of community service or educational seminars, but the ability to craft a specific sanction can sometimes lead to a more satisfying solution. A creative sanction may involve a specific meeting with an individual faculty or staff member, checking enrollment status of members, or placing specific time limits on some of the organization's functions. Allowing for flexibility in sanctioning can also provide the opportunity for the organization to propose its own solution, whereby the discipline process is more of a collaborative, educational effort.

Who Receives the Penalties

When an organization violates a university rule there are several ways in which discipline can be imposed. University penalties can be assessed against the organization, the individual members of the organization responsible for the violation, or both individuals and the organization.

Which option is best will depend on what university rule was broken, the seriousness of the violation, and the status of the organization at the time of the infraction. In most cases an organization that violates a rule will willingly accept responsibility and sanctions in place of university sanctions imposed upon individual members. For example, a university regulation prohibits any alcohol in university classrooms. Following an organization's weekly meeting a building manager reports alcohol was found in the room and you know no one else had access to the room. In this instance the group is called in and admits that the champagne was to celebrate their team's winning of an intramural championship. The officer admits it was an organizational activity and willingly accepts consequences imposed upon the group.

But in the instance where the organization representatives believe that the violation was not the responsibility of the group—an individual member smuggled the alcohol in for personal use without the knowledge or permission of the officers— organization officers will often prefer that individual members suffer university sanctions instead of the organization.

Student Group Self-Discipline

Often sanctions against both the group and one or more students is appropriate. Appropriate sanctions can be imposed upon individual perpetrators not only by the university, but also by the organization itself. It is important to allow organizations to take responsibility for their own actions. There are cases where an organization may be willing to suspend or even expel a member to show its own disapproval of a violation and to protect the organization from sanctions.

In many cases, organizations see the need to impose internal sanctions, but do not have procedures in place to do so. You can establish a working relationship with the group to help them handle this case and to write by-laws or guidelines for dealing with members in the future. Students find it very difficult to discipline their own members, but they can learn a lot about themselves and their organization in the process. Learning, not punishment should be the focus.

Individual and Group Discipline

There will be cases where the discipline process will be used to sanction both an organization and one or more individuals in that organization. This does not have to be complicated, but university officials need to be careful not to violate either individual or organizational due process. In cases where two different offices have jurisdiction, pertinent facts can be shared by those investigating or hearing the case. If possible the outcome of the organization's case should be delayed until the individual cases are adjudicated. This allows for new facts from each of the individual cases to be used in the case against the organization.

Hazing is an example where both individuals and organizations may need to be penalized. In serious cases where the organization officers have planned and carried out the hazing the officers are responsible for representing the organization, but must also face individual charges. In cases like this it is often difficult to separate the organization and the individual discipline processes and it may be best to have the individual discipline jurisdictional authority be responsible for both.

Confidentiality

Organizations do not have the same rights of privacy as do individuals. In *NAACP v. Alabama* (1958) and *Brown v. Socialist Workers '74 Campaign Committee* (1982) the Supreme Court granted organizations the right not to disclose membership information (Maloney, 1988). However, a California Court, while recognizing "the rights of rank and file members to remain anonymous" (*Eisen v. Regents of the University of California*, 1969), required the institution to release information about the organization, including a purpose statement and the names of officers (Maloney).

When a student newspaper was denied access to records and proceedings involving hazing charges against two social fraternities they sued under the state's Open Meetings and Open Records Acts. In *Red and Black v. Board of Regents* (1993) the Georgia Supreme Court ruled that the records which related to a student organization were "not of the type the Buckley Amendment is intended to protect, i.e., those relating to individual student[s]" (p. 852). The Georgia Court also added that the student organization court was covered by the state's Open Meetings Act, however this did not include the deliberations of the student justices (*Red and Black v. Board of Regents*).

It is important to be aware of the laws of your individual state regarding open records or open meetings. If no statute exists, review court cases. "In most states, courts recognize 'a common law tort of invasion of privacy which protects individuals against the disclosure of affairs considered private" (Ebbers, 1988, p. 325, quoting Kaplan, 1985, p. 359). When done carefully and thoughtfully, providing relevant information to the public about the status of a student organization is possible without violating the rights of any officers or individual members. The demonstration of a sincere willingness to work with the media can often prevent unnecessary and extraneous conflicts or lawsuits.

Media

When working with members of the media it is important to be honest and respectful. It is appropriate to explain the discipline process and to let them know that until you have had a chance to review all the information you prefer to have no comment. It is not appropriate to ignore the press. They have a job to do just like you do. Help them understand your position and decision-making process, while agreeing to keep them informed and they will usually be more patient.

If the media is interested in a case it is a good idea to work closely with the university's public relations office. It may also be helpful to identify one spokesperson as a contact. Let the press know in advance when you will have information and the nature of the information you will release. A generic discussion of university procedures, and concerns about following applicable state and federal laws on privacy, can help build a positive relationship with members of the media.

But it is important to protect individual privacy rights. When releasing information about a group, be careful to exclude information about individual wrongdoing. It is possible to release the names of officers of the club without implicating the individuals as having broken any regulation. A press release, reviewed by administration and legal counsel, can help avoid mistakes that might be made during an interview with the media. A general distribution of a press release can alleviate the problems of who finds out first in a large media market where sources compete to get the news first.

Always notify the student group about your conversations with the press. You not only avoid hard feelings by misrepresentations in the media, but you can provide advice on helping the group get prepared to make its response.

CONCLUSION

Students have the right to associate and form student organizations. Institutions of higher education may establish reasonable, content-neutral rules of time, place and manner to regulate student groups. The organization discipline process should be an extension of these reasonable rules, but it is just one additional tool we have to use when working with student leaders. Discipline should not take the place of providing appropriate resources to student organization leaders so those goals can be accomplish without violating university policy.

References

Barr, M.J. (Ed.). (1988). *Student services and the law.* San Francisco: Jossey-Bass Inc..

Binder, R. & Hauser, G. (Conference Issue, 1995). Due process in fraternity and sorority hearings: A response to the Middle Tennessee State case. *Perspectives,* p. 16.

Brubacher, J. S. and Rudy, W. (1976). *Higher education in transition.* (3rd ed.). Harper & Row, Publishers.

Burke, T. M. (November, 1995). Disciplinary hearings—NY court decision yields two important points. *Fraternal Law,* 54, 1.

Correnti, R. J. (1988). How public and private institutions differ under the law. In M.J. Barr & Associates, *Student services and the law* (pp. 25-43). San Francisco: Jossey-Bass.

Ebbers, L. H. (1988). Management and use of student records. In M.J. Barr & Associates, *Student services and the law* (pp. 323-333). San Francisco: Jossey-Bass.

Healy, P. (1996, February 9). Federal judge rejects Alabama law barring aid to gay-student groups. *The Chronicle of Higher Education,* p.A29.

Joint statement on rights and freedoms of students (1992). Washington DC: American College Personnel Association.

Kaplin, W.A. (1985). *The law of higher education : A comprehensive guide to legal implications of administrative decision making.* (2nd ed.) San Francisco: Jossey-Bass.

Maloney, G. W. (1988). Student organizations and student activities. In M.J.. Barr & Associates, *Student services and the law* (pp. 284-307). San Francisco: Jossey-Bass.

Shur, G. M. (1988). Contractual agreements: Defining relationships between students and institutions. In M.J. Barr & Associates, *Student services and the law* (pp. 74-97). San Francisco: Jossey-Bass.

Wright, C.A. (1969). The Constitution on campus. *Vanderbilt Law Review,* 22(5), 1027-1088.

Cases

Bayless v. Martine, 430 F.2d 873, (5th Cir. 1970)

Bazaar v. Fortune 476 F2d 570 (5th Cir. 1973); modified 489 F.2d 225 (5th Cir. 1973).

Brown v. Socialist Workers '74 Campaign Committee, 103 S. Ct. 416 (1982).

Clark v. Community for Creative Non-Violence, 104 S. Ct. 3065 (1984).

Eisen v. Regents of the University of California, 269 Cal. App.2d 696, 75 Cal. Rptr. 45 (1969).

Gruen v. Chase, 626 N.Y.S.2d 261 (A.D. 2 Dept. 1995).

Healy v. James, 408 S. Ct. 2338 (1972).

Iota Xi Chapter of Sigma Chi Fraternity v. George Mason University, 993 F.2d 386 (4th Cir 1993).

Jenkins v. Louisiana State Board of Education, 506 F.2d 992, (5th Cir. 1975).

Joyner v. Whiting, 477 F.2d 456 (4th Cir. 1973).

NAACP v. Alabama, 357 U.S. 449, 78 S. Ct. 1163 (1958).

Norton v. Discipline committee of East Tennessee State University, 419 F.2d 195 (6th Cir. 1969)

Papish v. Board of Curators of the University of Missouri, 410 U.S. 667, 93 S. Ct. 1197 (1973).

R.A.V. v. City of St. Paul, 112 S. Ct. 2538 (1992).

Red and Black v. Board of Regents, 262 Ga. 848, 427 S.E.2d 257 (1993).

Rosenberger v. Rector and Visitors of University of Virginia, 115 S. Ct. 2510 (1995).

Shamloo v. Mississippi State Board of Trustee, 620 F.2d 516 (5th Cir. 1980).

Students Against Apartheid Coalition v. O'Neil, 838 F.2d. 735, (4th Cir. 1988).

Tinker v. Des Moines Independent School District, 393 U.S. 503, 89 S. Ct. 733 (1969).

Widmar v. Vincent, 102 S. Ct. 269 (1981).

Chapter VIII

Changing Behavior in Greek Organizations

Timothy F. Brooks

Since their inception Greek organizations have fostered tremendous debate. The Greek movement started with the founding of Phi Beta Kappa in 1776 at the College of William and Mary. Begun as literary societies, Greek organizations developed clandestine ritual and lure which set them apart from other student organizations (Pavela, 1995). Many observers of Greek organizations feel that they have lost their literary roots and have been transformed slowly but inexorably into drinking clubs.

THE POSITIVES

Fraternity and sorority proponents will tell you that there are many positives for individuals involved in the Greek system. They revolve around sisterhood, brotherhood, character development, scholarship and leadership opportunities. In fact, many sorority and fraternity leaders have gone on to become leadership forces in business, education, law and medicine. Fraternities and sororities can provide a very positive educational and social environment that helps students to survive in the mega university environment.

In particular the leadership opportunities can be extremely valuable learning tools for students. In some instances, students learn to handle large budgets, maintain million dollar facilities, and administer organizations that have over one hundred members. The positive lessons learned in these situations can last a lifetime.

THE NEGATIVES

Sororities and fraternities have had a history of positive influence on their own members and their respective institutions. In general, most members of Greek organizations believe that they have gained immeasurably from their Greek experience, especially in the area of

149

leadership. Institutions tend to believe that members of Greek organizations are some of their best student leaders and most loyal alumni. Despite the very strong positive influences there are some negative aspects to Greek life which include hazing, alcohol and sexual assault.

HAZING

The media has been deluged with articles concerning the negative aspects of Greek life. For instance the *Chronicle of Higher Education* has published a series of articles over the years about incidents that have occurred in fraternities. In March 1986, the *Chronicle* published an article on hazing rituals plaguing campuses across the country (Meyer, 1996). The article depicted several unfortunate incidents including the suspension of two student organizations at the University of Texas who were caught branding freshman members with dry ice. The article emphasized that hazing has been practiced historically by many fraternities and student organizations. The article quotes a former president of the National Pan Hellenic Council who said, "In black fraternities this (hazing) happens in 100 percent of the chapters" (Meyer, 1996).

The March 1988 edition of the *Chronicle of Higher Education* contained an article on "Behavior of Students in Fraternities Worsens on Many Campuses, as Membership Soars" (Hirschorn, 1988). This article described excessive drinking, hazing, sexual abuse, and anti-semitic activity as the key problems in Greek life. The article discussed several negative events including a Rutgers University freshman who died after consuming excessive amounts of alcohol at a fraternity pledge program. It also mentioned a white fraternity at the University of Pennsylvania that was suspended after a pledge event involving two black strippers. Several other campuses were cited in the article for engaging in racist and anti-semitic activity.

In May of 1988 the *Chronicle of Higher Education* printed an article on two colleges which decided to withdraw recognition from all of their fraternities and sororities. The institutions Gustavus Adolphus College and Franklin and Marshall College decided to remove recognition because of unacceptable liability risks and the anti-educational nature of some of the Greek organizations (Hirschorn, 1988). The *Chronicle of Higher Education* published in December of 1988 an article on an effort to change the pledge education system within fraternal organizations so that the possibility of hazing would be reduced. Mr. Drury G. Bagwell, president of Phi Sigma Kappa Fraternity, was quoted as saying "Despite our best efforts, the hazing and death continue. Nothing seems to eliminate hazing and death from the structure of pledging" (Collison, 1988).

In a September 11, 1995, article that appeared in the *Chronicle of Higher Education* the University of Arkansas suspended its chapter of Sigma Phi Epsilon "after members were accused of throwing a chair at a black professor" ("Fraternity suspended after racial incident," 1995). The professor also said that members of the fraternity yelled racial epithets at him and cheered when he left. Perhaps the most discouraging recent event was the death of Michael Davis at Southeast Missouri State in February of 1994.

Davis went through several days of beatings at the hands of Kappa Alpha Psi brothers. He died after being hit in the head during one of these hazing sessions. Seven members of the Kappa Alpha Psi Fraternity were charged with involuntary manslaughter and fifteen more were charged with hazing. As a result of this tragic incident, the state of Missouri passed a bill classifying hazing as a felony and also removing consent as a defense to hazing (Thomas, 1995).

ALCOHOL

Alcohol has also had a very negative impact on the image of Greek organizations. In September of 1995, the publication *Fraternal Law* reported that "The Arizona Court of Appeals issued a disturbing opinion in a wrongful death case involving allegations of underage drinking at a fraternity party. The opinion concluded that a national fraternity can be liable" (Powell, 1995). This situation developed from a lawsuit brought on behalf of Ruben Hernandez. Mr. Hernandez died from an automobile accident that allegedly was the fault of a Delta Tau Delta fraternity pledge (Burke, 1994).

The pledge was driving home after drinking at a fraternity party. *Fraternal Law* quoted the Arizona Supreme Court as stating "We are hard pressed to find a setting where the risk of an alcohol related injury is more likely than from underage drinking at a university fraternity party the first week of the new college year" (Powell, 1995; Burke, 1994). This ruling could have a significant impact on other national fraternities that have chapters in the State of Arizona.

There have been a myriad of disciplinary problems and lawsuits associated with the misuse of alcohol in Greek organizations. Several lawsuits showed the danger of alcohol overindulgence. *Quinn v. Sigma Rho Chapter of Beta Theta Pi* (1987) fraternity was brought after Quinn became very intoxicated during a pre-initiating ceremony and suffered neurological damage. *Campbell v. Board of Trustees of Walbash College* (1986) was brought because Campbell was driven home after a fraternity event by a drunk member and they were involved in a serious accident. *Ballou v. Sigma Nu General Fraternity* (1986) was a situation where Ballou died of alcohol intoxication following a hell night in his fraternity (Zirkel & Tsai, 1990).

In *Fassett v. Delta Kappa Epsilon* (1986) a fraternity party took place at the residence of several chapter officers. Allegedly, the chapter also paid for the alcohol that was served to approximately 200 guests. Fassett was critically injured and another individual at the party was killed when they became involved in an automobile accident after the event (Paine, 1994).

In September 1995 the fraternities and sororities at the University of Colorado/Boulder voted to ban all alcohol at social functions. The alcohol ban was the result of several deaths in the half dozen years prior to the ban that were attributed to alcohol consumption at Greek parties and later resulting in accidents. In addition, law enforcement officers in Boulder, Colorado, tired of the continuing problems associated with alcohol, raided many of the Greek social functions and arrested hundreds of underage drinkers.

Dr. Henry Wechsler of the Harvard School of Public Health conducted a study on "Binge Drinking on American College Campuses: A New Look at an Old Problem" (Wechsler, 1995). This study included approximately 17,000 students on 140 college campuses. Wechsler examined who was binge drinking on these campuses. The startling findings indicated that Greeks drink significantly more than non-Greek students. Sorority members are nearly twice as likely to be binge drinkers compared to other female students (62 percent versus 35 percent, respectively). Among women who live in sorority houses, an astonishing 80 percent are binge drinkers. Similarly, fraternity members binge more than other male students (75 percent versus 45 percent, respectively) and 86 of fraternity house residents binge (Wechsler, 1995).

SEXUAL ASSAULT

Another major issue facing Greek organizations is sexual assault. The literature is replete with examples of unconscionable acts perpetrated on women by men involved in fraternities. For instance, gang rape in fraternities has received significant publicity. Allegedly about 70 percent of reported cases of gang rape have occurred in fraternity parties (Bryan, 1987).

In a study conducted by Martin and Hummer (1989), they concluded "that the organization and membership of fraternities contribute heavily to coercive and often violent sex" (p.469). They argued that fraternity peer pressure stereotyping of women and the immature environment in fraternity houses all contribute "to coercive sexual relations and the cover up of rapes" (Martin & Hummer).

PREVENTION

Colleges and universities have had a difficult time deciding on how to relate to Greek organizations. A variety of relationship statements have been developed across the country. Everything from a total "hands off" approach to one of strict supervision have been proposed. Many institutions have also struggled with how to take action against Greek organizations for behavior problems that occur off the campus property.

The American Council on Education (ACE) reviewed relationship statements and came up with their own position. In its report, "ACE Calls for Tighter Controls on Fraternities and Sororities," ACE recommended the following actions to deal with fraternity issues:

1. Require a minimum grade point average for students to apply for or maintain active membership.
2. Conduct regular reviews of the relationship between the institution and its Greek system to determine how best to align the organization with educational goals.
3. Establish policies and effectively enforce penalties for hazing violations.
4. Develop educational strategies and performance criteria to eliminate discriminatory behavior toward women, handicapped individuals, and racial and ethnic minority group members.
5. Defer rushing until the second term of the freshman year or later so that students may become familiar with the full range of social and academic opportunities on campus.
6. Establish standards for the fraternity and sorority houses to protect the heath and safety of all residents and guests including regular inspections to ensure compliance with institutional standards and community codes.
7. Encourage Greek organizations to eliminate pledge status as a requirement for institutional recognition or support" (American Council on Education, 1990).

Soon after the ACE report Bucknell University made some drastic changes. These included postponing rush to the sophomore year, a 2.5 grade point average in order to be eligible to rush, limiting rush to ten days, including a resident house manager in all fraternity houses, and requiring that all Bucknell students "would need university permission to live off campus" (*Bucknell World*, May 1990). Bucknell made these changes in an effort to eliminate exclusivity, sexism, anti-intellectualism, and a variety of behavioral and social problems.

Also in 1990, all eight historically black national fraternities who are members of the National Pan Hellenic Conference (NPHC) voted to eliminate pledging. This action came after a series of unfortunate hazing activities in all of the organizations. Consequently, in an effort to change behavior and reduce liability, pledge education was eliminated.

In May of 1992, the University of Delaware Faculty Senate, which has responsibility for promulgating all rules and regulations pertaining to student behavior, announced several reforms for the Greek system. They included phasing out pledge education programs by 1997-98, deferring Rush to the second semester of the freshman year, and implementing a comprehensive assessment and evaluation system for all Greek organizations. (University Faculty Senate, 1992).

In the fall of 1995, the University of Maryland at College Park developed a series of new standards in order to enhance Greek life. These standards include the following requirements. Every chapter must have a grade point average that is above the all-men's and all-women's averages. A new member orientation program will be put in place of the traditional pledging. Pledging itself will be totally abolished over the next four-year period. The university also will require both a chapter adviser and a faculty adviser. These two individuals, it is hoped, will help create a positive Greek experience for the members (Pavela, 1995).

In addition, each chapter at the University of Maryland will be required to develop a diversity program. Every chapter will be asked to "demonstrate its response to racial and cultural diversity by organizing and implementing programs and activities that encourage both an appreciation of diversity and a commitment to promoting diversity among its members" (Pavela, 1995). Furthermore, each chapter will be required to develop an effective internal judicial system. The chapters will be expected to deal with inappropriate behavior by chapter members and take immediate disciplinary action.

Finally, all fraternities and sororities at the University of Maryland that have housing must employ a live-in house director. These house directors need to be familiar with the policies and procedures of the university and the office of Greek life and work to create positive behavior within the chapters. It is also expected that each chapter will have a viable housing corporation that will support the live-in house director and help manage the chapter facility.

DISCIPLINE

In the 1970s and 1980s most colleges and universities sought to distance themselves from Greek organizations. It was believed that there would be less liability if schools maintained a hands-off approach to supervising Greek organizations. However, in the 1990s there has been a decided change that was most recently reflected in the programs developed at the University of Maryland, College Park. Despite these aggressive measures in trying to control inappropriate behavior through additional regulations and supervision there still are times when discipline needs to be utilized. There are basically four kinds of disciplinary approaches to handling violations of college and university code's of conduct in Greek organizations.

Fraternity and Sorority Chapter Discipline

Almost all national sororities and fraternities have systems for disciplining individual members in their chapters. Quite often, disciplinary measures are invoked when members violate chapter rules such as failure to pay dues or complete assigned tasks. Unfortunately, chapters rarely use discipline in dealing with bizarre and inappropriate behavior.

It apparently is very difficult for Greek organizations to discipline their own individual members for acts of alcohol abuse, violence, or sexual assault. Generally fraternity and sorority individual chapter disciplinary systems are rather ineffective in addressing behavioral issues.

National Sorority and Fraternity Judicial Systems

A review of national fraternity and sorority disciplinary processes indicates that in many cases there are no specific written procedures. Instead, serious chapter problems are investigated and sanctions are exercised on a case by case basis when a chapter fails to comply with the national's constitution or bylaws. Most national sororities will also take action against individual chapter members when these individuals demonstrate blatantly unacceptable behavior.

National sororities and fraternities may come on to campus with their investigators and insist upon cooperation from their chapters. Often they can obtain more accurate information concerning violations than colleges or universities who have to be careful about not violating individual and procedural rights. After reviewing many cases at the University of Delaware, it has been clear that nationals not only have excellent investigators, they tend to ferret out important information during their campus visits.

National Panhellenic and Interfraternity Council Judicial Systems

At many colleges and universities across the country, the student umbrella groups of NPHC (National Panhellenic Council) and IFC (Interfraternity Council) have developed their own internal judicial systems for handling violations of their regulations as well as university policy. For instance, at Rutgers University the "Greek Review Board" has the responsibility of hearing cases involving individual fraternity and sorority members and/or entire chapters who have been charged with violating fraternal policies or university rules and regulations.

The "Greek Review Board" is comprised of twelve fraternity and sorority members. The board also has two advisers from the office of fraternity/sorority affairs and an alumni individual. The procedures that the board follows are classic due process policies. The sanctions can go from a warning to the loss of university recognition (Rutgers University, 1993).

Cornell University has a similar Greek judicial committee. Cornell explains its Greek judicial committee in the following manner. "The advantage of a Student Judicial Committee lies in the ability of its members to influence the attitudes and subsequent behavior of other students through a formal judicial mechanism. Peer influence, exercised through the judicial process, is often more effective in redirecting the behavior patterns of students than other methods of discipline.

They go on to say "The goals of the Greek judicial process are to compel adherence to the basic expectations, the campus code of conduct, university policies, and the New York state law to resolve conflicts within the Greek community; and to improve the public image of the Greek system by promoting high standards of conduct. As in the Rutgers system, Cornell has an all student committee but the assistant dean of students is its adviser. Historically both of these university systems have worked very effectively.

College and University Judicial Systems

Many colleges and universities across the country have decided to treat Greek organizations in a similar fashion to all other recognized student groups. They have built into their judicial systems policies that allow them to adjudicate cases against recognized student organizations and chartered sororities and fraternities. The University of Delaware system is typical of many such systems. It states "Registered student organizations, including fraternities and sororities, may be charged with violations of the code of conduct. A judicial hearing for a registered student organization will be conducted in a manner similar to the judicial procedures used to adjudicate individual undergraduate and graduate students. Hearings shall be conducted with one spokesperson from the university community representing the organization (usually the organization's president).

The sanctions range from disciplinary warning to revocation of registration/chapter status. In addition there is the possibility of suspending some or all chapter privileges. This would mean the possibility of the University of Delaware removing an organization's right to Rush new members, eliminate the use of university services, or eliminate the use of university facilities for a variety of programs such as meetings, social functions, or membership recruitment. A college or university judicial system of this type can take severe action against registered or chartered organizations if they have been found to have violated the university's code of conduct.

College and university systems of this type can be relatively ineffective at times because of lack of evidence. Administrators who have worked in this area have often been thwarted in judicial cases because they are unable to get sufficient evidence to find a violation of the code of conduct. Because fraternities and sororities impress upon their members and pledges the importance of secrecy of rituals and chapter business, university officials investigating alleged violations often find the chapters and members uncooperative.

SUMMARY

Often the best disciplinary approach is a combination of the four that have been mentioned in this chapter. It can be particularly effective to involve a fraternity or sorority national office in investigating major violations like hazing, racism, or sexual abuse. In many instances, the national office would prefer to take appropriate action rather than leave the situation in the hands of the college or university. The institution should always reserve the right to adjudicate cases that violate their own rules and regulations.

IFC, Panhellenic and NPHC judicial boards can be extremely effective if they have the support and guidance of the institution. They can also work hand in hand with the national organization to obtain an appropriate resolution to violations of policy. In many situations the best tactic is to always involve the national office in the situation as early as possible and later proceed with the appropriate method of adjudication.

References

American Council on Education. (1990, January 17). ACE calls for tighter controls on fraternities and sororities NEWS. pp. 29-30.

Bryan, W. A. (1987). Contemporary fraternity and sorority issues. *Fraternities and Sororities on the Contemporary College Campus.* pp. 37-53.

Bucknell World. May, 1990.

Burke, T. M. (1994). Once out, fraternity defendants back on trial. *Fraternal Law,* 48, 1.

Collison, M. N-K. (1991, September 4). Judge cites First Amendment protection in overturning suspension of fraternity. The *Chronicle of Higher Education,* pp.45-46.

Collison, M. N-K. (1988, December 14). National interfraternity conference to weigh alternatives to pledge system in an effort to halt hazing excesses. The *Chronicle of Higher Education,* pp. 25-26.

Fraternity suspended after racial incident. (1995, September 11). The *Chronicle of Higher Education,* p. 3.

Hauser, G. F. (1995). University-IFC sanctions violate chapter rights. *Fraternal Law,* 52, pp. 1-3.

Hirschorn, M. W. (1988, March 16). Behavior of students in fraternities worsens on many campuses, as membership soars. The *Chronicle of Higher Education,* pp. 34-36.

Hirschorn, M. W. (1988, May 11). 2 colleges drop recognition of fraternities, sororities amid continuing concern over groups' behavior. The *Chronicle of Higher Education*, pp. 27, 29.

McKaig, R. (1992). *Can the college or university legally distance itself from fraternities and other "independent" organizations, or must it assume a duty to enforce a fraternity code of conduct?* Presented at the Stetson University College of Law CLE Program. pp. addendum not numbered.

Martin, P. Y., & Hummer, R. A. (1989). Fraternities and rape on campus. *Gender and Society*, 3(4), 457-471.

Meyer, T. J. (1986, March 12). Fight against hazing rituals rages on campuses. The *Chronicle of Higher Education*, p. 34.

Moss, D. (1994). On campus, wrongful rites. *USA Today*, p. 8A.

Paine, E. A. (1994). Recent trends in fraternity-related liability. *Journal of Law and Education*, 23(2), 191-210.

Pavela, G. (1995). Drury Bagwell on rebuilding the foundations of fraternity life. *Synthesis: Law and Policy in Higher Education*, 7(1), 489-508.

Pavela, G. (1995). Robert E. Manley on the benefits and responsibilities of fraternity life. *Synthesis: Law and Policy in Higher Education*, 7(2), 511-528.

Powell, G. E. (1995). Arizona court: fraternities are drinking clubs. *Fraternal Law*, 53, 1-2.

Rutgers University. (1993). Greek Review Board Policies and Procedures.

Shea, C. (1995, July 28). A question of liability: Are fraternities responsible for assaults on their premises? 2 courts disagree. The *Chronicle of Higher Education*, pp.39-40.

Taggart R. J. (1992). Recommendations from the Greek life task force. Newark, DE: University of Delaware, University Faculty Senate.

Thomas, N. (1995, Summer). The death of Michael Davis. *The Scroll*. pp. 128-131.

University Faculty Senate. (1992, May 6). University of Delaware.

Wechsler, H. A. (1995). *Binge drinking on American college campuses: A new look at an old problem.* Cambridge, MA: Harvard University, School of Public Health.

Zerkel, P. A., Tsai, D. A. (1990). Alcohol and fraternities: The lessons of modern case law. *Journal of College Student Development*, 31, 141-146.

Cases

Ballou v Sigma Nu General Fraternity, 352 S.E.2d. 488 (S.C. 1986).

Beach v University of Utah, 726P 2d 413 (Utah 1986).

Campbell v. Board of Trustees of Walbash College, 495 N.E.2d. 227 (Ind App. 1986).

Fassett v. Delta Kappa Epsilon, 807 F.2d. 1150 (3d. Cir. 1986).

Quinn v. Sigma Rho Chapter of Beta Theta Pi Fraternity, 507 N.E.2d. 1193. (Ill. App. 1987) appeal dismissed. 515 N.E.2d. 125 (Ill. 1987).

Part Four

Campus Community
Conduct Issues

Chapter IX

Addressing Academic Dishonesty and Promoting Academic Integrity

William L. Kibler

INTRODUCTION

Academic dishonesty is not a new issue for higher education or our society at large. Throughout this century the topic has been discussed on campuses and in professional literature. Explanations as to why cheating occurs have varied over time. In 1941, Drake concluded that the problem stemmed from competition for grades.

More recently the Carnegie Council (1979) and others (Levine, 1980; Pavela, 1981) have indicated that today's students value achievement and the ability to compete successfully more than they value independent scholarship. The academic community has not been able to develop the intellectual values associated with effective scholarship in all of its students. Morrill (1980) described these values as honesty, respect, truth, rigor and fairness.

ACADEMIC DISHONESTY AS A CONTEMPORARY PROBLEM IN HIGHER EDUCATION

Academic Dishonesty Defined

One of the troublesome problems encountered in reviewing literature and research on academic dishonesty in the absence of a generally accepted definition. Academic dishonesty generally refers to forms of cheating and plagiarism which results in students giving or receiving unauthorized assistance in an academic exercise or receiving credit for work which is not their own (Kibler et al., 1988).

Most instances of academic dishonesty fit traditional patterns: taking an exam for another student; altering or forging an official document; paying someone else to write a paper to submit as one's own work; arranging to give or receive answers on an exam; getting questions and answers from someone who has taken the exam; copying

161

with or without another person's knowledge; doing assignments for someone else; plagiarism; and padding items on a bibliography. Obtaining a copy of a test; using unauthorized notes; working together with other students on assignments (collaboration) when it is not allowed; using cribsheets; turning in lifted exams as tests taken in class; changing grades and answers; and using an instructor's manual are other examples of unethical practices (Barnett & Dalton, 1981; Nuss, 1984; Singhal & Johnson, 1983; Rafetto, 1985).

Pavela (1978) proposed the following general definitions for use in campus judicial codes:

Cheating: intentionally using or attempting to use unauthorized materials, information, or study aids in any academic exercise. The term academic exercise includes all forms of work submitted for credit or hours.

Fabrication: intentional and unauthorized falsification or invention or any information or citation in an academic exercise.

Facilitating academic dishonesty: intentionally or knowingly helping or attempting to help another to violate a provision of the institutional code of academic integrity.

Plagiarism: the deliberate adoption or reproduction of ideas or words or statements of another person as one's own without acknowledgement. (p. 68)

Extent of the Problem

Just how extensive is the problem of academic dishonesty? Research suggests students on most, if not all, campuses cheat on their course work and tests. Although campus-specific reports give us a sense of the extent of the problem in earlier years, Bowers (1964) did the first national scale research on academic dishonesty in the early 1960s. He surveyed over 5,000 students on 99 campuses. Nearly 30% of the students in Bower's survey admitted to cheating on tests or exams and to plagiarism. Over 11% admitted to unpermitted collaboration. Thirty years later, Donald L. McCabe of Rutgers University conducted national research on academic dishonesty that is widely credited with initiating renewed interest in academic integrity issues in the 1990s on many campuses throughout the country.

McCabe's (1993) first study was conducted in 1990-91 and focused on thirty-one small to medium size highly selective, largely residential colleges. He surveyed over 6,000 students and found that nearly 70% admitted to some form of cheating at least while in college. Over 40% of the students admitted to cheating on a test during college.

McCabe's latest research (1993) was reported by Pavela (1994). He studied the extent of self-reported cheating by 1,800 students at nine medium to large state universities, also surveyed in 1962 by Bowers. McCabe found that the level of cheating increased over the last

30 years. The number of students admitting to cheating on exams increased from 26% in 1962 to 52% in 1993. The number of students admitting to unpermitted collaboration went from 11% to 49%.

Why Students Cheat

Academic dishonesty is a complex behavior influenced by multiple variables. To effectively address the behavior, one must understand some of the factors that may contribute to a student's decision to cheat. Higher education today is characterized by intense competition and heightened stakes. Expectations, validation and sense of worth are all linked to performance (Ellison, 1990). Successful performance in college is measured by grades. In this environment of academic survival, students may utilize numerous "survival strategies," including study skills, tutoring, time management, academic advising, career planning, and cheating. As noted in the previous section, the choice to cheat is increasing.

Contextual or situation factors can influence the choice to cheat. Research has shown that cheating goes down as the perception of negative consequences rises. The certainty of being caught reduces cheating (Tittle & Rowe, 1973). The perceived probability of punishment reducing cheating (Michaels & Miethe, 1989); and the perceived severity of punishment reduces cheating (McCabe & Trevino, 1993). The "opportunity" to cheat also influences the decision to cheat (Uhlig & Howes, 1967). Classroom atmospheres that allow or encourage cheating behavior usually result in increased cheating (Vitro & Schoer, 1972). The perception that "everyone else is cheating" is also a common explanation offered by students (Gehring, Nuss & Pavela, 1986). Finally, the perception by students that cheating is not really taken seriously by the institution, results in higher incidents of dishonest behavior (Nuss, 1984; Pavela, 1981).

Gehring et al. (1986) listed six factors that have been cited as contributing most frequently to incidents of academic dishonesty:

1. Students are unclear about what behaviors constitute academic dishonesty.

2. Students believe that what they learn is not relevant to their future goals.

3. Students' values have changed. The ability to succeed at all costs is one of the most cherished values.

4. Increased competition for enrollment in high demand disciplines and admission to prestigious graduate and professional schools prompts students to cheat to improve their grades.

5. Students are succumbing to frequent temptation. Exams are not properly secured and faculty members are casual about proctoring. As-

signments and exams are repeated frequently from semester to semester.

6. The risks associated with cheating are minimal. Students believe that no one gets punished and faculty members often choose to avoid campus disciplinary procedures. (pp. 3-4)

Kibler and Kibler (1994) asserted that low self-esteem is an important consideration in determining the likelihood that a student will choose to engage in cheating behavior. A lack of self-confidence, a fear of failure, and external locus of control characterize low self-esteem. The lack of self-confidence results in perceptions that the person is incompetent, incapable, inadequate, and inferior. The fear of failure reinforces these feelings. The external locus of control results in students looking outside themselves and their own abilities to meet challenges. Thus, when faced with academic challenges, such as exams, students with low self-esteem may be more likely than other students to choose dishonesty or cheating as a means of survival.

In both the McCabe and Trevino (1993) study and the Michael and Miethe (1989) study, peer behavior and peer pressure to cheat were the most influential variables. Other related pressures cited in their studies were: (1) help or encouragement to cheat from friends; (2) failure to study or prepare properly; and (3) pressure from parents to raise grades.

THE INFLUENCE OF HONOR CODES

Precisely how many institutions have honor codes is unknown. The absence of a common definition of an honor code has made it difficult to compare institutions. In a Harvard study on honor codes, (Melendez, 1985) looked at the characteristics common to many honor codes throughout the country. He identified four characteristics: unproctored exams, a peer judiciary, non-toleration of offenses, and an honor pledge.

The author's 1991 survey (Kibler, 1992) of nearly 200 higher education institutions revealed that less than 25% reported that they had honor codes. The participating institutions were permitted to define honor code individually. The study revealed that many institutions have only a statement called an honor code, but few if any of the other components. It may be more descriptive to define an honor system, which includes the honor code as a component. An honor system may contain the following components: (Melendez, 1985)

- **Honor code.** A statement that establishes the expectations of the academic community regarding honor and integrity from all members.

- **Pledge.** All students affirm their obligation and commitment to comply with the expectations of the honor code.

The Administration of Campus Discipline . . .

- **Unproctored exams.** All examinations are unproctored due to the expectation that students will not cheat and will not tolerate cheating.

- **Non-toleration or obligation to report.** Expectation that students report themselves or others that are known to have engaged in a violation of the honor code.

- **Student governance.** Students govern the honor system. Students are actively involved in policy formulation, communication and enforcement necessary to maintain the integrity of the honor system and the honor code.

Bowers (1964) and McCabe (1993) compared code and non-code schools and generally found higher levels of dishonesty at schools without honor codes. However, McCabe did find some overlap in reported levels of cheating between honor and non-code schools. Self-reported levels of student cheating of some honor codes schools exceeded the level of cheating found at several non-code schools. Both Bowers and McCabe documented the critical role of the campus climate in communicating expectations and influencing student values and behavior (McCabe & Cole, 1996, p. 68).

Perhaps the most important value of an honor code is its role in establishing a campus ethos that promotes academic integrity. Bowers (1964) identified a strong relationship between institutional climate and students' predisposition to be honest or dishonest in their academic work (McCabe & Cole, 1996, p. 68). Bowers cited several important factors including institutional size, student perceptions of the campus disciplinary system, student perceptions of the level of cheating at the institution, and the presence or absence of an honor code. The positive influence of honor codes was reflected in Bower's (1964) study. His results showed 10% of students attending honor code schools felt there was a high level of cheating on their campuses while 80% of students at schools without honor codes perceived there was a high level of cheating on their campuses.

Research and writing by McCabe and others in the past few years and the creation of the Center for Academic Integrity in 1992 has resulted in what is perceived by many as a renewed interest in honor codes and their importance in promoting academic integrity on campuses.

ADDRESSING ACADEMIC INTEGRITY VIOLATIONS

Unfortunately, there is no quick fix, no single or simple solution to the problem of student cheating. Adopting an honor code and widely publicizing it is not enough. Institutions must adopt a comprehensive approach involving the entire campus community—students, faculty members, and administration.

Prevention of academic dishonesty must begin at the institutional level (Gehring et al., 1986; Kibler et al., 1988). Institutions must establish an environment that promotes a sense of responsibility and a general sense of morality, values and ethics in order to educate students about the issues involved in academic dishonesty (Bushway & Nash, 1977; Pavela, 1981; Gehring et al, 1986; Kibler et al., 1988).

Although the precise causes of cheating and the extent of the problem are not completely clear, colleges and universities need to utilize systematic and conscientious efforts to help students appreciate the fundamental values associated with effective scholarship and to embrace the standards of academic integrity.

A comprehensive framework for institutions to use in addressing academic dishonesty has been developed (Kibler, 1992). The framework is built on the concept that the most effective way to prevent cheating is to actively promote academic integrity, while at the same time confronting those who do cheat. Confronting cheating should include sanctions that respond to the behavior as well as educational programs or seminars that address developmental issues.

The first step is for institutions to establish an ethos that promotes academic integrity, one that defines it and holds it up as something to be revered. Such an ethos can be created or maintained through an honor code or honor system. It can also be created through a code of conduct or other strong, clear statements about what the institution expects from its students, exactly how cheaters will be punished, and why cheating actually hurts, rather than helps students.

After setting out its standards, the institution then must use all the tools it has to communicate its position on academic integrity and its intention not to tolerate academic dishonesty: direct correspondence to faculty members and students; mandated discussions about cheating during orientation meetings for student and faculty members, as well as during individual classes at the beginning of semesters; printed material such as handbooks; and the campus news media.

Faculty members are the most critical element in insuring the success of any campus-wide effort to promote academic integrity. They should reflect, communicate, and enforce the institution's values. They also should be involved in developing and implementing whatever system the institution creates; their participation will give them a sense of personal commitment to, and ownership of, the system.

Many faculty members refuse to address the problem of academic dishonesty, feeling the rules are too complicated and the procedures for enforcing them too time-consuming. Others try to minimize the problem for fear that it may reflect badly on their ability to teach. Institutions must help train faculty members in ways to prevent cheating and in how to create a classroom atmosphere in which honesty is clearly the expected standard.

It is also essential that students be involved in developing and carrying out systems to promote academic integrity. Failure to involve students creates an "us versus them" atmosphere, which tends to encourage cheating. Students can serve on honor or disciplinary boards and on review committees that assess how well an institution's process for assuring academic integrity is working.

Finally, an institution must coordinate its efforts to insure that all the elements of its system are implemented. One office should be responsible for monitoring relevant data, assessing the effectiveness of policies and procedures, coordinating communication efforts, and coordinating training programs on academic dishonesty and ways to prevent it.

Besides working to create a campus ethos of academic integrity, institutions must develop policies that deal effectively with students who still choose to cheat. Those policies should include:

- **Appropriate sanctions.** These might include a notation concerning academic dishonesty on a transcript, required counseling, and required attendance at a class or seminar on academic integrity.

- **A required educational program for offenders.** Such a program should include discussion of what cheating is and why it is unacceptable. It should also include education in moral development, to help students understand the relationship between moral reasoning and behavior. By using discussions, case studies, and role-playing exercises, students can be helped in responding to ethical dilemmas. Finally, the program or seminar should include training in academic skills to help students gain confidence in their abilities to succeed in the classroom without cheating.

- **Testing policies that emphasize prevention of cheating.** These could include procedures that protect the security of the tests before they are administered, proctoring services, assigned seating and the use of different versions of the same test during exams, and guidelines for making writing assignment that limit opportunities for plagiarism. More specific prevention strategies are listed in the chart in the next section.

- **Methods for reporting cheating that are not intimidating**—for example, that allow the person reporting the cheating to remain anonymous.

Prevention Strategies in the Classroom

Appendix I features a table that provides a brief, easy-to-follow chart of prevention strategies that may be used in a classroom or for assignments.

LEGAL AND POLICY ISSUES
ASSOCIATED WITH ACADEMIC INTEGRITY

This section offers responses to the most prevalent questions that seem to arise regarding legal issues and policy perspectives on academic integrity. (Gehring & Pavela, 1994; Kibler et al, 1988)

1. *Should I fear being sued for accusing a student of academic dishonesty?* A review of case law for the past 30 years shows no case in which administrators, faculty, or students have been assessed damages for reporting alleged acts of academic dishonesty.

2. *Should I be concerned about defamation accusations?* Faculty need not fear defamation suits where the student, after being accused by a faculty member of academic dishonesty, is found not to have committed the act. Faculty and administrators essentially enjoy a qualified immunity from suit and will not be held liable for actions taken in good faith in carrying out their assigned duties. Maintaining academic integrity is certainly a basic duty of every faculty member.

The U.S. Supreme Court developed a strict test in this regard: educators will not be held personally responsible for violating a student's constitutional rights unless they have acted with "impermissible motivation" or with such disregard of "clearly established constitutional rights" that their "action cannot reasonably be characterized as being in good faith" (*Wood*, 1975, p. 322).

3. *Isn't it just my word against his or hers anyway?* Many questions of fact come down to one individual's word against another. However, hearing panels may, for a variety of factors, attach greater weight to one person's word than they do another and the courts will generally not overrule a fact-finder's decision.

In *Abrahamian v. City University of New York* (1991), the court said, "As it is arguable that room for choice exists between conflicting testimony, the respondent's [university's] decision as to which version of events to accept should not be disturbed."

4. *These policies are a big hassle—so what happens if I just ignore them?* Faculty members who choose to ignore policies and procedures expose themselves to a real possibility of damages and actually encourage academic dishonesty. A faculty member who independently assigns an F to a student suspected of committing an act of dishonesty rather than going through proper campus procedures risks liability for violating the student's constitutional and contractual rights as well as abridging his or her contractual obligations to the institution (*James v. Wall*, 1989).

5. *What if I disagree with the outcome of the disciplinary proceedings?* Faculty must comply with the outcome of the procedures regardless

less of whether or not they agree. Having fair procedures for reporting and resolving offenses is worthless if faculty ignore the results. Thus, students who are found not to have engaged in academic dishonesty should not continue to be penalized by the accusing faculty member (*Lightsey v. King*, 1983).

6. *Are academic dishonesty decisions disciplinary or academic evaluations?* The pertinent legal standard was set forth by the U.S. Supreme Court in *Board of Curators of the University of Missouri v. Horowitz* (1978). Justice Rehnquist outlined two distinctions between disciplinary and academic determination:

a. An academic evaluation "is by nature more subjective and evaluative" than the "typical factual questions" encountered in the average disciplinary decision"; and

b. Disciplinary proceedings "automatically" bring "an adversarial flavor to the normal student-teacher relationship. The same conclusion does not follow in the academic context." (p.135)

Most academic dishonesty cases seem to involve disciplinary decisions rather than academic judgements. Contested cases of academic dishonesty usually require resolution of disputed questions of fact. Under these circumstances, imposing a serious stigmatizing penalty brings "an adversarial flavor to the normal student-teacher relationship" and will be regarded by most courts as requiring many of the procedural protections used in disciplinary cases.

7. *What due process is required in academic dishonesty cases?* The imposition of disciplinary sanctions for acts of academic dishonesty requires basic procedural protections for students. Such protection is desirable because it serves as a useful check upon the arbitrary interpretation and enforcement of campus regulations. Do not allow your institution to become paralyzed by a misconception of "due process." Due process in campus disciplinary proceedings does not require full adversarial hearings, technical rules of evidence, multiple appeals, or "beyond a reasonable doubt" standard of proof. Due process procedures for resolving allegations of academic dishonesty need not be complicated. A good outline of the basic requirements can be found in a New York appellate court case, *Mary M. v. Clark* (1984):

a. Provide a written notice of charges.

b. Make the student aware of the grounds that would justify expulsion or suspension.

c. Provide a hearing that allows the student the opportunity to hear and confront evidence and the opportunity to offer evidence.

d. Afford the student the right to have someone from the college community assist in the proceedings.

e. Inform the student in writing of the decision and any sanction imposed. A formal right of appeal need not be granted in disciplinary cases, although a senior administrative officer should review suspensions or expulsions.

8. *Are there uniform policies and procedures that should be followed by all units with the institution?* Different institutions have different missions based on different value systems. Each institution should be free to develop its own definitions, standards, policies and procedures for defining and resolving violations of academic integrity. All policies and procedures should comply with the basic concepts of fundamental fairness.

However, if the institution is to become a purposeful, just and disciplined community in which students are absolutely clear about the policies and standards, then they must be internally consistent. All members of the institution should agree on the definitions of various forms of academic dishonesty. Student must be included in the process of defining academic dishonesty or they may never really know what it is or be able to communicate the concept to peers. Students, faculty and administrators must be involved in identifying the range of sanctions to be imposed for violations.

Graduate and professional schools may legally hold their students to a higher standard than other students within the same institution. For instance, they may choose to hold their students accountable to professional standards or a code of ethics that do not apply to undergraduate students on the same campus.

9. *How should I respond to an act of academic dishonesty when it occurs?* Individuals who observe or are aware of an incident of academic dishonesty should report the matter to the faculty member or other appropriate institutional representative. Proctors or faculty members who observe academic dishonesty during an exam, lab or class should:

a. Promptly inform the student—privately if possible.
b. Remove unauthorized materials such as "crib sheets," if possible.
c. Note the names of the students in adjoining seats.
d. Allow the accused student to complete the exam.
e. Report the incident to the faculty member or the appropriate institutional representative.
f. Review campus procedures and initiate required action.

Some campuses permit anonymous reports of suspected academic dishonesty. Normally, official action is not based on anonymous reports alone, although such information might permit campus officials to identify common types of problems and encourage the faculty member to enhance prevention and detection efforts.

CONCLUSION

Faculty members, administrators and students cannot afford to ignore their responsibilities to promote academic integrity. Students must develop the values they need, to deal effectively with the moral and ethical dilemmas facing them. Clearly communicating an institution's expectation for academic honesty is an important way to foster students' development.

Frequent discussions about integrity provide the opportunity for academics to communicate the value they place on integrity, relative to other values such as achievement and competition. When cheating does occur, campus procedures should make students confront the ethical implications of their behavior, expose them to discussion of moral reasoning, and help them understand that effective learning depends on honesty, respect, rigor and fairness.

References

Barnett, D.C., & Dalton, J.C. (1981). Why college students cheat? *Journal of College Student Personnel*, 22, 545-551.

Bowers, W.J. (1964). *Student dishonesty and its control in college.* New York: Bureau of Applied Social Research, Columbia University.

Bushway, A., & Nash, W.R. (1977). School cheating behavior. *Review of Educational Research*, 47 (4), 623-632.

Carnegie Council on Policy Studies in Higher Education (1979). *Fair practices in higher education: Rights and responsibilities in a period of intensified competition for enrollment.* San Francisco: Jossey-Bass.

Cole, S., & McCabe, D.L. (1996). Issues in academic integrity. In W.L. Mercer (Ed.), *Critical Issues in Judicial Affairs: Current Trends in Practice.* San Francisco: Jossey-Bass.

Drake, C.A. (1941). Why students cheat. *Journal of Higher Education*, 12, 418-420.

Ellison, C.W. (1990). *The Foundations of self-esteem.* Unpublished manuscript. Westmont College.

Gehring, D., Nuss, E.M., & Pavela, G. (1986). *Issues and perspectives on academic integrity.* Columbus, OH: NASPA.

Gehring, D., & Pavela, G. (1994). *Issues and perspectives on academic integrity* (2nd Ed). Columbus, OH: NASPA.

Kibler, W.L., & Kibler, P.V. (1993, July 4). When students resort to cheating: Colleges need a comprehensive approach to the problem of academic dishonesty. The *Chronicle of Higher Education*, 39(45), B1-B2.

Kibler, W.L., Nuss E.M., Paterson, B.G., & Pavela, G.R., (1987). *Academic Integrity and Student Development: Legal Issues and Policy Perspectives.* Asheville, NC: College Administration Publications.

Kibler, W.L. (1993). A framework for addressing academic dishonesty from a student development perspective. *NASPA Journal*, 31(1), 8-18.

Kibler, W.L. (1992, Nov. 11). Cheating: Institutions need a comprehensive plan for promoting academic integrity. The *Chronicle of Higher Education*, 34(12), B1-B2.

Levine, A. (1980). *When dreams and heroes died: A portrait of today's college student.* San Francisco: Jossey-Bass.

McCabe, D.L., & Trevino, L.K. (1993). Academic dishonesty: Honor codes and other contextual influences. *Journal of Higher Education, 64* (5), 522-538.

Melendez, B. (1985). *Honor code study.* Cambridge, MA: Harvard University.

Michaels, J.W., & Miethe, T.D. (1989). Applying theories of deviance to academic cheating. *Social Science Quarterly, 70* (4), 872-885.

Morrill, R.L. (1980). *Teaching values in college.* San Francisco: Jossey-Bass.

Nuss, E.M. (1984). Academic integrity: Comparing faculty and student attitudes. *Improving College and University Teaching, 32* (3), 140-144.

Pavela, G. (1978). Judicial review of academic decision-making after Horowitz. *School Law Journal, 55* (8), 55-75.

Pavela, G. (1981, February 9). Cheating on campus. Who's really to blame? The *Chronicle of Higher Education,* p.64.

Pavela, G. (1994, October 17). New data reveal increase in test cheating. *Synfax Weekly Report,* 285.

Raffetto, W.G. (1985). The cheat. *Community and Junior College Journal, 56* (2), 26-27.

Singhal, A.C., & Johnson, P. (1983). How to halt student dishonesty. *College Student Journal, 17* (1), 13-19.

Tittle, C.R., & Rowe, A.R. (1973). Moral appeal, sanction threat, and deviance: An experimental test. *Social Problems, 20,* 488-497.

Uhlig, G.E., & Howes, B. (1967). Attitude toward cheating and opportunistic behavior. *Journal of Educational Research, 60,* 411-412.

Vitro, F.T., & Schoer, L.A. (1972). The effects of probability of test success, test importance, and risk of detection on the incidence of cheating. *Journal of School Psychology, 10,* 269-277.

Cases

Abrahamian v. City University of New York, 565 N.Y.S. 2d 511 (A.D. 1 Dept. 1991).

Board of Curators of the University of Missouri v. Horowitz, 55 L. Ed. 2d 124 (1978).

James v. Wall, 783 S.W. 2d 615 (Tx. Ct. App. Houston, 14 Dist., 1989).

Lightsey v. King, 567 F. Supp. 645 (E.D.N.Y. 1983).

Mary M. v. Clark, 473 N.Y.S. 2d 843 (A.D. 3 Dept. 1984).

Wood v. Strickland, 420 U.S. 308 (1975).

Appendix I

Summary of Prevention Strategies for Academic Dishonesty

Types of Cheating	Detection	Prevention Strategies
All types of cheating.	Constant attention to details of prevention strategies. Student help.	Stress student's moral and ethical responsibilities to avoid cheating and to help prevent others from cheating. Clarify policies regarding cheating and penalties for those who do cheat. Set up a "hotline" for students to report incidents of cheating. Individually counsel with students caught cheating or suspected of cheating.
Obtaining a copy of the test.	Student's responses seem beyond abilities. Pattern of wrong answers by students known to associate with each other.	Tests should be secured in a safe place from creation to administration. Avoid leaving the exam on the hard drive of the computer. If possible, place on a disk that can be secured. Tests should be originals, not repetitions of exams given in previous semesters.
Test Taking: Copying. Crib notes and other means of bringing answers into the exam. Passing answers.	Carefully proctor exams.	Instructors should walk around the room. When giving multiple choice or short answer tests, alternate test forms should be used. Spread students out using randomized seating so every other seat is empty. All books, papers and personal belongings should be stored or placed in the front of the classroom. Paper should be provided for the test answers and any scratch work. Staple the answer sheets and the scratch paper prior to distribution with answer sheet on the bottom. Do not permit papers to be unstapled. If "blue books" are being used, require students to turn them in blank during the class prior to the exam. The books can be distributed at the start of the test. Give essay exams rather than true/false or multiple choice exams. Do not permit any communication among students. Test pick-up—have students leave their test package on their desks upon completion.

Types of Cheating	Detection	Prevention Strategies
Test Taking ... *continued*	Carefully proctor exams.	This helps reduce switching papers and will allow detection of copying from neighbors by answer patterns.
"Ringer" taking the test for another student.	Carefully proctor exam. Check student IDs.	Have each student display his or her photo ID on the desk during the exam. Proctors can match students with IDs during the exam. Have each student hand in the test personally and present his or her ID. The instructor inspects the ID, checks the class roster, checks the name on the exam, and initials the exam paper.
"Stooge" who sits in on the exam and leaves with a copy of the test.	Be vigilant—try to have a proctor watch each exit, especially early. Check IDs early.	Number all tests before distribution. Be sure all tests are returned. If one is missing, be alert to whether it shows up later. If a student needs to leave the room during a test have him or her hand in the exam until returning.
Following the Test: Turning in a lifted exam as if taken in class.	Close observation.	Do not leave exams or grade sheet/book on the desk or unattended. Keep in a locked/safe place. If a test is discovered missing at the end of an exam, be alert to whether it shows up later.
Changing grades on exams. Changing answers on exams.	Photocopy the tests before handing them back. If there are too many, copy them randomly and copy any suspected of cheating.	Mark grades on grade sheet/book prior to returning tests. Inform students that exams will be photocopied before returning—to detect changes. Do not keep grades on hard drive on computer—place them on a disk and secure the disk.
Take-home test done by an "expert."	Solution done in a way not covered during the class. Looks "professional."	Avoid giving take-home tests. Require oral presentation about suspicious material.
Homework/Reports: Copy solutions from instructor's manual.	Compare solutions with manual.	Change to a book with no manual.

The Administration of Campus Discipline ...

Types of Cheating	Detection	Prevention Strategies
Copy solutions from fellow students. Copy from old homework sets from previous semesters.	Careful grading—look for similarities.	Count homework as only a small percentage of final grade or not at all. Give different homework assignments each semester.
Have report done by an "expert."	Solutions done in a way not covered in class.	Ask for oral presentations on suspicious reports.
Plagiarism	Look for significant fluctuations in writing style. Looks "professional." Look for work that appears to be clearly beyond student's ability. Compare with in-class writing assignments.	Place limits on topic selection. Avoid topics that are too general—decreases the likelihood of using a "paper mill." Change topic lists frequently. Establish precise format for paper and stick to it. Require a tentative bibliography early in the term. Require library location numbers. Require advance outline of the paper. Do not permit late topic changes. Give pop test on basic knowledge. Accept only originally typed manuscripts—no photocopies. Require notes and rough drafts. Keep original papers on file for five years. Use in-class writing assignments.

Reprinted from Kibler, W.L., Nuss E.M., Paterson, B.G. & Pavela, G.R. (1987). *Academic Integrity and Student Development: Legal Issues and Policy Perspectives.* Asheville, NC: College Administration Publications.

Chapter X

Use and Misuse of Computers

Brent G. Paterson

The information age has arrived in the student judicial affairs arena. A few short years ago, student judicial affairs administrators dealt with the occasional hacker who was attempting to see how far he/she could go in gaining access to the mainframe computer. Today, the easy accessibility to computer workstations in university computer labs, personal computers linked to the campus network from residence hall rooms, and modem and Internet access from anywhere in the world have resulted in misuse of computer resources and facilities by more than a few "computer nerds."

Legacy of the '60s Generation

The computer age of the 90s has its roots in the 60s. Stewart Brand, creator of the *Whole Earth Catalog* and co-founder of Hackers Conference, described in a *Time* article entitled, "We Owe it All To the Hippies," how four generations of hackers have revolutionized the computer world.

The first generation emerged from university computer science departments in the early 60s and 70s. These individuals provided widespread access to computers changing mainframes into virtual personal computers.

The second generation was the hard-core counter-culture type of individuals. They lived by the motto "Turn on, tune in and drop out." The personal computer was invented and manufactured by this group in the late 70s. Two people who symbolize this group are Steve Jobs, a Reed College dropout, and Steve Wozniak, a Hewlett-Packard engineer, who together founded Apple Computers. In earlier days, they manufactured and sold illegal devices for making free telephone calls.

The third generation is the software hackers of the early 80s. They developed application, education and entertainment programs for personal computers providing everyone with a use for a personal computer.

The fourth generation includes the thousands of "netheads" who have transformed the ARPAnet developed for the Defense Department into the information superhighway known as the Internet. They lead the way in making available "freeware" or "shareware," software that is not copyrighted and is thus available to anyone that wants it (Brand, 1995).

The Internet

The Internet is "a vast international network of networks that enables computers of all kinds to share services and communicate directly, as if they were part of one giant, seamless, global computing machine" (Elmer-DeWitt, 1994, p. 52). Originally designed and built for the Department of Defense over 25 years ago, what has evolved into the Internet has changed significantly. The original purpose of what was known as ARPAnet was to enable academic and military researchers to continue to conduct research and communicate with each other even if part of the network was destroyed by a nuclear attack. Later, universities, governmental agencies and corporations were linked.

Users quickly determined that there were more uses of the system than official business. They sent colleagues private messages (e-mail) and developed information postings (USENET news groups). Graduate students who had access and computer hackers developed tools for navigating the Internet like the University of Minnesota's GOPHER. Yet, the Internet remained relatively obscure to the general public and difficult to use (Elmer-DeWitt).

What happens with and on the Internet is a departure from most organized systems. Since it was designed to withstand a nuclear attack, it is without a central command authority. There are no owners, no administrators deciding what and how things happen and no censors. Besides these technical difficulties in operating a system that has become a communications system for the masses, there are also cultural problems (Elmer-DeWitt, 1994).

Steven Levy in his 1984 book, *Hackers: Heroes of the Computer Revolution*, reports that an anarchistic ethic exists among computer wizards, the persons who changed the Internet. They believe that access to computers should be unlimited and total, that all information should be free, and that you should mistrust authority and promote decentralization.

Students today have grown up in this culture which subscribes to anarchistic behavior. It almost sounds like the 60s when the adage was "don't trust anyone over 30". Today, students question why colleges and universities should have any interest in what they view, post and send across campus networks and onto the Internet. They cry that you are violating their free speech rights and rights to privacy when any attempt is made to address inappropriate use of computing resources.

ABUSE OF COMMUNAL RESOURCES

Computing resources and facilities should be considered products to be shared. Although the university owns the mainframe computer that processes e-mail and Internet connections, the computer work stations in computer labs, and the connections in the residence hall rooms that tie students' personal computers to university networks and beyond, users often fail to realize that these resources and facilities are communal resources.

Abuse of communal resources may be as simple as the person who sits at a computer terminal in a computer lab for endless hours. It may be a person who unintentionally sends a large mailing that creates a gridlock at the mailhub causing the system to shut down. It also may be the large print job sent that monopolize a computing center printer for an inordinate amount of time.

Improper Use of Systems / Invasion of Privacy

The improper use of computer systems is what we commonly consider when we hear about a computer violation. One area of improper use is breach of computer security systems. Any unauthorized access to a computer resource is such a violation. These violators are the hackers and crackers. In August 1994, the Computer Emergency Response Team Coordination Center at Carnegie Mellon University issued an alert about computer crackers (mean-spirited hackers) who were seeking ways to interfere with or disable the Internet. (Wilson, 1994). There are numerous examples at every institution of the student who has gained unauthorized access to a campus computer system.

The release of passwords or other confidential information about computer security are considered a breach of computer security systems. All the technological safeguards in the world are of no use if users share their passwords with others and leave passwords and access codes where others can easily access them. Many campuses have computerized registration systems. At Texas A&M University, the students register for classes by touch-tone phone. The passwords to register are a student's identification number (social security number usually) and date of birth.

Every semester we have a few students who find that their class schedules have been dropped or new fees added by someone else. Often, it turns out that a scorned former boyfriend or girlfriend who knows the id number and date of birth has taken the liberty of tampering with the registration. Student information systems have given faculty, staff and sometimes student employees access to vast amounts of confidential information about students. Although these trusted faculty and staff are usually sworn to secrecy and informed of the intent of the Family Education Rights and Privacy Act, the chances of information leaks are high. The educational need to know is replaced with the personal want to check the grades of the star athlete or check the schedule of the person you met at the local bar.

Harmful access includes activities that create a computer malfunction; interrupt computer operations; alter, damage or destroy data or a computer program; or inject a computer virus into a computer system. In November 1995, a sophomore at Monmouth University was alleged to have sent 24,000 e-mail messages to the university's computers in a deliberate attempt to disrupt use of the campus e-mail system. Supposedly, the student's actions were in response to the university suspending his Internet account after receiving complaints that the student was advertising business proposals inappropriately on the network. The student was charged with two counts of violating the federal Computer Fraud and Abuse Act of 1986 for allegedly causing the university's e-mail system to shut down for five hours with a "mail bomb" (Wilson, 1995, November 30).

Other forms of improper use of computing systems include forged mail or postings and use of computer resources for personal or commercial gain. A professor at Texas A&M University at Corpus Christi received death threats and over 1,000 e-mail messages after someone illegally gained access to his e-mail account and sent 20,000 racist messages nationwide under his name. The message had a white supremacist message that was offensive to many (Messer, 1994a). While defining use of computer resources for personal gain may be easy to identify, defining personal use is not quite so clear.

Since colleges and universities have as their primary mission education, it is very difficult to determine where educational purposes end and personal use begins. Is the student employee in violation of a code that prohibits use of computers for personal gain when he/she types a paper on the office computer and prints the final copy on the office printer? Is the secretary of a fraternity in violation for typing and printing minutes of fraternity meetings on university computers? What about the student who prints color pictures of military airplanes on the high-speed university color graphic printer? What if the student is majoring in aerospace engineering or is in Air Force ROTC?

With students, it seems when you look at personal use you begin to make content decisions that come dangerously close to violating the First Amendment. With employees, it is easier to define use as those activities necessary to perform the job. However, just like telephone use, incidental personal use of computers may be appropriate so long as it does not interfere with job performance or result in undue expense to the institution.

The Computer Fraud and Abuse Act of 1986 (18 U.S.C. Section 1030) prohibits most activities that could be considered improper use of systems. According to this act, it is a violation of law to (1) knowingly access a "federal interest" computer (defined to include any computers accessed from more than one state) with the intent to defraud and obtain something of value beyond use of the computer itself; and (2) intentionally gain unauthorized access to a "federal interest" computer whereby such conduct alters, damages or destroys information therein or prevents authorized use. With the wide availability of Internet access on campuses, virtually every computer connected to a network can be considered a "federal interest" computer. Most states also have computer crime laws that address improper use of computing resources.

MISAPPROPRIATION OF INTELLECTUAL PROPERTY

Unlicensed copying of copyrighted material and software piracy are examples of misappropriation if intellectual property. Federal copyright statues (17 U.S.C. Section 101 et seq.) govern copyrighted material on computers and the Internet in addition to the paper media. The Copyright Statues protect "computer programs from infringement" and address the rental, lease, or lending of unauthorized copies of computer programs. The Working Group on Intellectual Property Rights from the U.S. Department of Commerce has been working on what changes in the law are needed in this electronic age of information. The final report of the Working Group recommends that copyright laws be revised so that copies of intellectual works can be distributed to the public by electronic means, and that the exclusive distribution right of the copyright owner govern such transmissions. The Working Group, however, did not provide a recommendation on "fair use" of electronic documents

The current Copyright Act permits duplication of portions of materials that are copyrighted for purposes of commentary, criticism, news reporting, research, and teaching (Report on Intellectual Property, 1995). There is considerable disagreement about "fair use" of electronic documents between publishers and libraries. Publishers are seeking that a copyright would govern any access to copyrighted material. While librarians argue that individuals should be permitted to browse material before paying copyright charges, they compare the browsing of electronic material to glancing at a book before deciding to buy it. One can easily imagine the cost to university libraries if there was a charge every time a patron accessed a copyrighted document. Writing in the January 1996 edition of *Wired*, Pamela Samuelson, a visiting professor of law at Cornell University, states, "The only way the entrenched copyright industry can imagine marketing content electronically is through extensive technological locks that will make digital information less free than print information" (p. 191). In fact, copyright legislation (S1284 and HR 2441) for the national Information Infrastructure (NII) that would have placed under the exclusive right of the copyholder any transmission of a copyright work over an electronic network, stalled in the 104th Congress (Hold up . . ., 1996).

Meanwhile, the Consortium of College and University Media Centers agreed on "fair use" guidelines for the use of copyright material in a multimedia work. According to the guidelines, limited amounts of a copyrighted work may be used in a multimedia work. For music, up to 10 percent or 30 seconds, whichever is less, of an individual musical piece is considered "fair use." In distance learning, copyrighted material may be used if only enrolled students have access to the material and that access is protected by technological means such as a password. There are also restrictions on the number of copies of CD-ROMS or videos created for students and professors (Blumenstyk, 1996). A House of Representatives subcommittee on Courts and Intellectual Property has endorsed the Consortium's guidelines.

Students have little understanding of copyrights. When you add the electronic environment to the mix, the understanding or, at least, the ethical obligation of abiding by copyright laws seems almost non-existent. It is quite common to have software and other copyrighted material on your computer that was "borrowed" from someone else or acquired from the Internet.

Businesses and corporations are becoming more aggressive in pursuing copyright infringements. For example, Playboy Enterprises monitors web sites that might contain images of Playboy Playmates. When a copyrighted image is found, Playboy sends a message to the web site owner informing him/her of the copyright infringement and requesting removal of the copyrighted image. The web site owner who does not comply with Playboy's directive might find him/herself in legal difficulties.

A student at M.I.T. was alleged to have established a system on university computers that permitted Internet users to duplicate copyrighted commercial software. The student was charged with violating federal wire-fraud laws. A U.S. district judge dismissed the case by ruling that the student could not be charged under the federal wire-fraud law and that successful prosecution of the case under the Copyright Act could not occur since it could not be proven that the student had "infringed a copyright willfully and for the purpose of commercial advantage or private financial gain." The judge also stated, "if the indictment is to be believed, one might at best describe [the student's] actions as heedlessly irresponsible, self-indulgent, and lacking in any fundamental sense of values" (Federal Judge Dismisses Software-Piracy Case, 1995).

A ruling by a federal judge in California suggests that colleges and universities may be responsible for violation of the copyright law appearing on university computers. This widely publicized case involved the posting of doctrine from the Church of Scientology on an electronic bulletin board. Netcom On-Line Communication Services was sued by the Church of Scientology for disseminating what it claims are copyrighted scriptures. The judge ruled that the Internet provider, Netcom, could be sued for copyright infringement if it was aware that copyrighted material was placed on its bulletin board (Court Ruling Alarms Managers . . . 1995).

Obviously, university administrators are concerned that universities may be held liable for possible copyright infringements on their computers. One can imagine how many hours it would take to check all computers on a campus for copyright infringements not even considering what privacy rights might be violated while conducting such investigations.

HARASSMENT

Are communications in computer discussion groups and on e-mail protected speech or can they constitute harassment? The answer is—it depends. The law in this area is vague and there will need to be more court cases decided to establish a precedent. However, it seems clear that sexual harassment is much more likely to be upheld by a court than harassment due to race, age, national origin, religion or other protected classes.

The Office of Civil Rights (OCR) in the U.S. Department of Education conducted an investigation of a complaint of sexual harassment from three students at Santa Rosa Junior College. Two of the students, both females, claimed that they had been sexually harassed by communications about them circulated on a men-only computer conference. The third student, a male, claimed that the college had retaliated against him for sharing the content of the conference with the two female students. The conference had been established by an instructor for students who wanted to discuss gender-related issues (DeLoughry & Wilson, 1994).

OCR determined that sex-segregated computer discussion groups violated Title IX and that comments made on the conference by three men who worked with one of the female complainants on the campus newspaper constituted "hostile environment discrimination" (Pavela, September 22, 1994). OCR concluded that the conference was an "educational program" with limited participation and monitored by the college. It was not a public forum.

Specifically, as reported in the September 28, 1994 edition of The *Chronicle of Higher Education*, the letter from OCR to Santa Rosa College states, "[the conference] was not like a traditional bulletin board or a conversation in a locker room, that any student could use to add their expression to the 'marketplace of ideas'; [The conference] was more closely analogous to the campus mailbox system what was established for a limited purpose and subject to control by the College" (Deloughry & Wilson, 1994).

According to Pavela (1994), "OCR also seems to be making a distinction between computer bulletin messages that are likely to promote a pattern of on-going harassment, and conversations that are merely statements of personal opinion, albeit vulgar and offensive. The latter does not constitute what the courts have been defining as sexual harassment" (p. B274).

In 1995, the arrest of a University of Michigan student who wrote a fantasy about rape and murder of a fellow University of Michigan student, identified by name, and shared the stories on the Internet made national news. In one of the stories the student described the torturing of the female student with a hot curling iron and raping her while she is gagged and tied to a chair. The student was charged with five counts of using electronic mail to issue a threat to kidnap or injure. The U.S. district judge dismissed the charges and indicating that it is not a violation of the Constitution to express "musings, considerations of what it would be like to kidnap or injure someone, or desires to kidnap or injure someone" (Death Tale, 1995).

However, the judge commented that the incident was more appropriate for handling by the university as a disciplinary matter than by the courts. The University of Michigan had suspended the student. A three-judge panel of the Sixth Circuit Court of Appeals ruled in a 2 to 1 decision that the stories did not constitute threats (Young, 1997).

Some states have laws that specifically prohibit harassment by electronic means. Arizona enacted an anti-harassment law in 1992 that includes threatening or harassing statements made by electronic means. Michigan passed a stalking law in the same year that covers repeated and unwanted mail or electronic communications. In 1995 Connecticut made harassment by computer a crime. The Connecticut law simply extends the already accepted definition of harassment to include electronic communications (Connecticut Makes Computer Harassment a Crime, 1995). Several other states are considering similar legislation.

Cornell University was in the news when a message created by four students called, "75 reasons why women (bitches) should not have freedom of speech" was widely disseminated via the Internet. The university was flooded with phone calls and e-mail messages urging the university to take action against the students. Other e-mail messages threatened to overload Cornell's computer system and the students received death threats. The students issued an apology that was printed in the Cornell student newspaper. According to the printed apology, the students sent the list they had written to only a small group of friends. At least one of these friends distributed the list to others and eventually it was posted in USENET, an electronic bulletin-board system accessible through the Internet (Wilson, 1995, November 24).

After reviewing the facts of the case, Cornell decided not to pursue disciplinary action against the students. It determined that sexual harassment did not occur since the "75 Reasons" were not directed at an individual or groups of individuals and did not create a hostile environment. Cornell also concluded that there was not a violation of computer policies. In a public statement printed in the November 20, 1995 edition of *Synfax*, the Cornell student judicial affairs administrator stated, ". . . they [computer policies] reaffirm the concept of free speech and recognize that certain offensive messages may have to be tolerated in a community that values the right of all to speak freely" (Pavela, 1995, p. 423). Several persons, including survivors of sexual assault, took the time to explain to these four students why their words were so hurtful. The education that occurred with these students far exceeded any learning that may have come from a judicial penalty.

When is it harassment? Each college and university should turn to their harassment policies to determine if the actions that include use of a computer constitute harassment. M.I.T. has developed a three-prong test to determine if a reported behavior constitutes sexual harassment. Posters containing this test and how to report incidents of harassment are posted in computer labs on campus. The posters, titled "Don't Ignore Harassment" state,

Is it harassment? Ask yourself these three questions:
1. Did the incident cause stress that affected your ability or the ability of others, to work or study?
2. Was it unwelcome behavior?
3. Would a reasonable person of your gender/race/religion subjected to this behavior find it unacceptable/acceptable?

If you answer yes to these questions, please don't ignore the situation (Jackson, 1994, p. 34).

CENSORSHIP

The idea of censorship in electronic communications has created quite a stir. "computer geeks" who cry First Amendment at any mention of censoring material on computers and the Internet are squaring off against legislators and those pushing to restrict the type of information available through computers. What initially was intended as an anti-smut bill by Senator Exon was folded into the Telecommunications Competition and Deregulation Act of 1995. The bill, known as the Communications Decency Act, as passed by the Senate would have imposed fines of up to $100,000 and/or up to two years in prison for persons distributing or knowingly permitting individuals to distribute material that is obscene, lewd, lascivious, filthy, or indecent (Senate Bill 652, 1995).

Former lieutenant governor of Texas and current chancellor of the University of Houston System, Bill Hobby (1995), wrote in a *Houston Chronicle* editorial, "Under the guise of protecting children from smut, the Senate has adopted one of the most draconian invasions of privacy ever . . . Congress has decided it must control what you send over your personal computer. This is directly equivalent to opening your mail."

In June 1996, a three-judge panel in federal district court in Philadelphia struck down the Communications Decency Act (CDA) in *ACLU v. Reno*. Judge Slovitar concluded "that the CDA reaches speech subject to the full protection of the First Amendment." Judge Buckwalter wrote, "I continue to believe that the word 'indecent' is unconstitutionally vague, and I find that the terms 'in context' and 'patently offensive' are so vague as to violate the First and Fifth Amendments." Judge Dalzell commented, "The Internet is a far more speech enhancing medium than print, the village green, or the mails . . . the Internet may be fairly regarded as a never-ending worldwide conversation . . . As the most participatory form of mass speech yet developed, the Internet deserves the highest protection from government intrusion." (Cited from Pavela, 1996).

On June 26, 1997, the U.S. Supreme Court, in its first venture into cyberspace law, ruled the Communications Decency Act was unconstitutional. Authoring the court's majority opinion, Justice John Paul Stevens wrote, We agree with the three-judge district court that the statute abridges the freedom of speech protected by the First Amendment. The Communications Decency Act is a content-based regulation of speech. The vagueness of such a regulation raises special First Amendment concerns because of its obvious chilling effect on free speech (as cited in "Court Strikes Down CDA," 1997).

According to the court, filtering software and other means are available to protect children from harmful materials on the Internet ("Court Strikes Down Internet Smut," 1997).

The *New York Times*, in a June 16, 1997 article stated that the White House, in anticipation that the CDA would be ruled unconstitutional by the Supreme Court, was drafting a policy statement that would recommend regulation of the Internet be left to industry (Gehl & Douglas, 1997, June 17). On June 20, 1997, federal judges in New York and Georgia blocked those states "from enforcing laws intended to protect children from on-line pedophiles and to bar anonymous communications in cyberspace" (Haworth, 1997).

The landmark case in defining what material is obscene remains *Miller v. California* (1973). In this case the Supreme Court stated that material is obscene if: (1) The average person, applying contemporary community standards would find materials taken as a whole, appeal to the prurient interest (arouse immoral lustful desire); (2) the materials depict or describe, in patently offensive way, sexual conduct specifically prohibited by applicable state law; and (3) the materials, taken as a whole, lacks any artistic, political or scientific value.

Virtually every university that permits students to establish homepages or provides Internet access to its students has some material on its servers that is offensive. The offensive materials likely include nude images; derogatory comments about race, ethnicity, gender or sexual orientation; and numerous other written and graphic displays. One common issue is the nude images available on student web pages. Persons outside the university and those who do not understand computing systems believe that the university is endorsing these displays and demand immediate removal. Colleges and universities by their very nature encourage an open environment for scholarly inquiry and the sharing of information. Thus, thus colleges and universities must protect freedom of expression and guard against censorship merely because the content may be offensive to someone.

In Fall 1996, Texas A&M University was contacted by GE Motors and Industrial Systems about an unauthorized web page that appeared on the GE server. The web page which contained numerous images of nude women, some of the images displayed men and women engaged in sexual acts. The university rules for responsible computing prohibited the use of computing system for criminal and illegal acts including obscenity. The case was taken to the district attorney who indicated that some of the images were likely violations of the state law on obscenity.

The Texas Penal Code (paragraph 43.21) defines obscenity as material that depicts or describes patently offensive representations or descriptions of ultimate sexual acts, normal or perverted, actual or simulated; including sexual intercourse, sodomy, and sexual bestiality; or patently offensive representation or descriptions of masturbation, excretory functions, sadism, lewd exhibition of the genitals, the male or female genitals in a state of sexual stimulation or arousal, covered male genitals in a discernibly turgid state or a device designed and marketed as useful primarily for stimulation of the human genital organs . . ." (Texas Penal Code, 1996, p. 90). Based on the opinion of the district attorney, the university informed the student that he would need to remove the pictures identified as obscene from his web page or face discipline charges.

Even with the debate on censorship, the law, today, clearly prohibits the distribution of child pornography including the use of electronic communications. In September 1995, the FBI arrested twelve America Online subscribers for allegedly transmitting photos of nude children between the age of two and thirteen (FBI Porn Sting, 1995).

These arrests followed the conviction of a California couple on eleven counts of obscenity for placing sexually oriented images on a computer bulletin board system. Interestingly, the case was heard in Memphis, Tennessee where a postal inspector had worked with the U.S. Attorney in gathering evidence. Thus, the community standard for the indecency of the material on the computer bulletin board system became the community standard in Memphis not California where the computer was located.

CONCLUSION

The laws have not caught up with the realities of the electronic information age. Meanwhile, colleges and universities must deal with students who are still learning that responsibility comes with the freedom to make your own decisions. They will push the limits with the electronic environment as they do in other areas of the campus. We need to be proactive in teaching students about responsible use of computer resources and facilities.

We need to be teaching ethics for the information age and how they directly apply to how they use a computer everyday. They need to understand that while colleges and universities protect their freedom of expression, what they say, send and display may be offensive and even hurtful to others. They also need to understand that the work environment is not as tolerant and forgiving as the academic environment. When they leave the halls of academia and take that job with the Fortune 500 company, inappropriate use of computing resources will quickly lead to the unemployment line.

Not all communications and displays on web pages or via e-mail are protected by the First Amendment. Unlawful expression includes obscenity, harassment based on a protected class (race, sex, disability, religion, age, etc.), harassment in general, defamation, threats of violence, and disruption of the normal operations of the university. When these unlawful expressions occur, the student behavior should be addressed as would any other violation of the code of conduct.

Bill Gates, Chairman of Microsoft, is quoted in the February 1997 edition of *George* as saying, "It is always surprising how old concepts carry over into the new medium. It's overly idealistic to act like, Oh, the Internet is the one place where people should be able to do whatever they wish: present child pornography, do scams, libel people, steal copyrighted material. Society's values have not changed fundamentally just because it's an Internet page" (as cited in Gehl & Douglas, 1997, February 4).

If your campus has not already done so, it needs to review its computer policies. Do they address networks and Internet access? Do they cover sexual harassment and child pornography? How will you handle the posting of offensive material? The landscape, or should I say cyberspace, is changing so quickly that many campuses have a select group of faculty, administrators and legal counsel who meet regularly to discuss the latest inventive use of computing resources by students and the latest wrinkle in legislation or legal decision.

Computer misuse will be the topic of conference sessions and articles for years to come. Hopefully, Congress and the courts will give us direction in how to administer campus computer systems in a way that is feasible and recognizes the uniqueness of the academy.

References

Blumenstyk, G. (1996, October 16). Agreement reached on fair use rules for "educational media." *Academe Today* [On-line]. Available: http://chronicle.com

Brand, S. (1995, Spring). We owe it to all the hippies. *Time,* 145(12), 54-56.

Computer Fraud and Abuse Act of 1986, 18 U.S.C. section 1030.

Connecticut makes computer harassment a crime. (1995). *About Woman on Campus,* 4(4), 7.

Court ruling alarms managers of computer networks. (1995, December 8). The *Chronicle of Higher Education,* A21.

Court strikes down Communications Decency Act. (1997, June 26). *USA Today* [On-line]. Available: http://www.usatoday.com/life/cyber/tech/cta746.htm.

Court strikes down Internet smut law. (1997, June 26). *CNN* [On-line]. Available: http://www.cnn.com/US/9706026/sc.

Death tale by e-mail not a crime (1995, June 22). *Houston Chronicle,* 18A.

DeLoughry, T. J. & Wilson, D.L. (1994, September 28). Case of computer conference at California college pits free speech against civil-rights protection. The *Chronicle of Higher Education,* A26.

Elmer-DeWitt, P. (1994, July 25). Battle for the soul of the Internet. *Time,* 144(4), 50-56.

FBI porn sting nabs 12 nationwide. (1995, September 14). *c/net central* [On-line]. Available: http://www.cnet.com.

Federal Copyright statues, 17 U.S.C. section 101 et seq.

Federal judge dismisses software-piracy case (1995, January 6). The *Chronicle of Higher Education,* A4.

Gehl, J. & Douglas, S. (1997, February 4). Gates says old laws are good enough for the net. *Edupage* [On-line Serial]. Available: Educom, Washington, DC.

Gehl, J. & Douglas, S. (1997, June 17). White House does somersault on Decency Act. *Edupage* [On-line Serial]. Available: Educom, Washington, DC.

Haworth, K. (1997, June 23). Federal courts bar Georgia and New York from enforcing Internet-decency laws. *Academe Today* [On-line]. Available: http://chronicle.com.

Hobby, B. (1995, April 17). Danger lurking: Thought police in cyberspace. *Houston Chronicle,* 17A.

Hold up international negotiations on electronic copyrights until U.S. Law is decided in Congress, say educational associations, (1996, September 17). *Life Science* —as reported from the Washington Fax.

Jackson, G.A. (1994). Promoting civility on the academic network: Crime and punishment or the golden rule? *Educational Record,* 75(3), 29-39.

Messer, L. (1994, October 21). E-mail messages outrage networkers. The *Battalion,* 1, 10.

Pavela, G.M. (1994, September 22). E-mail and sexual harassment. *Synfax Bulletin,* B274.

Pavela, G. M. (1995, November 20). Sexual harassment and e-mail. *Synfax Weekly Report,* 423-424.

Pavela, G. M. (1996, June 17). The end of computer decency? *Synfax Weekly Report,* 497-498.

Report on intellectual property suggests minor changes in law. (1995, September 6). *Academe Today* [On-line]. Available: http://chronicle.com.

Samuelson, P. (1996, January). The copyright grab. *Wired,* 134-138, 188-191.

Wilson, D.L. (1994, August 17). "Crackers": A serious threat. The *Chronicle of Higher Education,* A23-A24.

Wilson, D.L. (1995, November 24). Misogynistic e-mail sparks controversy on Cornell campus. The *Chronicle of Higher Education,* A20.

Wilson, D.L. (1995, November 30). Student charged with fraud for flooding campus system with e-mail. *Academe Today* [On-line]. Available: http://chronicle.com

---

Cases

American Civil Liberties Union, et al. v. Janet Reno, 929 F. Supp. 824 (E.D. Penna. 1996), no. 96-511, slip op. (U.S. June 26, 1997).

Miller v. California, 413 U.S. 15 (1973).

Sable Communications of California, Inc. v. FCC, 492 U.S. 115 (1989).

Chapter XI

Responding to Students Manifesting Serious Psychological Problems*

William L. Kibler

Pavela (1995, July) effectively defines the concerns related to responding to students manifesting serious psychological problems:

> Many educators are increasingly concerned about the appropriate response of the academic community to suicidal students and to students who appear to have a mental disorder. Too often, that response entails the mandatory "psychiatric" withdrawal of students pursuant to broadly worded policies which provide for little or no procedural due process, and which reflect insufficient attention to the requirements of Section 504 of the Rehabilitation Act of 1973 and the ADA. While it is possible to draft psychiatric withdrawal policies which may avoid these difficulties, campus administrators should be alerted to the dangers of misusing any psychiatric withdrawal policy in an effort to remove students who are simply perceived "troublesome" or eccentric. (p.1)

When violations of student conduct regulations occur, regardless of the underlying issue that led to the misbehavior, it is always in the best interest of the student and the institution to use the student disciplinary process. Resorting to involuntary psychological withdrawal procedures, even when the misbehavior appears to be a manifestation of serious psychological problems, denies the student and the campus as a whole the important benefits and protections associated with formal student disciplinary processes (Pavela, 1995, July).

This chapter will address the issues and concerns that should be considered in developing procedures for the withdrawal of students manifesting serious psychological difficulties. The chapter will also identify those instances where it is appropriate to use these procedures and when it is more beneficial to use the student disciplinary process.

---

* The author acknowledges and credits the work of Gary Pavela, who wrote the most comprehensive and defining book on this subject; *The Dismissal of Students With Mental Disorders: Legal Issues, Policy Considerations and Alternative Responses*. Pavela's book and subsequent outlines have been utilized extensively in this chapter.

191

Finally, a comprehensive model policy that incorporates the safe-guards addressed in this chapter has been developed, including samples of associated correspondence. Existing institutional policies and context make it inappropriate for campus administrators to adopt the sample procedures "as is." They are intended, however, to provide a framework from which institutions may develop or modify their own procedures.

Substantive Due Process

Ill-conceived psychological withdrawal policies may inadvertently mirror campus conduct policies that existed during the pre-1960s "in loco parentis" era. A review of such policies reveals language that calls for students to be "withdrawn" because their "state of mind so recommends" or because their "mental health renders them undesirable" (*Aronson v. North Park College*, 1981, p. 781).

Broadly worded psychological withdrawal policies at public institutions may be unconstitutionally vague. In *Shamloo v. Mississippi State Board of Trustees* (1980), the court invalidated a campus regulation that authorized only "wholesome" demonstrations. The court observed that "[t]he regulation must not be designed so that people of common intelligence must guess at its meaning and differ as to its application" (pp. 523-524). It is imperative that such policies clearly define the characteristics that the institution considers "a manifestation of serious psychological problems." The model procedures at the end of this chapter define such manifestations as follows:

1. Instances where a student engages, or threatens to engage in behavior which poses a danger of causing physical harm to self or others; or

2. Instances that would cause significant property damage, or would directly and substantially impede the lawful activities of others, or would interfere with the educational process and the orderly operations of the institution.

The use of "medical" language in such polices is not a panacea. The fact that medical or psychological issues are being addressed does not justify a reduction in due process. See Chief Justice Burger, concurring in the Supreme Court decision *O'Conner v. Donaldson* (1975): "[w]here claims that the state is acting in the best interests of an individual are said to justify reduced procedural and substantive safeguards, this court's decisions require that they be 'candidly appraised'" (p. 586).

Procedural Due Process

A common characteristic of many involuntary psychological withdrawal policies is the almost complete absence of procedural due process for students (Bernard & Bernard, 1980). Appropriate procedural due process is vital to protect the interests of the student as well as the institution.

At public institutions, the imposition of a stigma associated with a finding of emotional or mental illness may constitute a deprivation of a protected "liberty" interest, thereby requiring some due process protection. In *Lombard v. Board of Education for the City of New York* (1974), the court stated:

> [Plaintiff was] deprived of his reputation as a person who was presumably free from mental disorder. Without his being given the right to confront witnesses, the termination of his probationary employment was recommended . . . on the primary ground: "Illogical and disoriented conversation, causing request for examination by the Medical Department, which found him unfit for duty." This is not only a finding but a stigma. If it is insupportable in fact, it does grievous harm to the appellant's chances for further employment, as indeed the record demonstrates, and not only in the teaching field. For that reason he was entitled to a full hearing. (pp. 637-638)

The Supreme Court decision *Vitek v. Jones* (1980) also provides guidance in this area: "[T]he questions whether an individual is mentally ill . . . 'turns on the meaning of the facts which must be interpreted by expert psychiatrists and psychologists . . .' The medical nature of the inquiry, however, does not justify dispensing with due process requirements. It is precisely 'the subtleties and nuances of psychiatric diagnoses' that justify the requirement of adversarial hearings." (p. 495)

It is possible to conceive of legally acceptable alternatives to formal "trial-type" proceeding which are better suited to the campus setting while also offering substantial protection to the student subject to the withdrawal (Pavela, 1985). The model procedures at the end of the chapter incorporate these recommended basic elements:

1. A clear statement of policy pertaining to involuntary withdrawal from the institution, or from the residence halls, for psychological reasons.

2. Clear definitions of the circumstances that would result in the student being under the jurisdiction of the involuntary psychological withdrawal policy.

3. Written advance notice provided to the student that he or she may be subject to the involuntary psychological withdrawal policy.

4. An appropriate evaluation by a mental health professional.

5. Reasonable access to the case file, including the evaluation.

6. An opportunity to meet with an impartial campus administrator or panel before any final determination is made. During that meeting the student should have the following:

a. An opportunity to view or hear all evidence in support of the withdrawal;

b. An opportunity to question those providing information in support of the withdrawal;

c. An opportunity to present verbal or written information and/or witnesses in support of the student's position.

7. A statement of reasons should be given to the student that is subject to involuntary withdrawal on psychological grounds. Also, conditions or requirements necessary to re-enter the institution should also be provided, if re-entry is an option.

Institutions may also wish to consider the opportunity for the student to be accompanied in the meeting by a family member, an advisor or mental health professional and whether or not to afford the student an appeal or an administrative review of the decision.

SECTION 504 OF THE REHABILITATION ACT OF 1973 AND THE AMERICANS WITH DISABILITIES ACT

Federal regulations issued pursuant to Section 504 of the Rehabilitation Act of 1973 (Section 504), as amended (29 U.S.C. §794, 1982) have defined the statutory words "physical or mental impairment" to include "any mental or psychological disorder" such as "emotional or mental illness" [45 C.F.R. 84.3 (j)(2)(I)(B), 1983]. Individuals addicted to drugs or alcohol are included. Comparable language is used in the Americans with Disabilities Act of 1990 (ADA) (Pub. L. No. 101-336, codified at 42 U.S.C. §12101 et. seq.), although there are exclusions for pedophilia and various gender identity disorders. Current users of illegal drugs and individuals who violate campus alcohol policies that apply to the entire campus community are not protected by these statutes.

Section 504 and the ADA have not been construed to mean that a college or university must ignore or excuse the behavioral manifestations resulting from a student's psychological problems or drug addiction or alcoholism. In *Doe v. New York University* (1981) the court stated "if the handicap could reasonably be viewed as posing a substantial risk that the applicant would be unable to meet [the institution's] reasonable standards, the institution is not obligated by the Act to alter, dilute, or bend them . . ." (p. 788). Section 504 and the ADA likewise, do not protect individuals who pose a "direct threat" to others, or who engage in behavior that violates reasonable standards of conduct (Pavela, 1993).

ADA and Section 504 do not preclude an institution from setting reasonable behavioral standards and holding students accountable for their behavior. It is important that the accountability focus on their behavior rather than the perception of mental dysfunction. Care must

The Administration of Campus Discipline . . .

also be taken, however, not to use disciplinary charges as a pretext for dismissing an individual with a mental disorder on the assumption the individual might be violent or violate the standards in some other way in the future. This same concept applies to admission or re-admission decisions regarding students with an actual or alleged mental disorder.

Decisions to exclude a student from an institution must be based on facts rather than on stereotypes of what the student may do in the future, based on a disability. It is not permissible to exclude a student based on "psychiatric" grounds. According to Pavela (1985) the following are impermissible reasons for excluding a student from an institution:

1. Simply because the student has a mental disorder, or had a mental disorder in the past; or
2. Because it is assumed, without sufficient supporting evidence, that a student with a particular mental disorder would be unable to meet the reasonable institutional standards; or
3. Because, out of paternalistic concern, it is hoped that a student with a mental disorder, who nonetheless continues to meet reasonable academic or conduct standards, will obtain treatment elsewhere. (p. 7)

Pavela (1985) concludes: In the context of mandatory psychiatric withdrawals that institutions of higher education should:

conduct a careful inquiry into whether a student suffering from a mental disorder has engaged in some demonstrable behavior which indicates that he or she can "reasonably" be viewed as posing a "substantial risk" of being unable to meet "reasonable [institutional] standards" (*Doe v. New York University*, 1981, p. 775). (p. 9)

THE LIMITATIONS OF PSYCHOLOGICAL EVALUATIONS

Most involuntary psychological withdrawal policies have been designed to remove students experiencing "emotional problems" who might "represent a threat to themselves or to others." Indeed, the model procedures at the end of this chapter cite that basis. However, it is important to understand that the notion that psychiatrists and psychologists are able to predict violent behavior, especially in the absence of a verbalized threat or a pattern of violence in the past, is not supported by the professional literature. Resnick (1993) indicated what appears to be the current thinking in the psychiatric field regarding violence prediction:

Confirming common sense, researchers have found that the best single indicator of future violence is past violent conduct. The younger a person is when first arrested for a violent crime, the more likely he or she is to commit more such crimes. People who have been repeatedly violent are likely to act violently again unless their attitudes or their circumstances change. (p. 8)

Pavela (1985) deems it "questionable whether mental health professionals can form any kind of a scientifically valid conclusion based upon the brief evaluative interview required in many mandatory withdrawal policies." (p. 37). Pavela quotes noted psychiatrist Karl Menninger, who was "especially critical of the legal profession for its expectations in this regard":

[m]ost lawyers have no conception of the meaning or methods of psychiatric case study and diagnosis. They seem to think that psychiatrists can take a quick look at a suspect . . . and thereupon be able to say, definitely, that the awful "it" . . . loathsome affliction of "insanity" . . . is present or absent. Because we all like to please, some timid psychiatrists fall in with this fallacy of the lawyers and go through these preposterous antics (Menninger, 1959, p. 137-138). (p. 37)

It is therefore important that the mental health professionals involved in a psychological withdrawal procedure recognize the limits of their own expertise. It is vital that these procedures not be misused by mental health professionals or others involved in the process to impose their own social or moral values (Gross, 1978). We may see more incidents or misbehavior due to mental disorders in the future. This may be due in large part to the decline of the family in our society, which is widely credited with the increases in emotional and psychological problems among college students. Another factor is that according to the American Psychiatric Association's *Diagnostics and Statistical Manual of Mental Disorders, 4th Edition* (DSM—IV) (1994) there are now more defined disorders than ever before.

Care must also be taken to ensure that psychological withdrawal procedures are not misused to dismiss students who are simply eccentric. In the Supreme Court decision *Wisconsin v. Yoder* (1972) the court stated: "A way of life that is odd or even erratic but interferes with no rights or interests of others is not to be condemned because it is different" (p. 205).

The discussion in this section is intended to support the assertion that it is always preferable to use the student disciplinary process to address student behavior. There may be extraordinary circumstances where campus administrators have no alternative but to rely on the diagnoses of psychologists or psychiatrists. Such a circumstance may exist when a student is unable to accept responsibility for his or her behavior; as in the case of repeated suicide attempts or some eating disorders. Such reliance, however, should not be based upon unrealistic expectations of the current capabilities of those professions, and must always be tempered by an awareness of the damaging stigma associated with the finding of a mental illness.

The Administration of Campus Discipline . . .

THE BENEFITS OF STUDENT DISCIPLINE

It has already been established earlier in this chapter that withdrawing a student based solely on a finding that the student has a mental disorder is precluded by Section 504 and the ADA. Pavela (1985) identifies the benefits of proceeding through the disciplinary process:

Accordingly, the focus of inquiry in any psychiatric withdrawal procedure must be upon specific, usually prohibited behavior, which indicates that the student poses a physical threat to self or to others, or is otherwise unable to meet reasonable institutional standards. With very few exceptions, these are precisely the forms of behavior which campus disciplinary systems should be designed to address. (p. 41)

Pavela (1985) further points out:

Perhaps the greatest benefit associated with the imposition of disciplinary sanctions on students is that the language used to define prohibited conduct can be relied upon to affirm a shared set of behavioral standards. Unfortunately, psychological withdrawal decisions are often based upon hidden value judgements disguised by "medical" language (p. 45).

Another benefit identified by Pavela (1995, July) to the student disciplinary process is that:

... school officials can properly impose sanctions for reasons of deterrence and retribution. Punishment imposed for those reasons focuses upon the community *and* the individual; it is designed to redress the unfair advantage which the individual acquired over those who "restrained themselves" and adhered to established behavioral standards; it "teaches" the student that self-control is a necessary part of living within a viable community; above all, it encourages students to regard themselves as being responsible for their own actions. The affirmation of personal responsibility is a critically important component of "personhood" which is denied to students withdrawn on psychiatric grounds. (Pavela, p. 5)

Students accused of a disciplinary violation may be able to discuss the fairness of the regulation itself with institution officials. Students subject to psychological withdrawal policies are usually not accorded the same opportunity, since the psychological diagnosis locates the source of the problem within the individual and encourages administrators to focus exclusively on the student's "pathology" (Pavela, 1995). Even though the result of a psychological withdrawal process may be comparable to a disciplinary suspension or dismissal, generally the "medical context" of the process does not allow a comparable discussion of justice, fairness or appeal. (Pavela, 1995, July, p. 5)

Even though the behavior is bizarre, if it is disruptive it can be handled as a student disciplinary case. The disciplinary process affirms that we care by attempting to help the student focus on and take responsibility for his or her own behavior, to learn how that behavior fails to meet community standards, and to learn how to adjust the behavior to be a more successful member of the community. Behavioral contracts, often used in conjunction with other sanctions, are generally an effective disciplinary technique for resolving these kinds of caseïn summary, although there are some instances where it is appropriate to use the psychological withdrawal process, care should be taken not to use it in any instance where the student disciplinary process can be used. Even if the student has a mental or psychological problem, the student and the institution are more likely to benefit using the student disciplinary process.

APPROPRIATE USES OF
PSYCHOLOGICAL WITHDRAWAL POLICIES

Pavela (1985) cautioned about diverting students from the disciplinary process:

> A student suffering from a mental disorder who did not violate the institution's reasonable standards of conduct might be offered some form of counseling or therapy, but should not be withdrawn on psychiatric grounds. Even though the student might be dismissed for academic deficiencies, the stigma associated with an academic dismissal is far less damaging than that which would result from a mandatory psychiatric or psychological withdrawal. (p. 53)

The most perplexing problem facing most campus administrators, however, is the student who apparently has a psychological problem or a mental disorder and engages in behavior which significantly disrupts the academic process or which threatens the physical safety of others. As recommended in the preceding section, administrators should rely upon a properly drafted student disciplinary policy to protect the campus community. In rare cases, however, it may be unjust to subject a student to disciplinary sanctions, even though the student had engaged in prohibited behavior.

Pavela (1985) asserts that "any decision to rely upon a mandatory withdrawal policy in lieu of disciplinary action must be guided by some articulated standard. Given the benefits associated with imposition of discipline, such a standard should be narrowly defined" (p. 54). Pavela (1995, July) concludes that "a student with a mental disorder who is accused of a disciplinary violation should not be diverted from the disciplinary process unless the student, as the result of a mental disorder, did not know the nature or wrongfulness of the conduct at the time of the offense" (p, 6). The standard might limit such a decision to those instances where a student's mental condition or disorder demonstrably impairs his or her perception or understanding of reality and is not attributable primarily to the use of alcohol or drugs. (APA, 1983, February)

Another appropriate use for an involuntary psychological withdrawal policy might be to remove suicidal students from campus. Pavela (1985) cautions that "it would be unwise, however, to adopt a policy that requires the automatic removal of all students who threaten to harm themselves." (p. 56) Educators should make a reasonable effort to counsel students in these circumstances, rather than simply withdrawing them from school on psychological grounds (Bernard & Bernard, 1980). It may be appropriate to require such students to submit to an evaluation to determine the best course of action for assisting the student.

Some campus administrators overreact to the risk of liability in cases involving suicidal students. In a California Supreme Court decision (*Nally v. Grace Community Church*, 1988) the court refused to extend a duty to care on the part of "non-therapist counselors" to take affirmative steps to prevent suicidal behavior. It is appropriate for the institution to take reasonable steps to ensure that a student who threatens suicide is referred for appropriate psychological care.

It may not always be reasonable or possible for campus officials to render ongoing assistance to a suicidal student in every case, especially if the student has made a serious suicide attempt or has made repeated attempts or threats. This may be particularly true if the student is deemed to have a psychological problem or mental disorder that might be exacerbated in the academic environment. Such a student may be likely to continue to engage in self-destructive behavior and could, eventually, contribute to a climate on campus that might encourage suicidal behavior in others. There may be no alternative under these circumstances but to withdraw the student on psychological grounds, unless the student chooses to leave voluntarily. In cases where the student withdraws voluntarily, it would be prudent for the institution to require a review of psychological care received while out of school and an updated evaluation prior to any consideration for re-admission.

If a suicidal student is involuntarily withdrawn from school for psychological reasons it will be imperative to make appropriate and reasonable efforts to refer the student for psychological care or to arrange for an involuntary commitment to a psychiatric facility. Pavela (1985) warns that "campus officials who would be quick to withdraw a student on the grounds that the institution might otherwise be liable for preventing the student's suicide should understand that their legal risks are substantially greater if they simply 'dump' suicidal students in the larger community" (p. 58).

CONCLUSION

Pavela (1985) identifies several factors for consideration in the context of involumtary withdrawal of students manifesting psychological problems:

It would not be administratively sound or legally sufficient to use vague and ambiguous labels (e.g., "disturbed," behavior of concern to others," "abnormal") to remove a student from a college or university. Instead, if "medical" language must be used, it is best to use words capable of at least some professionally accepted meaning, such as the term "mental disorder," as used in the current American Psychiatric Association Diagonstic Mannual [DSM—IV]. Furthermore, good administrative practice and (at public institutions) current constitutional standards, require some minimal due process protections before students can be removed on psychological grounds. Removal on the basis of a mental disorder alone, however, would be precluded by Section 504 of the Rehabilitation Act of 1973 [and the Americans with Disabilities Act], even with sufficient procedural due process. Consequently, the focus of inquiry must be on specific, usually prohibited behavior. It is recommended, on policy grounds, to rely upon the disciplinary process in response to incidents of such prohibited behavior, unless the student lacks the capacity to respond to the charges or did not know the nature or wrongfulness of the act in question. Furthermore, in cases of threatened or attempted suicide, or in cases in which students are suffering from eating disorders, an initial effort should be made to allow the affected student to remain on campus [while ensuring that appropriate evaluation and intervention take place]. If the student is to be withdrawn [for psychological reasons], school officials should refer the student to an appropriate [professional or] facility for professional observation, evaluation [and intervention].

The model procedures that follow attempt to take these factors into consideration. There is no intent to suggest that the model procedures and sample correspondence are the definitive policy or process for these issues. It may be more accurately referred to as a framework. It is intended to show examples of the types of information, procedures and correspondence that may be used in developing such a policy on individual campuses.

MODEL PROCEDURES FOR THE WITHDRAWAL OF STUDENTS MANIFESTING SERIOUS PSYCHOLOGICAL PROBLEMS

NOTE: The phrase "medical" withdrawal is used in these model procedures. "psychological," "psychiatric" or other terms may be substituted. These procedures assume the existence of a student health center, a student counseling center, a dean of students and a vice president for student affairs. Adjustments may need to be made to reflect different staffing patterns and organizations. These procedures assume "in-house" psychologists, psychiatrists, or physicians. Clearly many institutions have these staff only on a consulting basis or not at all. In such cases, procedures should be adjusted to reflect referral to appropriate resources outside the institution.

A. Students Manifesting Serious Psychological Problems

The university shall, through the student health center and the student counseling center, provide evaluation, referral, and appropriate treatment, within the available resources of the institution, for students manifesting serious psychological problems. The personnel of all departments of the university are expected to refer students with apparent serious psychological problems to the student health center or the student counseling center. Serious psychological problems include, but are not limited to:

1. instances where a student engages, or threatens to engage in behavior which poses a danger of causing physical harm to self or others; or
2. instances which would cause significant property damage, or would directly and substantially impede the lawful activities of others, or would interfere with the educational process and the orderly operation of the university.

The dean of students is responsible for the university disciplinary process. These procedures do not preclude a student's removal from the university, or any unit, class, or program, for disciplinary reasons in accordance with the student code of conduct. The dean of students and the student counseling center and the student health center may consult to determine whether a student accused of violating the student code of conduct should be diverted from the disciplinary process and be considered for involuntary medical withdrawal in accordance with these procedures. Conversely these departments will consult to determine whether a student referred for consideration for an involuntary medical withdrawal might be more appropriately handled through the disciplinary process.

B. Involuntary Referral for Evaluation

Students involuntarily referred for evaluation in accordance with the above shall be so informed in writing, and the student also shall be given a copy of these procedures. Delivery of these documents will be either by a personal delivery or by certified mail with return receipt requested and delivery restricted to the student only. (See attached sample documents.)

In order to facilitate the evaluation process, the student will be asked to sign a release of information (request and authorization to exchange information) so that all relevant parties can disclose information needed to make a decision regarding the evaluation and to delay, modify, or waive any disciplinary proceedings.

It shall be the responsibility of the directors of the student health center and the student counseling center to designate qualified staff professionals (physician, psychiatrist, psychologist, or counselor) to provide an initial evaluation of the student's condition.

The psychological/psychiatric evaluation of the student must be initiated within one university business day from the date the student received the referral letter unless an extension is granted by the director of the student health center. The student may not be accompanied by anyone during the evaluation.

Any student who fails to complete the evaluation process as required is subject to immediate interim withdrawal (see section H).

C. Recommendation for Involuntary Withdrawal

If the psychologist, counselor, psychiatrist, or physician recommends that it is in the best interest of the student or the university community that the student be involuntarily withdrawn from the university, or any unit, class, or program within the university, for psychological/medical reasons (hereafter referred to as medical reasons), this recommendation must be presented to the director of the student health center.

If the director of the student health center concurs that the student should be involuntarily withdrawn, the director shall make that recommendation to the vice president for student affairs, or designee. If the director of the student health center determines that the situation is imminently dangerous, he/she may recommend an immediate interim withdrawal (see section H).

D. Notification of the Student of the Recommendation and the Right to a Hearing

Upon receipt of a recommendation that a student be involuntarily withdrawn for medical reasons, the student shall be informed in writing by the vice president of student affairs, or designee, of this recommendation. This written notification shall be given to the student in person or sent by certified mail with return receipt requested and delivery restricted to the student only. In this letter the student will be informed of this recommendation and of his/her right to request a hearing to be held on a subsequent date prior to a decision being made about the recommendation.

The student shall also be requested to authorize the vice president for student affairs, or designee, and other participants in the hearing to have access to relevant documents and materials as are deemed essential for the hearing process. If the student refuses to grant access to the records for the parties involved, the hearing may proceed, but without the requested information.

If the student desires a hearing, he/she shall give written notice to the vice president for student affairs, or designee, within three university business days from the date of receipt of the notification letter. The hearing date should normally be set within seven university business days after the notification date.

E. Administrative Hearing

Students subject to an involuntary withdrawal shall be accorded a hearing, if requested by the student, before the vice president for student affairs, or designee, (hereafter referred to as the "hearing officer"). The following hearing guidelines will be applicable:

1. The student will be informed of the time, date, and location of the hearing, in writing, at least two university business days in advance.

2. The student's case file, including an evaluation prepared pursuant to these procedures, and the names of prospective witnesses, will be available for inspection by the student in the hearing officer's office during normal business hours at least two business days before the hearing. The file need not include the personal and confidential notes of any institutional official or participant in the evaluation process.

3. The hearing will be closed unless the student requests otherwise.

4. The hearing shall be administrative and non-adversarial. Formal rules of evidence and procedure will not apply. The hearing officer shall exercise active control over the proceedings to avoid needless consumption of time and to achieve the orderly completion of the hearing. Any person who disrupts the hearing may be removed from the hearing.

5. The burden of proof shall be upon the university to prove its case by a preponderance of the evidence.

6. The student shall have the right to be present during the presentation of all evidence, to present such witnesses and documentary evidence as may be pertinent, and to ask relevant questions of any individual appearing at the hearing.

7. The only exception to (6) is when, in the opinion of the hearing officer, the student becomes disruptive to the hearing process. In that case, the student may be removed and the hearing may proceed without the student present.

8. The hearing may be conducted in the absence of a student who fails to appear after proper notice.

9. The student may choose to be accompanied by a family member or advisor and/or a licensed psychologist or psychiatrist, although the role of this person is supportive, and this person may not represent the student or question witnesses. The student also may be accompanied by legal counsel, although the attorney will be limited to providing legal advice to the student and may not represent the student or question witnesses.

10. The student, all university personnel present in the hearing including the hearing officer, and/or any witnesses shall be afforded the opportunity for reasonable oral presentations and shall be permitted to file typewritten briefs.

11. The professional who conducted the evaluation pursuant to these procedures may be expected to appear at the hearing and respond to relevant questions, but only if the hearing officer determines that such participation is essential to the resolution of the case.

12. The hearing shall be recorded by a tape-recording device, and upon timely request by any party to the hearing the testimony shall be reduced to writing with the cost for transcription being borne entirely by the party making this request. All parties present should audibly identify themselves on the tape recording.

13. If the hearing is not conducted by the vice president for student affairs, the hearing officer will prepare a recommendation to the vice president for student affairs, based on the record, immediately after the hearing. The recommendation, along with the record, shall be forwarded to the vice president for student affairs by the hearing officer as soon as possible but in no case should it be more than five university business days from the adjournment of the hearing, unless the deadline is extended for the filing of briefs.

14. Within five university business days from the receipt of the hearing officer's recommendation, or within five university business days from the hearing if the hearing officer is the vice president, the vice president for student affairs shall make a decision regarding the case and implement appropriate action and notify all parties of the decision.

15. The decision of the vice president for student affairs shall be final and conclusive and not subject to appeal.

16. Reasonable deviations from these procedures will not invalidate a decision or proceeding unless significant prejudice to a student may result.

F. Decision Notification

Prior to making the decision, the vice president for student affairs shall certify, by letter to be included in the record, that he/she has reviewed the proceedings and read all attachments thereto.

The Administration of Campus Discipline . . .

If the vice president for student affairs, or designee, concludes that the student should be involuntarily withdrawn, he/she shall send to a student who has been involuntarily withdrawn from the university a letter outlining that the student is blocked from re-enrollment to the university until certain conditions are met. A notation shall be placed on the student's record that he/she is blocked from re-enrollment for medical reasons. A letter will also be sent to the registrar to request that a notation be placed on the student's transcript indicating a block for medical reasons. The block will remain on a student's academic record until the student's readmission is approved.

If applicable, the student should be informed in writing of re-enrollment procedures and conditions.

G. Re-Enrollment Procedure

Upon receipt of a completed "Application to Remove Enrollment Block" and "Treating Doctor's Re-Enrollment Questionnaire" and treatment summary from the treating professional(s), the vice president for student affairs, or designee, shall make an evaluation of the request. Consideration shall be given to any conditions for re-enrollment set forth in the student's letter of involuntary withdrawal and any other relevant information that the vice president for student affairs, or designee, deems necessary for a complete review. In conducting the evaluation, the vice president for student affairs, or designee, may ask the student counseling center or the student health center to assist in the review, and thereafter make comment on, the re-enrollment application.

The evaluation process shall normally be completed within twenty (20) university business days, after receipt of a complete application. Thereafter, the vice president for student affairs, or designee, shall make a determination to approve or disapprove the re-enrollment application. If the re-enrollment application is approved, it shall be within the discretion of the vice president for student affairs to require an additional letter of recommendation from the student's treating professional immediately preceding re-enrollment and/or class attendance to confirm that the opinion of the treating professional has not changed since the date of the initial letter of recommendation. If the re-enrollment application is disapproved, the vice president for student affairs shall notify the student in writing.

H. Interim Withdrawal

An immediate involuntary withdrawal on an interim basis can be recommended in the following circumstances:

1. Any student who fails to complete an evaluation in accordance with these procedures, may be immediately involuntarily withdrawn on an interim basis or referred for disciplinary action, or both.

2. If the director of the student health center determines that a student is manifesting serious psychological problems and the student's behavior poses an imminent danger of:

a. causing serious physical harm to the student or others; or

b. causing significant property damage, or directly and substantially impeding the lawful activities of others, or interfering with the educational process and the orderly operation of the university.

The vice president for student affairs or designee shall implement the interim withdrawal. In Pavela's (1985) model procedures, he proposed the following considerations related to interim withdrawal:

> A student subject to an interim withdrawal shall be given written notice of the withdrawal either by personal delivery or by certified mail, and shall be given a copy of these standards and procedures.

> The student shall then be given the opportunity to appear personally before the dean of students [vice president for student affairs], or designee, within two business days from the effective date of the interim withdrawal in order to review the following issues only:
> a. the reliability of the information concerning the student's behavior;
> b. whether or not the student's behavior poses a danger of causing imminent serious physical harm to the student or others, causing significant property damage, or directly and substantially impeding the lawful activities of others;
> c. whether or not the student has completed an evaluation, in accordance with these standards and procedures. (p. 67)

During this meeting the student may be assisted in the proceeding by a family member or an advisor and/or a licensed psychologist or psychiatrist. Legal counsel may also accompany the student, although the role of counsel will be limited to providing legal advice to the student. Students will be expected to speak for themselves whenever possible.

If the interim withdrawal is deemed appropriate, the student will remain withdrawn on an interim basis pending completion of the required evaluation (if needed) and the hearing, if requested by the student. A student who has been withdrawn on an interim basis will be allowed to enter the campus to attend the hearing, or for other necessary purposes, as authorized in writing by the vice president for student affairs, or designee.

Appendix I

Sample Documents

RELEASE OF INFORMATION

REQUEST FOR AUTHORIZATION TO EXCHANGE INFORMATION

{Date}

To: *{Student}*

We are concerned about your future emotional and physical health, and your ability to function positively within an academic and/or residence hall community. This concern is based on (describe incident and/or behavior). Therefore, a stipulation for you to continue to attend classes as a student at the university or to live in the residence halls is that the Dean of Students needs to know that you are completing medical or psychological evaluation as required by university policy. The Dean of Students also needs to be informed of the recommendations of this evaluation as well as the progress you are making. To obtain this information and communication, the Dean of Students requests that you sign the attached *Authorization to Exchange Information.*

Your signature simply authorizes the Student Counseling Center, the Student Health Center and the Dean of Students to communicate regarding your evaluation, your compliance with the treatment recommendations, and your progress in counseling. The Student Counseling Center, the Student Health Center and the Dean of Students are only authorized by your signature to exchange relevant information and only to university officials within these departments that have a legitimate need to know this information.

Please understand that your signature will in no way jeopardize the integrity of your university records and that no disclosure of your records can or ever will be made without your written consent. This authorization will be restricted only to those items indicated on the attached form. Please understand that you do have the right to refuse to sign the attached form. However, your refusal to sign could result in the Dean of Students pursuing disciplinary action against you for the behavior or incident(s) you were involved in without benefit of the evaluation information.

Sincerely,

{Name}

{Dean of Students}

RELEASE OF INFORMATION

AUTHORIZATION TO EXCHANGE INFORMATION

I understand that signing this form will in no way jeopardize the integrity of my university records and that no disclosure of my records can or ever will be made without my written consent unless otherwise provided for by the Family Education Rights and Privacy Act or other legal statutes. This authorization is restricted only to those items indicated below. I also understand that I have the right to refuse to sign this form, but refusal to sign could result in the Vice President for Student Affairs pursuing disciplinary action against me, related to the behavior or incident(s) I was involved in, without benefit of the evaluation information.

I, _____   _____
Student's Name   SS#

authorize the staff involved in my evaluation from the following departments:
Dean of Students
Student Counseling Center
Student Health Center

and _____

to release and exchange with each other, written and / or oral information *(circle one or both and check and initial items authorized)* concerning my:

	Initials		Initials
❐ results of evaluations	____	❐ disciplinary sanctions	____
❐ attendance in counseling	____	❐ contents of discipline file	____
❐ progress in counseling	____	❐ pending discipline case	____
❐ other (specify):			

I also understand that I may revoke this consent at any time except to the extent that action has already been taken upon this release. I hereby agree that a photocopy of this release is a legal equivalent of the original document.

_____   _____
Student Signature   Staff Member Signature

_____
Date

I acknowledge receipt of the following *(please initial)*:
____ Procedures For the Withdrawal of Students Manifesting Serious Psychological Problems.
____ Request for Authorization to Exchange Information explanation letter.

TREATING DOCTOR'S RE-ENROLLMENT QUESTIONNAIRE

On occasion, a student withdraws or is withdrawn from the University and is subsequently blocked from re-enrollment for manifesting serious psychological problems. This course is normally pursued only after available university resources have been used in attempting to reduce or remedy the student's medical/psychological problem.

The university reserves the right to determine whether the student, under certain conditions, may remain enrolled during a particular semester, or may re-enroll for a future semester. A decision to withdraw and/or block a student for medical/psychological reasons is made only after consideration of all pertinent information and appropriate consultation with the psychiatrists, other physicians, and psychologists.

Therefore, it is the practice of the university that any student blocked from re-enrollment for these reasons from this or any other institution must have information submitted by the treating psychiatrist, other physician, and/or licensed psychologist. The enclosed form, a brief statement of recommendation for re-enrollment on office letterhead, and a treatment summary must be submitted to the university before the student can be considered for re-enrollment.

* * *

NOTE: The student completes and signs a re-enrollment application which contains the following statements:

"I hereby tender my application for re-enrollment. I understand that I may be required to have a re-enrollment questionnaire and letter of recommendation completed prior to consideration of this application.

"I understand that said questionnaires, recommendations, and treatment summaries are confidential and not to be seen by me but may be used by officials at the University when considering my application for re-enrollment.

"Finally, I give my consent that my treating psychiatrist, other physician, and/or licensed psychologist may release any information to the University Vice President for Student Affairs and/or the Student Counseling Center needed for the evaluation of my re-enrollment application. I hereby agree that a photocopy of this release is a legal equivalent of the original document."

RE-ENROLLMENT

```
TREATING DOCTOR'S RE-ENROLLMENT QUESTIONNAIRE

Instructions: This form is to be completed by the treating psychiatrist, other M.D.,
or licensed psychologist. Please respond to the questions listed below and at-
tach a brief statement of recommendation for re-enrollment and a treatment sum-
mary on your office letterhead. Send the completed form and statement directly
to the following address:

Office of the Vice President for Student Affairs
{The University}
{City, State Zip}
```

Please Respond To All Questions

Full name of patient: _____

Are you a: ___ Psychiatrist   ___ Other M.D.   ___ Licensed Psychologist?

Did you provide treatment for the above named patient?   ___ Yes   ___ No

How may treatment sessions have you provided for the patient (relating to this matter)?   _____

Has the above patient completed treatment?   ___ Yes   ___ No

Are you continuing to provide treatment?   ___ Yes   ___ No

If not, was treatment terminated with your approval?   ___ Yes   ___ No

When did the treatment commence?   _____   Conclude?   _____

If the patient has not completed treatment, how frequently will the patient need to see you?   _____

Have you referred the patient for continuing treatment?   ___ Yes   ___ No

If yes, please indicate the name, address, and phone number of the individual or agency: _____

Why have you referred the patient for continuing treatment?   _____

_____

_____

If the patient is continuing treatment with you or someone else, do you believe he/she would be able to function appropriately as a student at this University without that continued treatment? ___ Yes ___ No

Do you consider that the patient presently, or in the reasonably foreseeable future, is likely to be a danger to himself/herself or others, or a threat to his/her own life or the lives of others? ___ Yes ___ No

If yes, please explain: _____

_____

_____

Do you think this patient is capable of carrying a full academic load (12 to 18 credit hours) at this University? ___ Yes ___ No

To your knowledge, are the parents and / or legal guardian(s) of the patient aware of the problem(s) for which you have provided treatment? ___ Yes ___ No

Other comments: _____

_____

_____

_____

_____

_____   _____
Signature of Treating Professional   Date

_____   _____
Name of Treating Professional (please print or type)   Phone Number

_____
Address of Treating Professional

Please remember to attach a brief statement of recommendation for re-enrollment on your office letterhead and a treatment summary. Return to: Office of the Vice President for Student Affairs, {The University, City, State Zip}. The student's re-enrollment application will not be accepted for review unless it includes these materials.

RE-ENROLLMENT

APPLICATION TO REMOVE RE-ENROLLMENT BLOCK

Name: _____
          Last   First   Middle

Mailing Address: _____

_____

Phone: (____) _____

Student I.D. Number: _____

Date of Withdrawal: _____

Semester desired for re-enrollment: _____ Year: _____

* * *

I hereby tender my application for re-enrollment. I understand that I may be required to have a reenrollment questionnaire and letter of recommendation completed prior to consideration of this application.

I understand that said questionnaires, recommendations, and treatment summaries are confidential and not to be seen by me, but may be used by officials at The University when considering my application for re-enrollment.

I understand that approval by the Vice President for Student Affairs of my re-enrollment meets only the conditions for removing the re-enrollment block from my records. I further understand that, if approved, I must contact the Admissions Office to complete the re-enrollment process.

Finally, I give my consent that my treating psychiatrist, other physician, and/or licensed psychologist may release any information to the Office of the Vice President for Student Affairs and/or the Student Counseling Center needed for the evaluation of my re-enrollment application. I hereby agree that a photocopy of this release is a legal equivalent of the original document.

_____   _____
Signature   *Date*

After completion of this form, submit it to:
    Vice President for Student Affairs
    {The University}
    {City, State Zip}

The Administration of Campus Discipline . . .

CORRESPONDENCE TO IMPLEMENT THE
PROCEDURES FOR THE WITHDRAWAL OF STUDENTS
MANIFESTING PSYCHOLOGICAL PROBLEMS

The following letters and memos are designed to serve as examples of correspondence to be used in implementing the Procedures for the Withdrawal of Students Manifesting Psychological Problems. There may be circumstances where it is appropriate to deviate slightly from the examples that are given. In those cases, these examples can serve to provide an outline of the types of information that should be transmitted and who should receive copies of each correspondence. Below is an overview of the documents, their titles and purposes:

A. Medical Block Notification Letter: Letter sent to a student who has already withdrawn from or left the university. Informs the student that he/she is blocked for medical reasons and explains the conditions for applying for re-admission.

B. Medical Withdrawal Recommendation and Right to Appeal Letter: Letter sent to a student who is still in school, but has been recommended for medical withdrawal. Informs the student of that recommendation and offers the student the opportunity to request a hearing.

C. Records Release for Administrative Hearing on a Medical Withdrawal: Release enclosed with document B. Allows the student's medical records to be used during the administrative hearing.

D. Hearing Officer Designation Memo: Memo used by the Vice President to appoint a hearing officer to conduct the administrative hearing regarding the recommendation to medically withdraw the student from the university.

E. Hearing Notification Letter—Student: Letter to the student from the designated hearing officer informing the student of the specifics of the administrative hearing.

F. Hearing Documentation Memo: Memo requesting records and representatives to each of the appropriate departments that may have records or information pertaining to the recommendation to medically withdraw the student.

G. Hearing Notification Memo—Staff: Memo from the hearing officer to the specific staff designated to present information or records at the administrative hearing.

H. Medical Withdrawal Notification Letter: Letter from vice president to the student informing him/her of the medical withdrawal as a result of the hearing. Conditions for applying for re-admission are explained.

I. Withdrawal and Block Memo: Memo from the vice president to the appropriate officials to implement the medical withdrawal from the university.

A. MEDICAL BLOCK NOTIFICATION LETTER

Send by Certified Mail—Return Receipt—Delivery Restricted to Adressee

{Date}

{Name}
{Address}
{City, ST ZIP}

Dear *{Name}*:

As a result of the serious incident(s) that you were involved in, we are concerned about your future emotional and physical health, and your ability to function positively within an academic community.

This letter is to officially follow-up on a recommendation that I received from the Director of the Student Health Center that you be blocked from re-admission to the university for medical reasons effective *{date}*.

You have been blocked from being re-admitted until you can establish that you are able to effectively function within this rigorous academic environment. Therefore, as a stipulation for you to re-enroll as a student, the university must have the opportunity to review and consider the evaluation and treatment you have undergone since the serious incident.

Enclosed are two forms that must be returned to the university if you wish to re-enroll in a future semester at the university:

1. Treating Doctor's Re-enrollment Questionnaire. You should provide this questionnaire to the professional who has been treating you. If you have seen more than one, please copy the questionnaire and provide one to each professional. The treating professional(s) must follow the completion instructions exactly and return the questionnaire and requested attachments directly to the address on the form.

2. Application to Remove Re-enrollment Block. You should fill out this request and return it to the address on the form.

Please understand that only by proper completion and return of these two forms can the university consider whether or not to remove your block and allow you to re-enroll for any future semester. If you have questions, please contact me.

Sincerely,

{Name}

Vice President for Student Affairs

Attachments: 1. Treating Doctor's Re-enrollment Questionnaire
                 2. Application to Remove Re-enrollment Block

xc: Director of Student Health Center
      Director of Student Counseling Center

B. MEDICAL WITHDRAWAL RECOMMENDATION AND RIGHT TO APPEAL LETTER

Send by Certified Mail—Return Receipt—Delivery Restricted to Adressee

{Date}

{Name}
{Address}
{City, ST ZIP}

Dear *{Name}*:

As a result of the serious incident(s) that you were involved in, we are concerned about your future emotional and physical health, and your ability to function positively within an academic community.

This letter is to officially follow-up on a recommendation that I received from the Director of the Student Health Center, that you be withdrawn from the university for medical reasons effective *{date}*.

In accordance with university policy, you may request a hearing to review the facts and circumstances of your case prior to a final decision being made on this recommendation. If you desire a hearing, you must submit a written request to my office within three university business days from the date you receive this letter. Attached is a copy of the procedures followed during an administrative hearing of this type. Your written request should include the following:

1. State your desire to appeal the recommendation that you be withdrawn for medical reasons.
2. State whether you intend to be accompanied by anyone to the hearing (see Section 7 of the attached Hearing Procedures for limitations).
3. Sign and enclose the attached Records Release for Administrative Hearing form.

Your failure to respond to this letter will be taken as an intent not to appeal the aforementioned recommendation. If you have any questions about this matter, please contact me at *{phone}*.

Sincerely,

{Name}

Vice President for Student Affairs

Attachments: 1. Treating Doctor's Re-enrollment Questionnaire
               2. Application to Remove Re-enrollment Block
               3. Records Release for Administrative Hearing

xc: Director of Student Health Center
       Director of Student Counseling Center

C: RECORDS RELEASE FOR ADMINISTRATIVE HEARING ON A MEDICAL WITHDRAWAL

Records Release for
Administrative Hearing on a Medical Withdrawal

I, ___{Student's name}___ ___{Social Security #}___ authorize the Vice President for Student Affairs, or designee, and other participants involved in the administrative hearing to have access to relevant documents and materials as are deemed essential for the hearing process.

I understand that the vice president, or designee, will determine which documents and materials are essential for the hearing process.

No disclosure of my medical records will be made without my written consent unless otherwise provided for by the Family Educational Rights and Privacy Acts or other legal statutes.

_____   _____
Signature   Date

NOTE: You may refuse to sign this form, however, your refusal to sign may result in the hearing proceeding without the benefit of the information contained in your records.

D: HEARING OFFICER DESIGNATION MEMO

{Date}

MEMORANDUM

       TO: *{Name of designee}*
                  {Title}

SUBJECT: Administrative hearing for student manifesting serious psychological problems

      This is to appoint you as my designee (hearing officer) for an administrative hearing for an appeal by *{student's name}*.

      The policy and procedures for this hearing are attached. Your recommendation must be received by me no later than five working days after the hearing. Also attached is the records release signed by the student. Thank you.

{Name}
Vice President for Student Affairs

xc: *{Student}*

E: HEARING NOTIFICATION LETTER

Confidential

{Date}

{Name}
{Address}
{City, ST ZIP}

Dear *{Name}*:

The Vice President for Student Affairs has appointed me as his designee to be the hearing officer for your appeal of a recommendation for involuntary withdrawal from the university for medical reasons.

I will closely follow the guidelines for how the hearing should be conducted as noted in an attachment you received from *{VPSA}*.

The hearing has been set for *{time}* in *{place}* on *{date}*. The case file will be available for your review *{times and date}* at my office *{location}*.

Sincerely,

{Name of designee}
{Title of designee}

xc: Vice President for Student Affairs
     Director of Student Health Center
     Director of Student Counseling Center

F: HEARING DOCUMENTATION MEMO

Confidential

{Date}

MEMORANDUM

> TO: Director of Student Counseling Center
> Director of Student Health Center

SUBJECT: Documentation for Administrative Hearing for *{Student's name}*

    The appeal hearing of *{student's name}* is scheduled for *{time}* on *{date}*. Attached are the release forms signed by *{student's name}*. Please have appropriate documents to be used in the hearing in my office by *{time, date}*. Please also inform me who will be presenting this documentation at the hearing. If you have no documentation to provide for this hearing, please notify me to that effect.

Sincerely,

{Hearing Officer}
{Title}

xc: Vice President for Student Affairs
    {Student}

G: HEARING NOTIFICATION MEMO—STAFF

{Date}

MEMORANDUM

TO: *{Staff designated to present information or materials at hearing}*

SUBJECT: Administrative Hearing

This is to notify you to appear for the appeal hearing of *{student}*. The purpose of this appeal hearing is to consider the recommendation that *{student}* be involuntarily withdrawn from the university for medical reasons.

The hearing is scheduled for *{date, time, room}*.

Sincerely,

{Hearing Officer}
{Title}

xc: Vice President for Student Affairs
       {Student}

H: MEDICAL WITHDRAWAL NOTIFICATION LETTER

Confidential

{Date}

{Name}
{Address}
{City, ST ZIP}

Dear {Name}:

I have received and reviewed the information presented to me by {name of hearing officer}, who conducted your administrative hearing. My decision is that you should be withdrawn from the university for medical reasons. You have been blocked from being re-admitted, and the block will not be removed until I receive a letter either from your attending psychologist(s) or psychiatrist(s) stating in effect that you have undergone the appropriate care and are deemed able to withstand the rigors of academic life.

Enclosed are two forms that must be returned to the university if you wish to re-enroll in a future semester at the university:

1. *Treating Doctor's Re-enrollment Questionnaire.* You should provide this questionnaire to the professional who has been treating you. If you have seen more than one, please copy the questionnaire and provide one to each professional. The treating professional(s) must follow the completion instructions exactly and return the questionnaire and requested attachments directly to the address on the form.

2. *Application to Remove Re-enrollment Block.* You should fill out this request and return it to the address on the form.

Please understand that only by proper completion and return of these two forms can the university consider whether or not to remove your block and allow you to re-enroll for any future semester.

If I can be of further service regarding this matter, please do not hesitate to call on me.

Sincerely,

{Name}
Vice President for Student Affairs

Attachments: 1. Treating Doctor's Re-enrollment Questionnaire
             2. Application to Remove Re-enrollment Block

xc: Director of Student Health Center
     Director of Student Counseling Center

I: WITHDRAWAL AND BLOCK MEMO

{Date}

MEMORANDUM

TO: Registrar

SUBJECT: Re-enrollment Block for Medical Reasons for *{Student}*

The above named student has been blocked from re-enrollment at the university for medical reasons. I will appreciate your assistance in implementing the following:

1. Enter block notation on the student's transcript.

2. Drop pre-registered course schedule

This student may not re-enroll at the university without obtaining clearance from this office. Thank you for your assistance.

Sincerely,

{Name}
Vice President for Student Affairs

xc: Director of Student Health Center
      Director of Student Counseling Center

References

American Psychiatric Association (1994). *Diagnostic and Statistical Manual of Mental Disorders* (4th Ed.) (DSM-IV). Washington, DC: Author.

Bernard, M.L. & Bernard, J.L. (1980). Institutional responses to the suicidal student: Ethical and legal considerations. *Journal of College Student Personnel*, 21 (2), 109-113.

Gross, M. (1978). *The psychological society*. New York: Random House.

Menninger, K. (1959, August). Verdict guilty, now what? *Harper's Magazine*, 60-64; cited in Murphy, J. (1973). *Punishment and rehabilitation*. Belmont, CA: Wadsworth.

Pavela, G.M. (1985). *The Dismissal of Students with Mental Disorders: Legal issues, policy considerations and alternative responses*. Asheville, NC: College Administration Publications, Inc.

Pavela, G.M. (1993, July 12). Mental disabilities and student conduct standards. *Synfax Weekly Report*, 114

Pavela, G.M. (1995, May 29). Predicting violence. *Synfax Weekly Report*, 368.

Pavela, G.M. (1995, July). *Responding to students with mental disorders*. Presentation at the Association for Student Judicial Affairs Campus Judicial Affairs Institute, Bellingham, WA.

Resnick, P. (1993, June). Can psychiatrists predict violence?, The *Harvard Mental Health Newsletter*, p. 8.

Third Branch. (February, 1983). American Psychiatric Association takes position on insanity defense. Washington, D.C.: Federal Judicial Center.

Cases

Aronson v. North Park College, 418 N.E. 2d 776 (Ill. App., 1981).

Doe v. New York University, 666 F. 2d 761 (CA 2, 1981)

Lombard v. Board of Education for the City of New York, 502 F. 2d 631 (CA 2, 1974).

Nally v. Grace Community Church, 253 Cal. Rptr. 97 (Cal. 1988).

O'Connor v. Donaldson, 422 U.S. 563 (1975).

Shamloo v. Mississippi State Board of Trustees, 620 F. 2d 516 (5th Cir., 1980).

Vitek v. Jones, 445 U.S. 480 (1980).

Wisconsin v. Yoder, 406 U.S. 205 (1972).

Part Five

Intervention Strategies

Chapter XII

Increasing Campus Judicial Board Effectiveness: Are Two Heads Truly Better Than One?

Diane M. Waryold

INTRODUCTION

This chapter focuses on enhancing the educational value of the judicial process through increasing campus judicial board effectiveness. The selection and training of effective judicial boards is thoroughly reviewed with special emphasis devoted to the "pro's and con's" associated with student peer boards versus student/staff/faculty combinations versus administrative boards.

It is a typical Monday morning in the dean of students office. You arrive at the office bright and early. You are well rested from a relaxing weekend and are eager to face the week. You glance at your calendar for the day and notice a familiar name. Megan McManus, a sophomore engineering student, has made an appointment to see you today to discuss her hearing that took place on Friday of the previous week. You meet with Megan and she expresses several concerns in regard to how her case was handled by her student peers.

She alleges that the student hearing panel adjudicating her case did not give her the opportunity to adequately state "her side of the story." She continues stating her concerns and indicates that she is angry because at one point during her testimony, a member of the panel laughed out loud at her response to a question, making her feel as if her case, or her opinion, were of little value. Her last concern focused upon the finding of responsibility. Evidently, the witnesses bringing forth the allegations were not present to testify at the hearing.

The rejuvenated feeling you enjoyed just moments before has suddenly turned into feelings of concern and dismay ... where did you go wrong you ask yourself? Did the panel receive adequate training? How were students selected to serve on the panel? Should an administrative hearing panel, composed of faculty and staff be utilized in place of a student hearing panel? Who advised this hearing? What is the role of the advisor? How could Megan's concerns have be avoided?

The effectiveness of campus judicial boards is directly dependent upon the amount of time, care, and nurturing put forth towards the proper selection, training, and maintenance of the hearing panel. This responsibility usually rests with the professional responsible for the administration of the student discipline system. Educationally sound processes do not just happen! Intentional efforts need to be directed towards the recruitment, selection, training, and supervision of panel members. Without these efforts, many students, like Megan, will walk away from the process feeling as if they have been treated unfairly, and thus, denying them of any opportunity to take advantage of teachable moments.

COMPOSITION OF THE HEARING PANEL

The composition of the hearing panel can take many forms and combinations. Hearing panels may be composed entirely of students, of staff, or of faculty members. Hearing panels may also be composed of a combination of students, staff, and faculty. The composition of the hearing panel best suited for any respective institution is based upon institutional philosophy pertaining to the degree of student involvement in the governance of the college or university, and the staff resources available to supervise and coordinate the operation of the panel.

All student panels, if adequately trained and supervised, can be the most effective means of affecting an educational outcome. Student development theorists support the notion that peer influence can be extremely pervasive for traditional aged students (Feldman and Newcomb, 1969; Astin, 1973; Chickering, 1969). Therefore, students dialoguing with students in a disciplinary hearing regarding the behavioral expectations of the university community can be the best method for redirecting behavior. Varied opinions exist, among professionals in judicial programs across the country, regarding the appropriateness of utilizing student hearing panels in cases that are of a sensitive nature such as cases of sexual assault.

This author supports the notion of granting properly trained student hearing panels with the responsibility to hear all type cases, regardless of their volatileness. Without proper training, however, sensitive cases such as these can quickly become high profile institutional nightmares, from a public relations perspective, in which the college or university is at the mercy of the press and may be facing possible litigation. It is important to emphasize that the real tragedy lies with the students, both the accused student and the alleged victim, who may have suffered emotional harm as a result of the institution being remiss.

Hearing panels, regardless of their composition, cannot and will not function effectively without proper training, and thus, will not yield the desired educational outcomes. Because of the nature and sensitivity of some cases, students may not be comfortable with their peers adjudicating the incident. Therefore, offering students who find themselves utilizing the system to seek a remedy, or navigating the system because of allegations directed towards them, a choice of an administrative hearing option may be worth consideration.

Hearing panels made up of individuals reflecting the diversity of the student population are perceived as being more fair and equitable in the adjudication of student cases. Therefore, careful consideration should be directed towards designing panels that are balanced by race and gender. Panels should be composed of an odd number of individuals in anticipation of the necessity to reach a decision by a majority vote. A group of three or five panelists is ideal. It is important to note, that a positive attribute of the larger panels is that they offer more perspectives to draw from in formulating a conclusion regarding a case. However, larger panels tend to be less efficient. Simply stated, there are more personalities to contend with in establishing positive dynamics in the larger panels, and therefore, it usually takes longer to come to a consensus.

SELECTION

Well designed selection processes are vital to ensure the effectiveness of the hearing panel. Selection processes vary from campus to campus and the procedures included within the selection process tend to also vary by the population targeted in the recruitment effort. For example, student panel members may be required to submit a written application and may be asked to proceed through an interview process, whereas faculty members might be appointed by the president or vice president for student affairs. The recruitment and selection process is an effective vehicle by which the educational philosophy of the discipline system can be conveyed.

A carefully crafted philosophy statement needs to be included in all recruitment materials in an effort to attract panel members with the right intentions. Candidates need to possess strong interpersonal skills, they must be able to assert themselves, and to hold their ground within a group. Other positive attributes include good listening skills, a personal philosophy that embraces diversity, a temperament that does not pre-judge people based upon first impressions, and a maturity level necessary to make difficult decisions regarding the fate of their fellow peers.

The written application should include questions which emphasize the educational purpose of the disciplinary system. Examples of application questions are noted below.

1. Briefly describe why you would like to serve on the student hearing panel?

2. Describe what you believe to be the purpose of student discipline in a university setting?

3. Are there any rules or regulations in *The Code of Student Responsibility* that you think should be altered or eliminated?

4. What are the pro's and con's associated with an all-student hearing panel?

It is beneficial to establish a minimum criteria for application for selection to the student hearing panel. An example might include a minimum of a 2.5 cumulative grade point average (4.0 scale), a minimum number of hours completed towards graduation, and good judicial standing.

The selection of members is best coordinated by the administrator responsible for student conduct on campus in consultation with the student leadership of the hearing panel. Written applications can be screened by these individuals with selected students being granted an invitation for an interview. Interviews can also be conducted by representatives from the student hearing panel and the administrator responsible for student conduct. The interview is yet another means for emphasizing the educational purpose of the process. Face-to-face interviews are effective in clarifying statements made on the application and eliciting the motivation for application. Semi-structured interview questions might include the following.

1. Why would you like to serve on the student hearing panel?

2. What is the purpose of rules and regulations in a university setting?

3. To what extent should a student be held accountable for their behavior if they were under the influence of alcohol or other drugs?

4. How comfortable are you with persons who are different from you?

5. How do you react when others challenge your opinion?

6. What is it about you as a person that sets you apart from other students who may have applied for this position?

TRAINING

As already emphasized, there is no substitute for a carefully planned training program which addresses basic knowledge, skills and attitudes of the judicial process. It is foolhardy to assume that any panel can become proficient at adjudicating cases effectively without arming them with the tools needed to conduct business. A comprehensive training program may consist of a core training program that would be offered to each panelist just prior to their service. This core program would include a blend of lecture and experiential exercises designed to equip the panelists with the foundational material needed to get started. A sample training program for students and faculty and staff is included in *Appendix A*.

The core training experience needs to be supplemented with opportunities to observe and practice skills. Therefore, mock hearings and the opportunity to observe seasoned panelists in a hearing setting are crucial to the development of an effective panelist. An in-service training program consisting of topical areas such as communications skills, alcohol and other drug education, relationships with police/public safety, Myers-Briggs and other personal style type programs, diversity issues, legal issues, hazing, sanctioning, questioning, etc. are but some examples of areas that may be presented on a monthly basis.

A carefully crafted procedural manual is also vital to teach the basic nuts-n-bolts of the process. As previously mentioned, certain cases of a sensitive nature, or cases involving large groups require additional training, above and beyond what is taught in the core training session. Panelists need to be sensitized to the intricateness involved in cases of a sexual nature and cases that are far more complex than what those with which they are accustomed to dealing. The Association for Student Judicial Affairs (ASJA) has produced a training videotape entitled *Adjudicating Cases of Campus Sexual Assault* to assist panels in exploring the issues that frequently complicate the hearing process. Commission XV of the American College Personnel Association (ACPA) offers a resource packet on the selection and training of judicial board members. Both resources are highly recommended by many practitioners in the field.

MAINTAINING

Like any other organization or group, once members are recruited, selected, and trained, efforts need to be set forth to maintain their membership and to continue their group and personal development. Devoting a portion of the core and in-service training programs towards team building activities is important for building the foundation necessary to promote positive working relationships. Keeping the leadership within the organization motivated and well informed by meeting with them regularly and by rewarding them with praise is but another important aspect. The wide-reaching influence that positive leadership has on the organization can be very beneficial. Publishing a monthly newsletter with organizational news, personal tidbits and a review of cases is very effective in maintaining positive dynamics and keeping people informed within an organization.

The role of the advisor is crucial to the maintenance function of the organization. Members should be able to view the advisor in a consultative role during hearings to clarify procedural questions and to offer feedback on the dynamics of the proceedings. Advisors are in a key position to offer feedback in a non-threatening manner. Devoting ten minutes to "processing time" at the close of each hearing allows the advisor to offer feedback while the case is still fresh in the mind of the panelists. Comments should focus upon the panelist's verbal and non-verbal behaviors and whether or not the student appeared to learn from his or her experience before the panel.

CONCLUSIONS

This chapter was designed to give a brief overview of the selection, training, and maintenance of effective judicial panels. Although judicial systems vary from institution to institution, intentional efforts need to be directed towards these boards or panels in order to ensure their effectiveness.

Appendix A

Sample Core Training Programs

STUDENT HEARING PANEL

Time	Event
5pm	Welcome
	Review of training schedule
	Ice breakers
	Pizza party
—NEXT DAY—	
8am	Philosophy
	Conflicts students face
	Judicial stats
	• discipline as an educational tool
	• why students behave the way they do
	• campus statistics
8:30am	Social barometer exercise
	• how personal attitudes influence decision-making
9am	Legalities
	• how campus discipline differs from a court of law
	• procedural due process standards
10am	The Code of Student Responsibility
	• understanding the code
	• quiz of frequently asked questions
11am	Flow chart of student judicial process
	• where does the student hearing panel fit in
BREAK FOR LUNCH	
2pm	Communication skills
	• verbals and non-verbals
	• role play exercises
2:30pm	Group dynamics and decision-making
	• why are group dynamics important
	• the role of chairperson and advisor

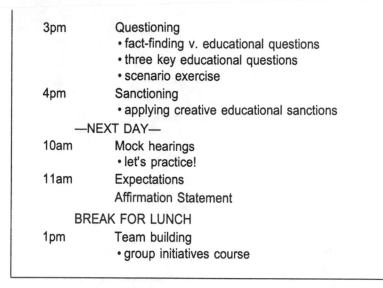

3pm	Questioning
	• fact-finding v. educational questions
	• three key educational questions
	• scenario exercise
4pm	Sanctioning
	• applying creative educational sanctions
	—NEXT DAY—
10am	Mock hearings
	• let's practice!
11am	Expectations
	Affirmation Statement
	BREAK FOR LUNCH
1pm	Team building
	• group initiatives course

ADMINISTRATIVE HEARING PANEL (FACULTY / STAFF)

Half day session to include:
- Philosophy
- Statistics
- Social barometer exercise
- Structure
- The Code of Student Responsibility
- Questioning
- Sanctioning
- Mock hearing

The Administration of Campus Discipline . . .

References

American College Personnel Association Commission XV—Model Judicial Board Selection and Training Manual (undated).

Association for Student Judicial Affairs. (1996). *Adjudicating cases of campus sexual assault.* [Video]. (Available from Dean of Students Office, University of North Carolina–Charlotte, Charlotte, NC 28223-001).

Astin, A.W. (1973). The impact of dormitory living on students. *Educational Record, 54,* 204-210.

Chickering, A.W. (1969). *Education and Identity.* San Francisco: Jossey-Bass.

Feldman, K.A. and Newcomb, T.M. (1969). *The impact of college on students.* 2 vols. San Francisco: Jossey-Bass.

Chapter XIII

Alternative Dispute Resolution: A New Look at Resolving Campus Conflict

Eugene L. Zdziarski

INTRODUCTION

The preceding chapters of this book have focused on the student judicial process as the primary means by which to address student conduct. However, while some types of student conduct may be clearly perceived by the campus culture as inappropriate, such conduct may not be a violation of the student conduct code. Such perceived inappropriate conduct may be legally protected, as is the case of free speech issues. Yet, these types of campus conflict are very real problems for colleges and universities, and the campus judicial officer frequently is expected to respond. To deal with these situations the campus judicial officer must have access to some alternatives to the traditional student judicial process.

The purpose of this chapter is to encourage judicial affairs professionals to look beyond the student judicial process and explore methods that can enhance or supplement their student conduct system. First, a general overview of the various types of alternative dispute resolution (ADR) methods is provided, with particular emphasis on mediation. Because of it's unique characteristics, mediation is an ideal starting point for incorporating ADR methods into a student conduct system. Second, mediation is compared and contrasted with the traditional judicial affairs approach followed by a discussion of the types of cases which are conducive to a mediated resolution. Lastly, three potential approaches for applying mediation to a student affairs program are reviewed.

ALTERNATIVE DISPUTE RESOLUTION

In the 1970s, there was growing concern about increased litigation and the negative impact it was having on American society. This interest in finding alternatives to the traditional adjudication process spawned the alternative dispute resolution movement (Goldberg, Sanders, and Roger, 1992; Nolan-Haley, 1992). Today, ADR methods encompass a wide range of processes, the most common of which are negotiation, conciliation, mediation, and arbitration. While there are similarities among each of these processes, the primary differences lie in the involvement and role of a third party neutral.

Negotiation is probably the most familiar process for resolving disputes, and simply involves discussion and bargaining between the parties themselves. It is voluntary and does not involve a third party. Negotiations occur everyday in both the general public and the academic community. Student negotiations may range from minor logistical issues such as what time to go to lunch with a group of friends, to more significant concerns like the division of monthly bill payments.

When people are unable to resolve a dispute between themselves, usually a friend or other third party will intervene to try to assist the two parties in working out the situation. Such negotiations, conducted with a third party that attempts "to bring the parties together or shares information between the two parties," are called conciliation (Girard, Rifkin, and Townley, 1985). A typical example of conciliation is when a residence hall staff member works with two residents to resolve a roommate conflict. While many might state that the residence hall staff member mediated the dispute, there are subtle, yet significant differences between conciliation and mediation.

Mediation involves a neutral third party that assists the disputing parties in resolving their dispute through participation in a structured process designed to achieve a mutually acceptable agreement. One of the key differences between mediation and conciliation is the involvement of a neutral third party. The neutrality of the individual facilitating the process is a significant factor in developing trust and getting the parties to be open and discuss their real needs and interests in the dispute. While a residence hall staff member may perceive themselves to be entirely neutral, the residents involved may have a much different perception of this individual's neutrality. Such student perceptions can be a significant barrier to dispute resolution.

Arbitration is similar to mediation in regards to the involvement of a neutral third party, however the role of the neutral is distinct from that of the mediator. Unlike the mediator, the arbitrator has decision-making authority. In essence, the parties agree to submit their dispute to a neutral third party to make a decision. While the issues and interests of the parties play an important role in the decision-making process, the arbitrator ultimately decides how the matter will be resolved. Although arbitration may loosely resemble some existing conflict resolution or grievance procedures used by student affairs administrators, neutrality may again be a distinguishing factor. In most institutional grievance processes, the third party decision-maker is identified by organizational position or hierarchy rather than being selected and agreed upon by the parties themselves. Again, the student's perceptions of the administrators neutrality may be a stumbling block to achieving long term resolution of the situation.

The student judicial process might be the next step along this continuum of dispute resolution processes, but the characteristics of student judicial proceedings tend to make it more analogous to adjudication than a formal ADR process. Student judicial affairs processes are governed by rules or policies; have sanctions issued by hearing officers or boards; and tend to be adversarial in nature. In contrast, "the various ADR approaches emphasize cooperation, direct involvement of the parties in decisions, and the reduction of tensions" (Girard, Rifkin, and Townley, 1985). These differences do not imply that ADR approaches are better than the judicial affairs approach or even litigation. Instead, alternative dispute resolution processes are alternatives to traditional approaches. For the legal community, ADR provides lawyers with alternative methods for resolving their clients disputes. In addressing the need for law students to study ADR methods, Jacqueline M. Nolan-Haley (1992) notes that:

> For law students to focus exclusively on the litigation process is like medical students studying only surgery as a means of curing illness. Of course this is not what medical students do. They study an extensive range of subjects for the treatment and cure of illness (p. 3).

Student judicial affairs professionals likewise, should consider alternatives For years student judicial processes have served as the primary process and in some cases the only process for addressing student conflicts and disputes. With students as our ultimate clients, the question should not be does their dispute involve a violation of university policy and therefore meet the needs of our process, but rather what university process meets the needs of our students in resolving the particular dispute.

WHERE TO BEGIN

Mediation tends to be the first distinctive step in providing students with alternatives to the traditional student judicial process. Before discussing the organization and structure of mediation programs on college campuses, it is important to have a clearer understanding of what mediation is, and when it should or should not be used to resolve student disputes.

A more formal definition of the mediation process is provided by the Texas Alternative Dispute Resolution Act (1987), "Mediation is a forum in which an impartial third person, the mediator, facilitates communication between parties to promote reconciliation, settlement, or an understanding among them" (Sec. 154.023). Unlike arbitration, the mediator has no decision-making authority. The involvement of the mediator as a neutral and impartial third party is one of the significant distinguishing factors between mediation and negotiation. The role of the mediator is to assist the disputing parties in reaching a mutually acceptable settlement of the issues, with the decision-making power left to the parties directly involved in the dispute.

When confronted with the option of mediation, many individuals assume that what they will be asked to do is compromise—if one person gives in a little the other will do the same, and eventually a middle ground is reached. This approach is commonly referred to as distributive bargaining (Haley, 1992, p. 15). It assumes that there is a fixed set of resources that will be distributed between both parties. The more one party receives, the less that is available for the other party. Bargaining in this type of zero-sum game usually involves both parties taking up positions on what they want or expect from the other party. Recognizing that it is unlikely that they will get everything they ask for, parties frequently present extreme positions, hoping that they can ultimately get what they want. Such situations become win-lose battles, where the winner is often the person with the greater endurance.

While most disputes involve a central issue that has brought the parties into conflict, there typically are one or more related issues that are impacting the dispute. Without addressing and resolving the related issues, the parties are unable to obtain movement on the central issue. The mediator's role is to assist the parties in identifying these interests and develop alternatives for mutual gain. This approach, called integrative bargaining, shifts discussion from positions and wants, to interests and needs, and focuses the parties on generating mutually beneficial solutions (Haley, 1992, p. 16).

Take, for example, a dispute between a student and the university library. The student has been assessed past due and book replacement charges which exceed $1000. The student indicates that she did not receive several of the past due notices the library staff claim to have sent. Further, all the books for which she is being assessed a replacement charge have been returned to the library. The circulation desk manager, on the other hand, indicates that the student is responsible for the past due fees regardless of whether or not she received the notices. In addition, the deadline for returning the books has passed and he has already placed an order for several of the new books.

From a distributive bargaining approach there is a fixed set of resources—the amount of the bill. To reduce the bill by any amount means a loss to the library staff member and a win for the student. Yet, no reduction in the bill will be a loss to the student and a win for the library staff member.

However, from an integrative bargaining approach the situation is analyzed beyond the obvious fixed dollar amount. For example, why is the circulation desk manager so rigid in his enforcement of library policies in this situation? Why is there so much hostility between the student and the staff member? In exploring these areas the mediator begins to uncover some underlying issues. The student has been extremely rude and difficult with the library staff. The student has a history of ignoring library policy and then argues and debates the matter each time an incident is addressed. The circulation desk manager and his staff are tired of dealing with her. Yet, the student responds that the library staff is always throwing some new policy at her and no one ever bothers to explain. She feels she is being taken advantage of because of her lack of understanding about their library processes.

With these underlying interests brought to the surface, the focus of the dispute is broadened beyond the original positions to include issues that directly impact the participants' perceptions of the conflict. Recognizing her attitude toward the library staff, the student may make an apology to the circulation desk manager and his staff and agree to be more respectful in the future. The manager, on the other hand, might acknowledge that some library procedures are not widely understood by the student body and agree to provide the student with more specific information concerning these processes. Having reached a new understanding, the student and the circulation desk manager could develop a set of guidelines by which similar conflicts between them could be resolved in the future. Resolution of these interests may now allow both parties to approach the central issue of the dispute, the amount of the bill, from a different perspective.

Through an integrative bargaining approach, the mediation process encourages the parties to look beyond the obvious issues in their dispute, and explore the real nature of the conflict. By identifying and understanding all of the issues impacting the dispute, and focusing on interests and needs, rather than positions and wants, both parties have the opportunity to achieve equitable gains and reach a win–win solution.

THE MEDIATION PROCESS

There are a variety of mediation models and each typically describes the process as a series of steps or stages (e.g., Beeler, 1986; Folberg & Taylor, 1984; Girard, Rifkin & Townley, 1985; Goldberg, Sander & Rogers, 1992; Lovenheim, 1989). As a brief summary of the process based on these earlier models, mediation will be described in terms of the following stages: (1) Opening Statement; (2) Story-Telling; (3) Identification of the Issues; (4) Generation of Options; and (5) Agreement.

- **Opening Statement:** Generally a mediation session begins with an opening statement being made by the mediator. The opening statement provides the mediator with the opportunity to present a brief explanation of the process and his or her role as the mediator. The mediator will also discuss basic ground rules concerning matters of courtesy, time constraints, as well as remind the participants of the confidential nature of the process. Lastly, the mediator will reaffirm with each party their willingness to participate and bargain in faith.

- **Story-Telling:** Discussion concerning the actual dispute involved begin with what is often referred to as story-telling. This initial stage of discussion between the parties is an opportunity for each participant to tell his/her side of the story without interruption. Participants are asked to actively listen to each other and refrain from rebutting each other's story on a point by point basis. Instead, the parties are encouraged to share their personal perceptions and feelings concerning the dispute. The story-telling process can be a very powerful stage of the process for many disputants because it may be the first time they have actually listened and considered the other parties perceptions of the situation.

- **Identification of the Issues:** Once the opening statements have been made by each party the mediator will assist the parties in exploring and identifying the specific issues involved in their dispute. Ultimately, the goal is for the parties to develop a list of specific issues which they believe must be addressed in order to resolve their dispute. This list will serve as an outline for the remainder of their deliberations.

- **Generation of Options:** Having developed a specific list of the issues, the parties then select one of these issues on which to focus. The mediator assists them in exploring a variety of options for addressing this particular issue. In this brainstorming process it is important that the parties recognize their common interests and evaluate options they might not have previously considered.

- **Agreement:** Once a suitable alternative is identified, the mediator assists the parties in developing and writing an agreement that is mutually beneficial to both sides. It is important that the agreement on each particular issue is written with sufficient specificity so as to avoid creating a future dispute about the interpretation of the agreement.

With a satisfactory agreement reached on one particular issue, the parties will return to their list and begin to tackle a new issue until an agreement is reached on each of the issues they identified. Throughout this process the mediator is careful to keep the parties focused on the particular issue being discussed at that time, and avoid discussion of other issues identified. If new issues arise, these issues can be added to the list so that they can be addressed through the mediation process.

Occasionally, parties will reach an issue where it appears agreement cannot be reached. Often such a stalemate is a good indication that an underlying issue exists which has not been acknowledged by the participants. While ideally the goal is to openly discuss and address each issue in joint session with both of the participants, some situations may require some individual discussion with the mediator before a participant is comfortable discussing the matter in joint session. Such individual or private discussions with the mediator are commonly known as caucuses.

Caucusing involves the mediator meeting privately with the parties during the course of the mediation. All information discussed with the mediator during private caucus is confidential and will not be disclosed to the other party unless the party providing the information expressly approves its disclosure. Rogers and Salem (1987), note that private caucuses are used to:

> provide an opportunity for a party to vent and cool down when emotions flare; encourage candor and get to the root of the dispute; clarify an issue; spend time alone with a party to build trust; provide time to review issues and alternatives; encourage movement when a party is unyielding; help a party determine if a position is unrealistic; remind a party of the consequences of not reaching an agreement; get information that may help generate or shape new alternatives; check whether a party has thought through the potential consequences of a probable agreement or separate one party from the threatening or intimidating conduct of the other. (cited in Goldberg, Sanders & Rogers, 1992, p. 110)

Generally a mediator will caucus with both parties, paying close attention to the time spent with each, before returning to joint session. Despite the advantages caucusing may provide, it also presents some dangers. Folberg and Taylor (1984), point out that it is difficult for a mediator to maintain the appearance of absolute impartiality when private caucuses are utilized. If a party in a dispute is aware that the mediator knows some "secret" information that is not shared with each side, the party may perceive some partiality between the mediator and the other side.

Further, private caucuses create problems of confidentiality, because although a party may agree that the mediator may disclose specific information, the same party may disagree with the way in which the mediator presents the information in joint session. Whether or not a mediator chooses to use private caucuses depends on the individual dispute being mediated and the mediator's style, but it is an important mediation tool which should be considered.

Overall, the mediation process provides the disputing parties with an opportunity to have a direct impact on the outcome of the conflict. It not only provides the parties with an opportunity to be heard, but an opportunity to develop a better understanding of the other side's point of view. Such an understanding may provide a framework from which future disputes may be resolved, and in this way, serves as an educational process for students. According to Folberg and Taylor (1984), "unlike the adjudicatory process, the emphasis is not who is right or wrong or who wins and who loses, but rather upon establishing a workable solution that meets the participant's unique needs" (p. 10).

MEDIATION VERSUS THE JUDICIAL AFFAIRS PROCESS

Although mediation can provide significant advantages over traditional judicial processes, it is equally important to recognize that not all conflicts are appropriate for mediation. Both in society and the college community, violent or criminal behavior must be addressed and should entail appropriate consequences. Thus, in addition to understanding the mediation process, it is also necessary to understand when a case should be mediated.

Lovenheim (1989), identifies a series of factors which were adapted from *A Student's Guide to Mediation and the Law* (Rogers & Salem, 1987) to consider when determining whether a case should be mediated. A number of these factors are applicable to the student affairs setting and are worthy of discussion. One of the most significant factors favoring the use of mediation is when the law, or institutional policies do not provide a remedy. For example, two roommates might decide to share long distance telephone service.

One of the roommates establishes the service in his/her name, and the other roommate agrees to pay his/her portion of the monthly bill. At some point in the semester, the roommate in whose name the service was established stops receiving payments from the other roommate, and the long distance company threatens to cut off service.

In most cases, university policies would offer no solution, because there is no regulation addressing the payment of debts to other students. Yet, left unchecked, the situation might escalate and result in a fight or some other altercation which would be a violation of university policies. Mediation would provide an opportunity for the roommates to sit down and work out an agreement before the situation escalated to a disciplinary matter.

Another factor identified by Lovenheim (1989) is parties wanting to end a problem, not a relationship. When by choice or circumstance the parties involved are likely to have a continuing relationship, mediation may be a more desirable solution. Consider the case of two residence hall students that live in adjacent rooms and have an on-going dispute about how loud a stereo should be played. One resident claims that the other student plays the stereo too loud. Whenever the resident attempts to contact a residence hall staff member to report a violation of the hall's "quiet hours policy" the resident is unable to find a staff member. Further, none of the other residents on the floor seem to be experiencing any difficulties with the other resident's stereo. Although the staff could be placed on "alert" to try and catch the noisy resident in the act, and address the matter through the student discipline process, such a resolution is unlikely to assist the residents in resolving any future conflicts that might arise because of their close living arrangements. Mediation, however, could provide a more lasting solution.

Lovenheim (1989) also notes that when the dispute is no one else's business—and you want to keep it that way, mediation may be the best alternative. Although student disciplinary records are confidential and protected by the Family Educational Rights and Privacy Act of 1974, some disputes are of a very personal nature and may be difficult for both the parties and any hearing board or panel to discuss. One example might be a relationship dispute. The girl-friend discovers that her boy-friend has been intimate with another woman, and she tells him she never wants to speak with him again. The boy-friend calls her repeatedly, sends her flowers and candy and continues to ask for the opportunity to explain the situation. The boy-friend's actions might be just enough to be considered harassment, but the girl-friend really doesn't want him to face any disciplinary action. She just wants him to leave her alone, and she certainly doesn't want to discuss the matter in front of a hearing panel or any other group of people. Again, mediation may be a more desirable approach to dealing with this situation.

Having considered a number of factors which favor mediation, let's turn to the factors which oppose mediating a particular case. According to Lovenheim (1989) a case should not be mediated when the dispute involves a serious crime. Violence or abusive behavior should not be mediated. Lovenheim (1989) notes that "in Massachusetts, for example, district attorneys are instructed that no crime for which the state would normally recommend a jail sentence should go to mediation" (p. 29). However, misdemeanor offenses such as simple assault, personal harassment, and minor property damage might be appropriate cases to mediate.

Mediation is also not an alternative when it is important to prove the truth or set a precedent (Lovenheim, 1989). Some cases may be of such a nature or importance that the student/institution may determine that mediation is not a viable alternative. From the student perspective this situation may be readily apparent—a student is accused of some wrong-doing and wants to clear his/her name. Therefore, mediation may not be the best alternative in the student's case. From the institutional perspective, however, the situation is a little less clear and requires careful consideration.

For example, in an acquaintance rape situation, where the case has not been accepted for criminal prosecution, and the survivor as well as the accused would prefer to address the incident through mediation, should an institution proceed with mediation or adjudicate the case through the student judicial process? Some institutions may view such cases as inappropriate for mediation. Because of the prevalence of acquaintance rape on college campuses, there may be a need to send a clear message to the campus community that acquaintance rape simply will not be tolerated. Further, some administrators may fear that handling such cases through mediation may be perceived as an attempt to hide such incidents from the campus community, and in no way want to support such a perception.

On the other hand, some institutions may feel that acquaintance rape situations are slightly different from other incidents of sexual assault, although none the less serious. Since the case was not accepted for criminal prosecution, and since acquaintance rape cases often revolve around the interpersonal communication of the students, or lack thereof, then the rights of the victim are paramount. Sometimes victims will indicate that they do not wish to pursue formal action, but they do want their assaulter to know how they feel and understand the hurt the assaulter has caused.

Provided that the survivor has voluntarily decided to address the incident through mediation after having been fully informed of the alternatives available, mediation of the case may be appropriate. Obviously, sexual assault cases are very serious, and the implications of utilizing mediation in such situations should be carefully considered by administrators before choosing a particular course of action.

It is also important to note that the choice between the student judicial process and mediation does not have to be an all or nothing decision. The two processes can work together. A case may originate as a judicial matter, such as a simple assault between two students, but during the course of the hearing process an underlying conflict which was the root of the inappropriate behavior may be identified. Mediation of this conflict could become a part of, or a factor in the sanctioning process. The hearing officer or board could decide to require the parties as a part of the sanction to participate in mediation to attempt to resolve the conflict which was identified. Such a requirement would be similar to court ordered mediation, where a judge or magistrate requires parties to mediate their dispute. Generally, court ordered mediation requires the parties to participate in at least one mediation session, and make a good faith effort to resolve the dispute. The mediator assigned to the case would report to the judge only whether the parties appeared for the session and made a good faith effort to resolve the dispute, and whether or not a settlement had been reached. All other information pertaining to the dispute would remain confidential.

While this type of forced mediation is used, and can produce results, mediation under these types of conditions is extremely difficult. Ideally, mediation is a voluntary process in which both parties agree to participate. With a sincere willingness and interest in participating in a collaborative process to resolve their dispute, participants are much more likely to achieve a settlement that is mutually beneficial. Instead of requiring students to mediate a dispute, it could be offered as an alternative to some other sanction, or a hearing could be stayed pending a mediation session allowing the students to reach their own resolution of the dispute.

To illustrate this approach, we can use the situation mentioned earlier in which two residence hall students live in adjacent rooms and are involved in an on-going noise dispute. The problems has now risen to the point where it has become disruptive to the rest of the residence hall community and must be addressed. A hearing officer could sanction one or both of the parties for a noise violation, but this does not resolve the underlying dispute between them. Instead, after hearing both parties side of the situation, the hearing officer could offer the students the opportunity to participate in a mediation session where they can attempt to work out their differences in a positive and structured environment.

Similar to court ordered mediation, the hearing officer would only be informed of whether or not the parties participated and a settlement agreement was reached. With this information the hearing officer would issue a final disposition for the case. Obviously, such an approach would require the involvement of another individual as the mediator, but it can be a tremendous educational experience for the students and is likely to produce a more lasting solution than the hearing officer might be able to develop.

Campus judicial processes are necessary and valuable components for resolving student conflict. Serious student misconduct must be addressed, and should incur appropriate consequences. Yet mediation, whether independent of or in conjunction with the student judicial process, may offer an alternative for addressing some types of student conflict in a more effective and lasting way.

APPLYING MEDIATION TO THE STUDENT AFFAIRS SETTING

The literature concerning college mediation programs is growing, but is still fairly limited, and offers few models for the application of a mediation program to a student affairs setting. Based upon a review of a variety of campus mediation center brochures and training materials from institutions across the United States, three potential approaches for applying mediation to a student affairs setting appear to exist.

Peer Mediation

One potential approach to mediating student disputes is through peer mediation. Peer mediation programs may be totally student operated, or they may receive some assistance from the university administration. Students mediate disputes, as well as coordinate some of the other related functions of the program. In a peer mediation program, students would be trained in basic mediation skills and techniques, but generally would not receive state certified mediation training. A staff or faculty advisor with some background in mediation would be beneficial. The program could be associated with a particular office in a division of student affairs or with an academic department.

Peer mediation provides an excellent training ground for students. Nowhere is the concept of a community dispute resolution center more alive than when students mediate student disputes. Peer mediation programs could be extremely effective in resolving roommate disputes and simple student conflicts. Particularly in connection with a residence life office or commuter student services center. Referrals from such offices could represent a significant portion of a peer mediation program's caseload.

One disadvantage to peer mediation programs can be the credibility of the program with students. Students involved in serious disputes, which may involve large sums of money or have the potential for litigation, may feel that their situation is beyond what a peer mediation service can handle and seek out other avenues for resolution of their case. In addition, a student run peer mediation service might experience difficulties with the visibility of its program. Such programs could be overlooked as a viable means for resolving serious disputes.

Mediation Service

Another approach is the creation of a separate office or center offering mediation services for students. A student mediation center could be staffed by one to two professional staff members that would coordinate the operations of the office. These professional staff would not only conduct intake sessions, but also personally serve as mediators in student disputes. Although their individual academic backgrounds might vary, staff in such offices could complete state certified mediation training programs, and may even become mediation trainers. If establishing such a mediation center within a student affairs division is not feasible, it could be established jointly between a segment of student affairs and an academic department, such as a speech communications or psychology department or even a school of law.

A separate mediation service would provide students with a centralized office where a dispute may be brought and staff in these offices could devote full attention to student disputes. Because the center would be operated by professional staff, perceived credibility of the center with students may be much greater than with a peer program. Such a center could also provide training to members of the campus community (faculty and staff, as well as students) and utilize these individuals in various mediation cases.

The combination of professional and peer mediators could enhance the program by capitalizing on the advantages of both approaches. The availability of trained mediators from throughout the campus community may not only serve to reduce the caseload of the professional mediators, but might provide other advantages in situations where such mediators may offer a greater perceived level of impartiality or where their individual technical knowledge or experience could be beneficial to a particular dispute.

As with peer mediation, students must be informed about the separate office or center offering mediation services. To seek out the service, students must not only be cognizant of the service, but be familiar with the mediation process and the types of disputes for which it is best suited. Mediation services could increase their effectiveness if relationships can be built with other offices and services that would be likely to make referrals. Such offices or services might include: judicial affairs, student legal services, university police, residence life offices, and commuter student services centers. Without such referrals and a well publicized program, it may be only by accident that students find their way to mediation.

Campus Dispute Resolution Center

The third approach is to integrate mediation services with other dispute resolution services already available on campus to create a campus dispute resolution center (see *Figure I* on p. 249). This approach is based on what has been termed "The Multi-Door Courthouse". This concept was first introduced in 1976 at the Conference on the Causes of Popular Dissatisfaction with the Administration of Justice (National Institute of Justice, 1986). In "The Multi-Door Courthouse," a variety of alternative dispute resolution services are housed in one facility. Individuals with a dispute or grievance can go to the "courthouse" and meet with a trained intake clerk. The clerk reviews their individual cases and refers them to the process most appropriate for their situation.

One of the significant advantages that may be offered by a campus dispute resolution center established on "The Multi-Door Courthouse" approach, is that it could reduce the "run-around" students can experience in attempting to get their conflict or dispute resolved. Knowledge of, or familiarity with, any one particular service is not vital since such a program could connect a student with any one of a variety of dispute resolution processes that would be appropriate to their needs. Not only could a campus dispute resolution center increase the likelihood of students utilizing mediation services, but it might also decrease the demand and caseload of more traditional services. A campus dispute resolution center using the "Multi-Door Courthouse" approach might include judicial affairs, legal services, ombudsperson, as well as mediation services. It could be staffed by professional staff and peers.

Certainly, one of the key difficulties to "The Multi-Door Courthouse" approach is obtaining the space to house all the various components of the center in one facility. Further, each of the components that might make up the campus dispute resolution center may be operated by a different department or division within a given institution. Assimilating each of these components into one unit may pose a number of practical or political difficulties. However, where two or more components exist in one department or division, a campus dispute resolution center offers an opportunity for more comprehensive and collaborative approach to resolving campus conflict.

SUMMARY

The student judicial process is an important and necessary part of any student affairs operation. However, the judicial process is not equipped to address all conflicts that arise on today's college campuses. In addition to a well-developed judicial system, campuses need to explore and utilize alternative methods to support and supplement the judicial system. Mediation is one particular form of alternative dispute resolution that is well suited for the campus environment. In mediation the students, rather than the administrators, are responsible for resolving the dispute. Because they develop the solution, students tend to be more satisfied with the process and are more likely to adhere to the agreement that is reached. Whether available through a separate campus service or an integrated component of a campus dispute resolution center, mediation is an important option with which student judicial affairs professionals should become familiar as an alternative to the traditional hearing process.

Figure I

Campus Dispute Resolution Center Model

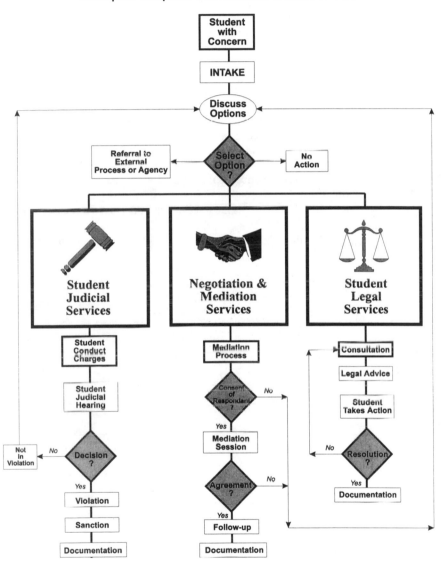

References

Beeler, K. D. (1986). Campus mediation: A promising complement to student judicial processes. *College Student Affairs Journal, 7*(1), 38-45.

Folberg, J. & Taylor, A. (1984). *Mediation: A comprehensive guide to resolving conflicts without litigation.* San Francisco: Jossey-Bass.

Girard, K., Rifkin, J., & Townley, A. (1985). *Peaceful persuasion: A guide to creating mediation dispute resolution programs on college campuses.* The Mediation Project, Waskiewicz House, University of Massachusetts, 425 Amity St., Amherst MA 01002.

Goldberg, S.B., Sander, F. E., & Rogers, N. H. (1992). *Dispute resolution: Negotiation, mediation, and other processes* (2nd ed.). Boston: Little, Brown & Co.

Lovenheim, P. (1989). *Mediate, don't litigate. How to resolve disputes quickly, privately, and inexpensively—without going to court.* New York: McGraw Hill.

National Institute of Justice. (1986). *Toward the multi-door courthouse—Dispute resolution intake and referral* (Reprinted from NIJ Reports/SNI 198). Washington, DC: U. S. Department of Justice.

Nolan-Haley, J. M. (1992) *Alternative dispute resolution in a nutshell.* St. Paul, MN: West Publishing Co.

Rogers, N. & Salem, R. (1987). *A student's guide to mediation and the law.* New York: Matthew Bender.

Texas Alternative Dispute Resolution Act, Chap. 1121, S.B. No. 1436 (1987).

Synthesis

Chapter XIV

What Does the Future Hold for Student Judicial Affairs? Just Discipline?

Donald D. Gehring

Trying to predict what the future holds for student judicial affairs is like trying to look into a crystal ball—you get a very distorted picture. However, student judicial affairs exists within the context of the university and there are some indicators of the challenges higher education will face and the environment in which it will exist. Student judicial affairs, existing within the university, will be affected by those challenges and that environment.

This chapter describes the complex issues higher education may face in the future and the environment in which it may find itself beyond 2000. Trends in the case law are examined to determine if they provide a harbinger, when linked with predictions of higher education's overall future, of what student judicial officers may expect in the years to come. Finally, the chapter offers suggestions for those in student judicial affairs to meet the challenges of the future.

Before embarking on this discussion, however, a caveat is in order. Although general predictions, based on some fairly reliable trend data, may be made about the challenges higher education will encounter and the environment in which it will exist, this does not predict how higher education will respond to these challenges or to that environment. As Fincher (1993) reminds us, universities are ". . . the outcome of subtle and complex interactions among historical events partially and adaptive, effective responses to changing public perceptions, expectations and values" (p. 28).

With this caveat in mind, it appears that higher education will face four primary types of challenges in the 21st century—economic, demographic, political, and technological. Levine (1989) captured these trends when he noted that a Ford Foundation Symposium was premised on the belief that, . . . The world of higher education is changing dramatically. Our nation is increasingly becoming part of the global society. Our economy is moving from an industrial to an informational and service base. Our population is undergoing a demographic metamorphosis. New technologies are burgeoning. The relationship between higher education and the federal government, state governments, industry and other external patrons is shifting. The financing of colleges and universities is undergoing a change. Critical research on learning is multiplying, and experiments applying this research to instruction, particularly in the business world, are mushrooming. (Levine, 1989, p. xi)

Fincher (1993) echoed Levine's comments in his perspective on the university in the 21st century. His list includes:

1. the changing sociocultural context;

2. continuing demographic shifts and the aging baby boomers;

3. simulation of international competition and cooperation;

4. the rapidity of cultural and technological change; and

5. the continuing influence of public perception, expectations and values.

FUTURE ISSUES FACING HIGHER EDUCATION

As the astute philosopher Casey Stengle once observed, "You can see a lot just by looking." If we look about us we can observe the changing cultural context of higher education and the changing demographics. We all know the demographics. The African-American population "represents a younger and faster growing population than do whites" (Thomas & Hirsh, 1989, p. 76), but, according to *The Economist* ("People-Power," 1992), the Asian-American population will rival the African-American population by the middle of the 21st century and Hispanic-Americans will outnumber African-Americans in about 20 years.

Baby-boomers are now in their 50s. They are the most well educated generation this country has produced and if there is one thing we know for sure from adult education research, it is that the more education you have the more you are likely to want (Cross, 1981; Long, 1983). Anyone who works in a two-year college will verify that they are seeing more and more students who already have an undergraduate degree taking classes, particularly in the technology areas. Even today more students live off-campus and at home than live in residence halls (G. Schwartzmueller, personal correspondence, December 3, 1996).

Somehow higher education will have to adapt to this changing demographic picture while responding to what Fincher (1993) calls the "continuing influence of public perception, expectations and values" (p. 28). The recent reports on higher education, like that produced by the Wingspread Group (1993), evidence little confidence in higher education and call for greater accountability. The very first paragraph of the report is the harbinger stating that, "A disturbing and dangerous mismatch exists between what American society needs of higher education and what it is receiving ... The American imperative for the 21st century is that society must hold higher education to much higher expectations or risk national decline" (p. 1).

Learning will be the centerpiece of higher education. But, learning will be viewed as a broad concept including personal development and not confined simply to classrooms, labs and libraries. Evidence of this can be seen in the recent call of student affairs to become more engaged in the learning enterprise with the publication of the *Student Learning Imperative* (ACPA, 1994).

Because learning will be demanded by the public and because the cultural mix of students will be greater, faculty will face challenges never before even envisioned. However, with faculty retirements increasing, higher education will have an opportunity to focus on learning in new ways.

The rapid changes in technology present both an opportunity and a problem—an opportunity in providing new ways to teach that can provide greater emphasis on the individual learner and can be used to link learners and learning guides no matter where they are, as well as providing almost instantaneous facts and data to researchers. However, technology may also pose a problem for higher education. The rapidity with which technology is changing will make it more difficult to "keep up to speed" and it will be expensive to do so. Technology also has the potential problem of keeping people out of touch with other real people. Although virtual communities have sprung up through the Internet, people seem to need face to face contact with other human beings. Without that contact students may experience more emotional problems. The rapid changes in technology will provide challenges for higher education not even envisioned today. Problems never imagined ten years ago are already becoming commonplace (see *Chapter X*).

The fact that keeping up with the rapid changes in technology can be very expensive coupled with the fact that about 80% of state and federal budgets are already allocated to mandated programs presents yet another challenge for higher education. There simply will not be a great financial windfall in the near future for higher education.

The federal government will also continue to cost higher education money with expensive mandated programs and no funds to carry them out. Not only will the government add additional costs to higher education, but it will continue to intrude upon the autonomy of higher education even more directly and more frequently. The federal government will no longer be satisfied with telling higher education what to do, but it will in the future want to mandate how to do it (Lowery, 1995). Attempts at federal direction are already taking place. Evidence the Hyde bill which attempted to tell private colleges how to respond to speech on their campuses (Gehring, 1991), the OCR finding at U.C. –Santa Cruz that a one-year suspension from college was not sufficient in a sexual assault case (J. E. Palomino, personal communication, April 29, 1994), or the President's Model State Drug Law which would require specific sanctions for off-campus student groups who violate a code of conduct mandated by law, and allowing for 24-hour inspections of the off-campus facility (Julian, 1994).

Finally, higher education will face all these challenges in a global society. A society in which international efforts such as NAFTA are already taking place. Probably this country's greatest export is education and the nation will be called upon to deliver it to increasingly diverse students while responding to insistent demands for accountability in a rapidly changing technological environment with less money and greater federal control.

If that were not enough of a challenge, colleges and universities will also be faced with the lingering problems of this decade including poor secondary preparation for college as well as equity and access issues.

THE EVOLUTION OF CAMPUS JUDICIAL ISSUES

Do these complex issues and the future environment of higher education have any relationship to what might be expected for the future of student judicial affairs? Campus judicial affairs are certainly affected by what takes place in the university, but is that impact primary or peripheral? How do the issues faced by higher education interrelate with the trends in student judicial affairs? To answer these questions requires an analysis of where student judicial affairs has been and the trends in that evolution.

In the early 1960s public college and university administrators were condemning the courts because institutions were now being required to provide a notice and hearing at which students could defend themselves before being suspended or expelled (*Dixon v. Alabama State Board of Education*, 1961). Prior to that time administrators acted *in loco parentis* without much concern for due process or formal hearings.

In 1969 the courts said that not only did students at tax supported institutions have the right to notice and hearing under the 14th Amendment, but that they were persons entitled to all constitutional rights and they do not leave those rights at the schoolhouse gate (*Tinker v. Des Moines Independent Community School District*, 1969).

Just as institutions wondered how they would deal with constitutional challenges, students began to assert their rights as consumers. They began to demand that institutions deliver everything they promised in all those slick brochures and catalogs. The courts agreed that students did have a contract with the university and the terms and conditions were generally to be found in the institution's publications (see, for example, *Steinberg v. Chicago Medical School*, 1977, *Dizick v. Umpqua Community College*, 1979 and *Joyner v. Albert Merrill School*, 1978).

Along with this consumer movement came an increase in the number of tort liability suits. These types of suits and other consumer issues were linked to the economic decline experienced by this country after 1975 (Elkhawas, 1975; Stein, 1980). Levine (1980) also noted this consumerism led to a "meism" or individual ascendency. Samuelson (1980), an economist, has suggested that in periods of economic decline individuals are more interested in promoting their own rights as consumers rather than asserting the rights of others or group ascendancy.

The mid-seventies also brought another new trend. Beginning in that period, institutions not only faced students asserting individual constitutional and consumer rights, but a new thrust of government protective policy laws beginning with the Family Educational Rights and Privacy Act (FERPA). In 1984, the federal government forced the states to raise the legal drinking age from 18 to 21 under penalty of losing federal highway funds (23 U.S.C. 158). In 1989, Congress enacted the Drug Free Schools and Communities Act Amendments mandating that institutions, at their own expense, inform students of what they already knew (Palmer, Gehring, & Guthrie, 1992). In the 90s, the government imposed the Campus Security Act requiring more record keeping and publications. In this same era the media perceived that student judicial officers were hiding information which made students on campus more vulnerable to crimes (Bernstein, 1996).

The first half of this decade has seen all these issues affecting student judicial affairs come together in ways that have created complex questions of moral and ethical concerns juxtaposed to legal and regulatory parameters. The issues in student judicial affairs seem to be very much interrelated with the complex changes predicted for higher education in general.

One example that illustrates how student judicial issues are interrelated with the changes predicted for higher education is the economy and the competition for resources it engenders, as well as the demographics of increased numbers of minority students coming from inner city schools where they were underprepared for college (Levine, 1989) and the emphasis on political correctness. Taken together, these issues have generated a backlash of reverse discrimination suits and violence in the form of hate speech and behavior.

In 1990, there were two racial harassment cases, one suit challenging an all minority organization, and one reverse discrimination admissions case. In 1991, one reverse discrimination case was reported involving financial aid. But in 1992, there were four racial harassment cases, two reverse discrimination cases involving financial aid, one involving the denial of admission and one dealing with the dismissal from a program. Three cases involving hate speech or hate crimes were reported in 1993 in addition to a reverse discrimination suit.

In 1994, five cases were reported that involved challenges based on race. Two involved race based scholarships, one the use of racial epithets, another was a challenge to an affirmative action plan and the final case challenged a disciplinary action on the basis of race. The year 1995 saw the Supreme Court reject an appeal of a case striking down race-based scholarships, a California speech code challenged and a coach dismissed for using a racial epithet. Finally, in 1996 a federal court of appeals said that an institution's affirmative action plan for admission of minority students to law school was unconstitutional and the Supreme Court refused to review the decision.

Racial tensions, however, have not been the only way that the streams of economic, political, demographic and technological changes in higher education have affected judicial affairs. While there have always been crimes of violence on campus (Rudolph, 1962), it seems that this problem is more prevalent today (Palmer, 1996). The political process has become involved in campus crime with Congress finding that:

1. students and employees of institutions of higher education should be aware of the incidence of crime on campus and policies and procedures to prevent crime or to report occurrences of crime;

2. applicants for enrollment at a college or university, and their parents, should have access to information about the crime statistics of that institution and its security policies and procedures; and

3. while many institutions have established crime preventive measures to increase the safety of campuses, there is a clear need to encourage:

   a. development on all campuses of security policies and procedures;

   b. uniform and consistent reporting of crimes on campus; and

   c. development of policies and procedures to address sexual assaults and racial violence on college campuses (P.L. 101-542, Title II 202, 104 Stat. 2384) and newspapers seeking access to campus hearings. Uses of the Internet on campus have been regulatedby the government (J. E. Palomino, personal communication, April 29, 1994)

The Administration of Campus Discipline ...

and a federal Communications Decency Act attempted to control the medium. Colleges and universities have been required to compile, publish, and distribute to every student and other adult on campus information they already know about alcohol, drugs and crime (Palmer, Gehring, & Guthrie, 1992). The public has sought accountability of the campus judicial process through the news media (*Red and Black Publishing Co. v. Board of Regents*, 1994) while the government has declared those records not open to inspection, and the Justice Department was directed to compile data on "the adequacy of policies and practices of educational institutions in addressing campus sexual assaults and protecting victims" (P.L. 103-322 §40506).

Each of the situations described represents a manifestation of the economic, political, demographic and technological changes occurring in higher education and each has had an effect on the administration of campus judicial affairs. This connection between the environment of higher education and campus judicial affairs thus provides a basis for predicting what the future holds.

FUTURE ISSUES FACING STUDENT JUDICIAL AFFAIRS

The complexity of the problems that will face judicial affairs on campus will demand that the judicial affairs administrator become a professional specialization within student affairs. The issues this individual will encounter will simply be too complex and too intense for a generalist to undertake. The consequences of errors in judicial affairs are also too great to assign the task to anyone but a well trained, knowledgeable professional.

The problems of hate speech and behavior will not soon disappear. Tensions between the current majority and the increasingly large minority population in higher education will continue to be explosive. Judicial affairs administrators will need to be skilled mediators and understand how to effectively respond to hate speech and behavior in ways that defuse it and expose it to the light of truth.

Consumerism will continue to be a major issue for judicial administrators to deal with, but in addition to the current concern of getting what they paid for in the classroom, students will be looking to judicial affairs to ensure a safe, hospitable environment in which to learn. Judicial administrators will need to become skilled investigators who can access, interpret, and apply confusing regulations and conflicting judicial opinions (Department of Education, 1996; and *Davis v. Monroe County Board of Education*, 1996; contrast with *Rowinsky v. Bryan Independent School District*, 1996).

The disciplinary process will become more "federalized" as the government's mandates continue to proliferate. The distinction between public and private institutions will become blurred as private institutions are required to include in their codes of conduct federally mandated offenses, adjudicate those offenses in federally mandated ways and impose sanctions in accord with what the government believes to be appropriate.

Judicial affairs administrators will be faced with an array of new dilemmas caused by the increased accessibility to computers. Almost every student will have a web page causing concerns over whether the information displayed is covered by the First Amendment and how time, place, and manner restrictions apply. Information available on the web will raise new questions about copyright violations, trademark infringement, and academic honesty (Brady, 1996).

Being faced with a weak economy and an emphasis on student learning and assessment may cause faculty to concentrate more on teaching and grant writing. This possibility along with the problem of plagiarism enhanced by the Internet will result in more and more institutions turning over responsibility for resolving academic integrity cases to campus judicial affairs administrators where it is now handled by academic administrators or faculty.

Finally, the changes in the economy, politics, demographics and technology affect others just as they do higher education. I believe that local governments, also suffering from a weak economy, political pressure and changing demographics will defer to the campus judicial process rather than prosecuting students who commit criminal acts on campus. This will cause campus judicial administrators to be caught in the middle between local government and the news media and lobby groups pushing to open campus hearings.

THE FUTURE STUDENT JUDICIAL ADMINISTRATOR

Dealing with problems as complex as those outlined above will call for individuals with a secure professional identity. Most of us have studied Freud, Erikson, and more recently Chickering and find that each of them has included the core construct of identity in their theory of development. Identity is central because we each need to have some sense of who we are in order to progress through our lives meeting the millions of daily challenges, decisions, and situations that confront us—and do so in some purposeful way. Without a good sense of who we are—as Chickering would say, knowledge of our competencies, an awareness of our emotions, our social, historical and cultural context and our interdependence with others—we cannot live a very purposeful life (Chickering, 1993).

Reflecting on a professional identity for judicial affairs administrators requires that several questions be asked. What competencies
must judicial affairs administrators possess? What does it mean professionally to manage emotions? What is the social, historical and cultural context in which judicial affairs is practiced?

Ed Stoner in his excellent article, "Harnessing the 'Spirit of Insubordination' A Model Student Disciplinary Code," (1990) took his title
from a quotation of Thomas Jefferson. In a letter to Thomas Cooper,
the second president of what is now the University of South Carolina,
Mr. Jefferson said:

> The article of discipline is the most difficult in American Education.
> Premature ideas of independence, too little repressed by parents,
> beget a spirit of insubordination, which is the great obstacle to science
> with us and a principle cause of its decay since the revolution. I look
> to it with dismay in our institution as a breaker ahead, which I am
> far from confident we shall be able to weather.

Of course, what Mr. Jefferson means by "science" is rationality.

This statement of Mr. Jefferson is important in understanding the
historical context of the judicial affairs profession, but it becomes even
more significant when it is analyzed. Scholars say that whenever Jefferson was unsure of how a problem or issue should be resolved, he
would describe it using nautical metaphors such as "a ship without
a rudder" or "tossed at sea." Notice here that in reference to discipline Mr. Jefferson uses the metaphor of "a breaker ahead, which I
am far from confident we shall be able to weather." A nautical reference

He used this nautical description of the "spirit of insubordination"
to describe disciplinary problems in the year 1822. This provides some
insight into the historical context of judicial affairs. Discipline has been
a major issue for administrators for more than 170 years-longer than
most academic disciplines taught in our colleges and universities today. Furthermore, it challenged one of the brightest men the country
has known.

But the social context of judicial affairs is not, as some on campus
would tell you, "just discipline." Mr. Jefferson recognized that there
was a basis for this "spirit of insubordination" without the benefit
of Freud, Erikson, Chickering and others. He saw the connection between this "spirit of insubordination" and the "premature ideas of
independence, too little repressed by parents." Most would agree that
discipline problems today have a similar foundation—both premature
ideas of independence and too little repressed by parents. It can be
added that Ernest Boyer in his book, *Campus Life* (1990) said that students ". . . bring a determined independence to campus." Not much
changes!

Another aspect of the professional identity of judicial affairs is what Chickering (1993) calls managing emotions. This vector includes an awareness of emotions, appropriately channeling them and balancing control and expression. What this means professionally for judicial affairs is that we recognize the tendency for the purpose of discipline to become simply a means to uphold the norms of the community by punishment, but then channeling that tendency in a way that helps students to grow too; as Pavela (1985) has said, students need to "behold themselves," thereby creating an appropriate balance between punishment and education, and ideas of independence and interdependence.

But the professional identity of judicial affairs is more than understanding the context and managing emotions—it is knowledge of the competencies that must be possessed and acquiring them. The knowledge and competencies a judicial affairs administrator must possess are as demanding as any scholarly discipline. Judicial affairs administrators are expected to be well versed in constitutional law, including the rights guaranteed by the 1st, 4th, and 14th Amendments. They must know federal and state laws and regulations. Mediation and other alternative dispute resolution techniques constitute another competency they must have while computer skills are also a necessity. Because judicial affairs administrators work with students, they must be aware of developmental theories, cultural differences, and environmental/personal interaction theories.

If this knowledge base were not enough they must also possess at least some rudimentary public relations skills. Judicial affairs administrators will deal with parents more often in the future as well as nontraditional students who have a high degree of consumer mentality. The press and other media will also need to be reckoned with as will victim advocacy groups. Judicial affairs administrators need to understand governance systems and organizational and political structures as they attempt to build bridges with the faculty in resolving matters of academic integrity, with the campus police and local agencies in deciding on jurisdictional matters, and with coaches and A.D.'s in dealing with student-athletes.

The skills and competencies outlined above are necessary not only to be able to perform the day-to-day tasks of administering campus judicial affairs, but also to develop a sound philosophical basis upon which policies, practices and procedures may be grounded. Without such grounding administrators will find themselves acting inconsistently and creating mistrust and anxiety within both the student body and the administration.

Thus, understanding the historical and social context within which judicial affairs operates, having an awareness of emotions and knowledge of the skills and competencies necessary to carry out the daily tasks and developing a philosophy to guide practice can all aid in defining a professional identity for judicial affairs, an identity which will be necessary if judicial affairs administrators are to deal effectively with the complex problems that will arise in the future. However, identity is only a necessary precursor to purpose. What is the purpose of judicial affairs on campus? Is it just discipline—a reactive stance in keeping students under control? Or is it proactive, existing in an interdependent way with other campus units in ways that help build community? Chickering (1993) has suggested that we need to develop purpose and that this involves finding what energizes us and the ability to unify different goals within the scope of a meaningful purpose.

THE FUTURE OF STUDENT JUDICIAL AFFAIRS

What then can be the meaningful purpose of professional judicial affairs administrators as they face the complexity of the future. Erik Erikson (1968) has suggested that once you have established identity, you must resolve the polarity of "Generativity v. Stagnation." In other words, you become generative and give to others or you stagnate and become self-absorbed.

I suggest that generativity can become the meaningful purpose for one's professional life in judicial affairs. The question now becomes generative in what way. I propose that higher education desperately needs to develop a sense of community and that professional judicial administrators can contribute greatly to the building of that community.

How can judicial affairs administrators help to develop a purposeful community—a place where everyone works together to enhance teaching and learning? As judicial administrators you have the opportunity to turn misconduct into a "teachable moment" in which students can learn more than responsibility—you can help them learn how to become, in Don Schon's (1983) terms, reflective learners.

Your contribution to Boyer's second principle—an open community where freedom of expression is uncompromisingly protected and civility is powerfully affirmed—seems almost unnecessary to discuss except to point out as the former president of the University of California reminded, "The University is not engaged in making ideas safe for students. It is engaged in making students safe for ideas" (cited in Boyer, 1990, p. 22). We must counter incivility with civility and intolerant speech with more speech.

Judicial affairs administrators probably more than anyone else on campus, are central to the task of building what Boyer calls a just community and a disciplined community. Programs must be designed that are proactive attempts to combat campus racism and sexism with the idea of creating a community where each individual is respected, but individuals also accept their obligations to the community.

Building a caring community where the well-being of each member is sensitively supported and where service to others is encouraged is Boyer's fifth principle. In discussing this idea, Boyer tells us that "in a caring community students should make a connection between what they learn and how they live" (p. 54). Judicial administrators are in a position to help students make that connection, but it takes purposeful effort on their part to do this. Too often we attend to the legal to the exclusion of the learning.

Finally, Boyer has suggested that a college community is a celebrative community in which the heritage of the institution is remembered and where rituals affirming tradition and change are widely shared. Certainly judicial affairs administrators have a role here also. Beyond the individual institutional traditions, they can, through academic integrity programming and consciousness raising, help to maintain the historical traditions of academic excellence, scholarship and integrity.

The future for student judicial affairs is inexorably tied to the future of the university. Both will face complex problems created by the streams of change in the economy, demography, politics and technology. Judicial affairs administrators must, if they are to meet these challenges, develop their own professional identity as a means of achieving community on campus. The future demands that judicial affairs administration can no longer be just discipline.

References

American College Student Personnel Association. (1994). *The student learning imperative: Implications for student affairs.* Washington, D.C.: Author.

Bernstein, N. (1996, May 5). With colleges holding court, discretion vies with fairness. *New York Times,* pp. 1, 16.

Boyer, E. L. (1990). *Campus life: In search of community.* Princeton, NJ: Princeton University Press.

Brady, S. (Executive Producer). (1996, September 30). *Freedom of speech in the cyberspace university.* Bowling Green, OH: WBGSU TV.

Chickering, A. W., & Reisser, L. (1993). *Education and identity* (2nd ed.). San Francisco: Jossey-Bass.

Cross, K. P. (1981). *Adults as learners.* San Francisco: Jossey-Bass.

Department of Education Office of Civil Rights. (1996, August 14). *Sexual harassment guidance: Peer harassment.* Washington, D.C. : Author.

El-Khawas, E. (1975). Consumerism as an emerging issue for postsecondary education. *Educational Record,* 56, 126-131.

Erikson, E. H. (1968). *Identity: Youth and crisis.* New York: Norton & Company, Inc.

Fincher, C. (1993). The idea of the university in the 21st century: An American perspective. *British Journal of Educational Studies*, 41(1), 26-44.

Gehring. D. (1991). Abreast of the law. *NASPA Forum*, 11(7), 5-6.

Levine, A. (1989). *Shaping higher education's future: Demographic realities and opportunities, 1900-2000*. San Francisco: Jossey-Bass Publishers.

Levine, A. (1980). *When dreams and heroes die: A portrait of today's college student*. San Francisco: Jossey-Bass Publishers.

Long, H. B. (1983). *Adult learning*. New York: Cambridge.

Lowery, J. W. (1995). Complying with Congressional mandates and the practice of student affairs. *College Student Affairs Journal*, 15(1), 16-25.

Palmer, C. J. (1996). Violence and other forms of victimization in residence halls: Perspectives of resident assistants. *Journal of College Student Development*, 37(3), 268-277.

Palmer, C. J., Gehring, D. D., & Guthrie, V. L. (1992). Student knowledge of information mandated by the 1989 amendments to the drug free schools and communities act. *NASPA Journal*, 30(1), 30-38.

Pavela, G. (1985). *The dismissal of students with mental disorders: Legal issues, policy considerations, and alternative responses* [Monograph]. The Higher Education Administration Series, 2, 1-97.

People-Power. (1992, December 5). *The Economist*, 323, p. 29.

Rudolph, F. (1962). *The American college and university*. New York: Knopf, Inc.

Samuelson, P. (1980). *Economics* (11th ed.). New York: McGraw-Hill.

Schon, D. A. (1983). *The reflective practitioner: How professionals think in action*. United States: Basic Books, Inc.

Stein, R. (1980). The consumer movement in higher education: Past, present, and future. *NASPA Journal*, 18, 8-14.

Stoner, E. N., & Cerminara, K. L. (1990). Harnessing the "spirit of insubordination": A model student disciplinary code. *Journal of College and University Law*, 17(1), 89-121.

Thomas, G. E., & Hirsh, D. J. (1989). Blacks. In A. Levine (Ed.), *Shaping higher education's future: Demographic realities and opportunities, 1900-2000*, pp. 62-86. San Francisco: Jossey-Bass Publishers.

Violent Crime Control and Law Enforcement Act of 1994, Pub. L. No. 103-322, §40506 Stat. 1946 (1994).

Wingspread Group on Higher Education. (1993). *An American imperative: Higher expectations for higher education*. United States of America: The Johnson Foundation, Inc.

Cases

Davis v. Monroe County Board of Education, 74 F. 3d 1186 (11th Cir. 1996).

Dixon v. Alabama State Board of Education, 294 F. 2d 150 (5th Cir. 1961).

Dizick v. Umpqua Community College, 599 P. 2d 444 (Or. 1979).

Joyner v. Albert Merrill School, 411 N.Y.S. 2d 988 (Civ. Ct. City of NY 1978).

Red and Black Publishing Co. v. The Board of Regents, 427 S.E. 2d 257 (Ga. 1993).

Rowinsky v. Bryan Independent School District, 80 F. 3d 1006 (5th Cir. 1996), cert. den. 65 L.W. 3249 (1996).

Steinberg v. Chicago Medical School, 371 N.E. 2d 634 (IL. 1977).

Tinker v. Des Moines Independent Community School District, 393 U.S. 503 (1969).

Case Studies

Editor's Note: Special thanks to Dennis Gregory for editing the case studies. These case studies and the accompanying commentary are designed for discussion and analysis among colleagues. They are not intended to be comprehensive descriptions or models that fit the uniqueness of every institution of higher education. Legal advice should be sought from institutional counsel when addressing specific situations on your campus.

Case Study I. THE BASKETBALL STAR AND FERPA

Mr. Joseph Thomas is the center on the University of South Eastern Tennessee basketball team. The 7'2" Thomas is a senior and is half way through the basketball season with a chance to set virtually every record in the history of USET basketball. He has the most points scored in a game, and has six triple doubles (double figures in points, rebounds and assists) so far for the season. There is talk of his selection as a first team All-American and he will certainly be drafted during the first round of the post-season NBA draft.

One Sunday evening, February 18, at 3:00 a.m. campus police stop Mr. Thomas' car as it sped away from the athletic complex. Upon stopping the car and asking Thomas to exit the vehicle the police officers detect an odor of alcoholic beverage about him. They give him a field sobriety test that he passes, although he admits to having consumed two beers earlier in the evening. Mr. Thomas has turned 21 several weeks before. While shining a flashlight in the back seat, Officer Jones notices what appears to be a semi-automatic pistol lying on the seat. The gun is seized and Mr. Thomas says that the gun is not his, but his brother's. Reportedly the brother has had Mr. Thomas' car over the weekend while Mr. Thomas was playing in a basketball game away from home. The officers know that Mr. Thomas was away and that

269

the car, which is distinctive in appearance, has been seen driving on campus this weekend.

The officers choose not to arrest Mr. Thomas, but indicate that they will file an "incident report" with the judicial affairs office and they will log the incident in the campus police log. They indicate that the gun will be confiscated and that Mr. Thomas' brother may pick it up if he brings the registration to the police station. They indicate that they will file charges against Mr. Thomas for felony possession of a firearm on the grounds of an educational institution if his brother does not bring the permit. Monday morning Mr. Thomas' brother does bring in the permit and admits to inadvertently leaving the gun in the car. The gun is released to him.

Later that day, a reporter from the campus newspaper comes to the police department to scan the "police log." He notes the incident with Mr. Thomas. The reporter goes to the police chief and asks for a copy of the "incident report" written by the officers. He also goes to the Judicial Office and asks for a copy of the same "incident report." Finally, he goes to the basketball coach and asks for a comment on the situation with Mr. Thomas. Coach Norton says, "Yes, we understand that Mr. Thomas will be charged with student conduct violations and may be charged with criminal violations as well. I have suspended him from the team pending the results of these charges." The reporter writes his article and it is published on Tuesday. On Wednesday, the reporter receives a letter from the judicial officer indicating that he has violated the "Buckley Amendment" and is, thus subject to a lawsuit under section 1983 of the U.S. Code.

What problems exist in this situation?

Can the "incident report" be released? If so, by whom?

Did the reporter violate FERPA? Did anyone?

Does Mr. Thomas' status as a "public figure" change the matter?

Commentary

The Family Educational Rights and Privacy Act was passed by Congress in 1974 primarily as a way to assure that parents could get access to the educational records of their children. Since that time it has been used within the higher education setting to assure the privacy of records of college students. In the present case, the privacy of the student judicial records of a student is at question.

As a result of several court decisions, the increase in campus crime and the Student Right to Know and Campus Security Act of 1990, the records of campus police have been excluded from those records defined as "educational records" by FERPA. Thus, they have become public and are eligible for release without the permission of the involved student. Legislation currently before Congress (the Accuracy in Campus Crime Reporting Act) would require that all actions by campus police be logged and available for review within 24 hours. This act would also open campus student conduct hearings and records in cases that related to an alleged crime.

Since this case involves requests for access to both the incident report written by police and the copy of that report which has been sent to the Judicial Office, there may appear to be some conflict. However, The Family Compliance Office of the U.S. Department of Education has indicated that the copy of the report housed in the Campus Police Department is not an "education record" and can be released. The copy of the same report housed in the Judicial Office is an "education record" and may not be released without the permission of the student. Since the initial report was written for a "law enforcement purpose" it is not protected.

The campus newspaper has not violated FERPA. This is true for several reasons. First of all, only institutional officials can violate the act. Unless the newspaper is deemed to be acting as an "agent" of the university, it cannot be deemed to be in violation. Secondly, if the newspaper quotes the statement from Coach Norton, they are not dealing with anything other than public documents and public statements, each of which would be protected by the First Amendment.

If anyone has violated FERPA it is Coach Norton. As the basketball coach he may have a "legitimate educational interest" in knowing about the incident and the fact that campus charges are pending. He does not, however, have the right to release educational records to the media without permission from the student. If he has received such permission from Mr. Thomas, then he is free from violation and this goes even further to protect the report released by the newspaper.

Section 1983 has been used by plaintiffs in several cases in which they believe that institutions improperly released, or refused to release when requested, information in student records. Federal judges in several states have granted rights to private action under this section despite the fact that FERPA itself states no private right to action. A number of other judges, however, have relied on the law itself and have refused access to the courts through this section. In any case, it does not appear that the campus newspaper would be liable under this section since it is not a state entity. If the newspaper released false information it could possibly be liable under other statutes (i.e. libel), however, Mr. Thomas' status as a public figure may protect them unless it was determined that such action was done with malice.

—*The case study and commentary were written by Dennis Gregory, Assistant Vice President for Student Development and Student Life at Francis Marion University.*

Case Study II. **DISTURBANCE AT BASKETBALL GAME**

Collum University (CU) is a public, four-year institution that is located near a mid-size Midwestern metropolis. The student body's racial balance is roughly 50% white and 50% black, providing the university with a very diverse campus environment. CU is extremely popular for its success in NCAA Division I basketball as they have consistently stayed in the top 10 of the national polls. The distinct feature of the basketball team is that the 13 players, 4 coaches, and 2 managers are black. Presently ranked #2 in the country, a critical game versus Jefferson University, ranked #5, is coming up.

In the last few weeks, despite the team's success, an increasing number of articles have appeared in the school newspaper about the ethnicity of the team. As a result of these articles, there have been small rallies on the campus protesting the basketball team. Although there have been minor racial incidents in the school's past, the number of these incidents have declined each year.

A game between CU and another top 10 team is to be played and is also scheduled to be on national television. Organizations including the Pro-white Activists, Nation of white Brothers, and the Anti-black Pilgrims have made public protest on the campus. Representatives from these groups have also purchased 300 tickets to the game and rumors are floating around that some sort of protest is being planned to take place inside the game site but no one is sure what it is.

The university has a policy allowing signs in the arena as long as they are not on sticks or other objects that can be used dangerously. They also have a policy that prohibits the actions of any persons that will impede the progress of the event. A fan can be removed if their action is deemed dangerous to other fans or participants in the events. The regulation specifically states that actions such as throwing objects, fighting, or obstructing views of other fans are forbidden.

As the start of the game approaches, the group of pro-white advocates show up with a much larger crowd than earlier anticipated. Over 500 people are present and many are wearing traditional racist gear, including white hoods and sheets, rebel flags, anti-black T-shirts and other apparel. Several also hold cardboard signs that are racist-oriented, with messages such as "We Need Whites not Darkies," "Take the Niggers off our Teams," and "Stop Taking over our sports Black Jellybeans." As they enter the stands, many black fans notice them and are visibly upset at their presence.

The game starts and the racist group begins yelling racial epithets at the Collum players and coaches. They are not physically accosting anyone, throwing objects, nor obstructing the view of other fans, thus they are not breaking the university regulations. However, it is clear other fans and the players are disturbed by their actions.

The Administration of Campus Discipline . . .

As half-time arrives and the players and coaches from Collum head to the locker room, the group increases the volume of their shouting and yelling as they get closer. As a result, several players head for the stands to confront the group but are restrained by security personnel before they get there. Half time is 20 minutes long and the shouting of racial epithets continues at a higher volume.

The president summons the vice president for student affairs along with the athletic director, the chief of campus security, and the building supervisor to meet in an emergency conference. In the conference, the president states that he wants these people removed from the game because they are embarrassing the university on national TV, and wants disciplinary action taken against any students involved.

Does the university have the right to remove the group of people from the game?

Can disciplinary action be taken against students who participated in the protest?

Commentary

The first amendment of the Constitution was implemented to protect the right of free speech of individuals in America. Over time, the limitation on the restriction of hate speech has prevailed in the courts. In *Doe v. University of Michigan* (1989), the court ruled that certain speech cannot be prohibited because the university disagrees with the ideas being conveyed or because individuals find speech to be offensive. In a similar decision, the court ruled in *UWM v. Board of Regents of the University of Wisconsin* (1991) "that freedom of speech is almost absolute in our land." The court stated that it was not likely that all discriminatory remarks are intended to be violent and disruptive. Thus, the appropriate position in this case would be that the racist group has a right to remain in the arena and continue their actions even though others may not like it. Their actions are not intended to cause a violent or disruptive environment, although others may disagree and be offended.

The signs that group members are holding is similar to signs that have various Bible verses written on them being held by fans. Although, many people are against the messages on the signs, the First Amendment protects the freedom of these people. It appears that it would be illegal to force these people to stop their actions because of their personal beliefs in opposition to the messages.

An issue the university should consider in the decision-making is the forum in which the individuals are located. A point that could be argued by the university is that they can control speech in a limited forum, based on time, place and manner restrictions. Attempts to regulate speech in a limited forum are very difficult, to prove in a court of law. Clear and present danger must exist before the university can attempt to control freedom of speech. In this situation, the group is not presenting an environment in which danger is present, they are simply voicing their opinion. Referring to the *Michigan* decision, the only danger that would be present is the potential reaction from those opposed to the protected speech. In this case, it appears that this is not a valid reason for termination of the activity.

Also, the concepts of public, limited, and private forums are related to organized protests and demonstrations. In a legal sense, the group's actions are not a "public protest or demonstration." They are no different than others who are yelling insults at the referees and the opposing team. In this situation, embarrassment on national TV is not a valid reason in the eyes of the court for limitations on First Amendment freedoms. The First Amendment is the central force behind the establishment of the United States.

Removal of individuals in the group would constitute a violation of their freedom of speech protection as long as they did not commit violent or threatening acts. The possibility and likelihood of some or all of the individuals suing the university is very strong and their case in court would also be strong. Having not violated any of the conditions stated in university facility regulations, the university has no basis for removing them. If the decision is made to remove them, the university may be liable for First Amendment violation and the damages to the institution may be great. Losing a publicized case such as this would cause financial as well as reputation damage. On the other hand, the university may be willing to accept these risks in order to establish a public policy statement.

> —*This case study and commentary were written by Rudy Cullom, a graduate student in student affairs administration at Texas A&M University.*

Case Study III. STUDENT CHRISTIAN FELLOWSHIP AND THE TRAVELING EVANGELIST

Student Christian Fellowship (SCF), a recognized student organization at Eastern State University, has invited an evangelist to campus to speak about the word of God. SCF requests outdoor space in front of the student union from university scheduling, for the evangelist to preach to students and faculty. SCF wants to use this space because of the student and faculty pedestrian traffic that passes through this area on the way to the bookstore, food court and services located in the Student Union. Student organizations regularly use this space for their activities. SCF is granted a permit to use space in front of the Student Union on the day and at the time (11 a.m. to 2 p.m.) requested.

On the day of the event, Joe Preacher arrives at the site and begins "sharing the word of God." Students stop to listen as they pass by on their way to class or the Student Union. About 100 students and faculty gather to listen to the evangelist during the noon hour. Joe Preacher, in the course of his preaching, makes some comments about non-Christians. A student in the crowd asks Joe Preacher why he does not recognize non-Christian religions. Joe Preacher asks the student if she is Jewish. She responds that she is Jewish. Then, Joe Preacher tells the student that because she is Jewish, she is going to "burn in Hell." Joe Preacher asks if there are other Jewish students in the audience. Some persons in the audience reply yes. Joe Preacher, then says that Hitler did not go far enough. Angered students and faculty leave the area while others remain and continue to listen to Joe Preacher.

Within a few minutes the dean of students receives a call from an angry faculty member who wants to know what is going to be done to stop this antisemitic preacher. One of her students had just come into her office in tears after being verbally harassed by Joe Preacher. Students and faculty who witnessed the encounter between Joe Preacher and the Jewish students also call to complain.

As dean of students how do you respond to the complaints about Joe Preacher?

What are the free speech issues involved in responding to the complaints?

Does the location of the activity have any bearing on the content?

What responsibility did the sponsoring organization have for the speaker's comments?

If the sponsoring organization had responsibility, what action should be taken against the organization?

Commentary

In responding to complaints from faculty, students and other administrators, it is important to clarify that by permitting a person to speak does not mean that the university endorses what is being said. It appears that the area in front of the student union is a public area used by student organizations to host various events, likely including speakers. Such areas typically permit students, faculty, student organizations and, perhaps, the general public to reserve the space in order to espouse their views on virtually any topic unless the expression "materially and substantially interferes with the normal operations of the university or invades the rights of others."

In a non-public forum such as a classroom or a residence hall, the universities have greater latitude in regulating the content of the speaker. The students in the classroom or the residence hall (non-public forum) are "captive audiences" who do not deserve such treatment. (See *Chapter VI* for discussion of the type of forums) While members of the university community may be offended by the evangelist's comments, the university cannot prohibit the expression of ideas because of a disagreement with or dislike for its content. The university can, however, establish reasonable time, place and manner regulations. It appears that Eastern State University requires individuals and groups to reserve the space, limits the number of days, and limits the amount of time each day to use this space. It would also be reasonable to limit use of amplification equipment as well as the size of any displays.

The rights of the students who were personally offended by the evangelist's statements to them were not violated. That is, the students were not forced to listen to the message and had an opportunity to express their opinions, even if counter to the evangelist's message. Further, the students could have avoided the area or, if it was necessary to go to the Student Union at that time, they could have entered the building through other entrances.

While the Student Christian Fellowship is not responsible for the comments of the speaker, it is important that it understands the concerns from students and faculty about the evangelist. The dean of students might arrange for a meeting between the leadership of Student Christian Fellowship and the offended students. The purpose of the meeting would be to permit the offended students to express their feelings and for the Student Christian Fellowship leadership to express the intent of inviting the evangelist.

Every institution should have a policy on freedom of expression activities. The policy might begin with a philosophical statement regarding protection of the rights of freedom of speech, expression, petition and peaceful assembly while maintaining the university's right to regulate reasonable time, place and manner restrictions concerning acts of expression and dissent. Other components of the policy might include registration and use of free speech areas (if designated on the campus) and other campus facilities and guidelines for expression.

—*This case study and commentary were written by Brent Paterson, Director of Student Life, Texas A&M University.*

Case Study IV. **SPOOF ON THE REGENTS**

The Society for Improvisational Theater (SIT) is a registered student organization at Southwest Alabama State University (SWASU). They regularly perform at the coffeehouse in the student center. During one of their performances they perform a parody about the board of regents. The parody makes fun of one regent's African-American heritage and implies that another regent is a homosexual.

The chair of the board of regents contacts the president at Southwest Alabama State and demands that SIT be disbanded and that the students involved in the parody be punished. The president contacts the dean of students and demands that she suspend the group immediately. The suspension also means that the group will not be permitted to host a booth during the all-campus fair the following week.

The student members of SIT are outraged. They call the student newspaper and the local media complaining that the university has violated their rights as students. A reporter from the student newspaper contacts the dean of students to get her side of the story. The dean tells the campus reporter that the student organization violated university regulations and was suspended. She also told the reporter that Carlos, Harold, and Victor (members of the group who did the skit) will also face disciplinary action.

Has the group broken any campus rule?

By punishing the group did the dean violate its right to free speech?

Has the group been provided due process?

Commentary

The most likely charge against the student organization and the students would be slander, a form of defamation. Defamation is defined as oral (slander) or written (libel) expression that tends to injure a person's reputation. In order for a statement to be slanderous, a person must make a false statement about a third person to another person(s) that ridicules or disgraces the third person. The false statement must also injure the third person's reputation. However, the Regents are considered "public figures." Statements referring to public figures would need to have been made with intentional malice in order to be considered defamatory.

Performing groups have wide latitude in the content of their performance under the First Amendment. At a public institution, there would be no cause for disciplinary action against the student organization or the individual students. While the First Amendment does not apply to private institutions not engaged in state action, taking disciplinary action simply for dislike for the content would seem problematic, especially when everyone in attendance understood it was a spoof on the regents.

Based on the action of the dean of students, it appears that the student organization was not provided with any due process. Fundamental due process requires at least that the student organization be informed of the charges against it (letter of charges) and be provided with an opportunity to respond to those charges (hearing). More detailed information on hearing procedures can be found in the *Model Code* and in *Chapter VII.*

While the dean might issue an interim suspension to the student organization prior to a hearing, such action usually is reserved for situations where there is a continuing danger to persons or property. Even with the interim suspension, a hearing would need to take place as soon as practicable.

> —*The case study was written by Glenn Maloney, Associate Dean of Students, University of Texas at Austin. The commentary was written by Brent Paterson, Director of Student Life, Texas A&M University.*

Case Study V. THE FRATERNITY NIGHTMARE

This is a case study of a fictional incident that theoretically occurred at a mid-sized urban state university in the south. The university has a large, strong Greek system with over a hundred-year-long tradition. Both fraternities and sororities own houses that are adjacent to but not on university property. The vice president for student affairs is an alumnus of both the university and the Greek system, as are the mayor of the city, the local prosecutor and five of the nine city council members. The university code of conduct has no code section that specifically refers to sexual assault. The section used to adjudicate allegations of sexual assault and related issues is, "Removal from the university or any lesser penalty may result from the following—Physical abuse of any person, or other conduct which threatens or endangers the health and/or safety of any person whether any such conduct occurs on or off university property."

A female student, Jane, comes to the judicial affairs office and reports that she believes that she has been sexually assaulted and wishes to press campus charges against the alleged assailant. She reports the situation on Wednesday, November 21. The situation is alleged to have occurred on the night of Saturday/Sunday, September 15-16. The allegation has not been reported to any police agency nor has Jane sought any medical treatment as a result of the assault.

Jane is accompanied by her roommate, Sarah, who has encouraged her to report the incident, and a male member of the psychology faculty, Professor Smith, who is the victim's advisor and a close personal friend of Jane's parents. Jane's father is a faculty member in the astronomy department at the university. Jane is a junior psychology major who is 20 years-of-age, lives off campus in an apartment, and pays all of her expenses for school from a job at a local restaurant which she has held since the age of 16.

According to Jane, the incident occurred after she attended a fraternity party at the ABC fraternity house. She and her roommate went to a party at the invitation of the fraternity president. At the party Jane met Robert, who is a fraternity member and lives in the house. Jane had brought a pint of 100 proof vodka with her and reportedly drank all of the vodka during the party. Jane indicated that she does not remember much after the first hour or so of the party. She does remember waking up at approximately 3:00 a.m. in bed naked and by herself. She then remembers waking up again at approximately 8:30 a.m. and finding herself still naked in bed in the fraternity house with Robert, who is also naked. At that time she awakened Robert and asked him what happened.

Robert reportedly indicated that they had partied until about 1:00 a.m. after which they had come up to his room. According to Robert, they talked for approximately an hour during which time Jane had become sick once, began to become sexually intimate and then had intercourse. Robert reportedly asked if he should use a condom, to which Jane answered yes. After intercourse Robert reportedly left the room for some time to check on a fraternity brother who was sick and then returned to the room and fell asleep.

After the morning discussion Jane dresses and left the house. Robert called her several times over the next two weeks, seeking to ask her out on a date. She refused. Jane finally informed her roommate of the incident after three weeks and Professor Smith after four weeks.

As the judicial officer at this university, discuss how you would handle the following issues:

What additional information would be important before proceeding?

Should campus police be called? If so, why? If not, why not?

What, if any, federal laws are related to how this case is handled?

If upon confronting Robert, he indicates that yes, he had intercourse with Jane, but that it was completely consensual, and that on occasion during the evening she had initiated sexual contact, would that impact how you treated the case? If so, how?

Is the fraternity in any way implicated in this case?

Commentary

Before proceeding it would be important for the judicial officer to have the answers to the following questions. Has Jane discussed the sexual assault with her father? Does the university judicial officer have Jane's permission to speak with her father about her complaint if he contacts? What does Jane wish to see as the outcome of this process? Does Jane know of any other person with whom the judicial officer should speak that could provide information that would prove useful in the investigation? Does Robert know of any other person with whom the judicial officer should speak that could provide information that would prove useful in the investigation? Are there neutral individuals with whom the judicial officer can speak who may have observed Robert and Jane at the party on the evening of September 15 at the ABC fraternity house? The judicial officer should speak with Sarah, without Jane present, about the events of September 15/16 as she recalls them. The content of the conversation during which Jane first told Sarah that Robert had sexually assaulted her would also be asked of Sarah. Also, the judicial officer should speak with Professor Smith, without Jane present, about his conversation with Jane during which she first told him that Robert had sexually assaulted her.

The campus police should be informed that a female student had reported to the university judicial officer that she had been sexually assaulted in a fraternity house off-campus by another student. It is assumed in this case that an individual in the campus police department has been identified by the institution to collect the data necessary to comply with the campus security provisions of the Student Right-to-Know and Campus Security Act. Under the provisions of the legislation, the judicial officer should inform Jane of her right to report the sexual assault to campus police or the appropriate law enforcement agency in the city.

The campus security provisions of the Student Right-to-Know and Campus Security Act of 1990 (20 U.S.C. §1092) as amended by the Higher Education Amendments of 1992 set up certain guidelines for the development of institutional policies for responding to sexual assaults which will impact the handling of this case.

The Family Educational Rights and Privacy Act of 1974 (20 U.S.C. §1232), commonly known as the Buckley Amendment or FERPA, relates to this case to the extent that this legislation prevents the release of personally identifiable information from a student's education record without his or her consent subject to certain exceptions and limitations. In this case, FERPA would impact the potential release of information to Jane's father regarding the case and to the public at large.

Under the provisions of the Family Educational Rights and Privacy Act of 1974, Jane appears to meet the criteria of an independent student as defined by the IRS. As such, information from her education record can not be shared with her father without her permission. FERPA does allow institutions to share information with university officials with legitimate educational interests without the student's consent. However, this does not extend to Jane's father in this case, even though he is a member of the faculty. If the judicial officer received Jane's permission to share information with her father, I would encourage him to speak with her prior to addressing his questions. It would also be important to bear in mind Robert's rights under FERPA as well.

There also exists an inconsistent body of rulings which would indicate that Title IX of the Education Amendments of 1972 (20 U.S.C.

The Administration of Campus Discipline . . .

§1681) has bearing on this case. At least one regional office of the Department of Education's Office of Civil Rights has criticized several institutions' handling of sexual assault cases based upon the Title IX prohibition against sexual harassment and the associated institutional obligation to respond in a manner deemed appropriate by OCR.

The fraternity is implicated based on the information at hand because it allowed a minor to consume alcohol openly within the fraternity house during a fraternity party, in violation of state law and university policy, not to mention the risk management policy of the ABC national office. It is clear that Jane was an invited guest of the fraternity and by inviting a guest, the fraternity must recognize that it accepts certain responsibility for its guests' actions while at the event. It would be important to separate to some extent this violation of the university's alcohol policy from the alleged sexual assault in dealing with the fraternity. It would be helpful to attempt to work with representatives of the ABC national office to develop a joint response to this violation of university and national policy.

Given the relevant facts and circumstances of the case, the judicial officer would find that Robert had violated the provision of the university code of conduct which prohibits "Physical abuse of any person, or other conduct which threatens or endangers the health and/or safety of any person, whether any such conduct occurs on- or off-campus." Based upon the information presented in the case study, it seems unlikely that it would be determined that Robert "sexually assaulted" Jane as defined by state law. However, it would seem that he had engaged in behavior that threatened her health and safety. This decision would likely be subject to significant criticism on campus and in the media, but this decision seems to be the appropriate one given the information available.

Because it had not determined that Robert "sexually assaulted" Jane, as this term is commonly defined, he would not be separated from the university. However, a set of sanctions that would be educational for him should be developed for him. These sanctions could include:

1. University probation for the remainder of Robert's university career;

2. A prohibition against Robert having any contact with Jane and Robert's fraternity brothers or friends contacting Jane, on his behalf. Failure to comply with this sanction would be interpreted as a violation of his university probation.

3. A requirement that Robert complete community service with an agreed upon community service provider. He would also be required to complete a reflective exercise on his community service that serves as a form of confirmation of the completion of the sanction and encourages the practice of reflective judgment.

4. A requirement that Robert meet with a staff member in the Office of Alcohol and Other Drug Education to discuss his use of alcohol and to follow the staff members recommendations for additional action, if necessary.

Disciplinary action should not be taken against Jane. Reasonable people would interpret the university taking disciplinary action against a student in Jane's situation as "victim blaming." Furthermore, such action would have the potential effect of discouraging other victims of sexual assault from reporting the incident to the appropriate university official. In this case the university's goal of education can better be achieved by other means. Furthermore, campus judicial systems tend to be complaint driven. The case study does not indicate that anyone has filed a complaint against Jane regarding her underage consumption of alcohol.

> —*This case was developed by Dennis Gregory for the 1997 ASJA Graduate Student Case Study Competition. The commentary was written by John Wesley Lowery, doctoral fellow at Bowling Green State University, winner of the ASJA Graduate Student Case Study Competition.*

Case Study VI. JOHN AND KYLE

John and Kyle were devoted friends and collaborators. Unfortunately, one of their instructors at a public university suspected that their collaboration extended to cheating during a classroom examination. The course instructor became suspicious of John and Kyle's activities at the outset of the examination, when she observed them sitting next to each other, contrary to her instructions to sit "every other seat." The instructor asked Kyle to move, but noticed a few moments later that he had not done so. It was necessary for her to reiterate her instructions, and to point out a number of vacant seats. Later, during the first portion of the examination, Kyle walked to the front of the room to ask the instructor a question. She then observed him returning to his original seat next to John. Again, for a third time, she insisted that Kyle sit in a different location.

The instructor decided to compare John and Kyle's examination papers after the papers were submitted for grading. She discovered that both students' answers to fifty short answer questions were identical, including four wrong answers not commonly answered wrong by the rest of the class. Also, while both John and Kyle had done *A* work on the short answer questions, neither student did very well on the essay portion of the examination, which covered the same material. Finally, the instructor noted over a dozen erasures on the short answer section of Kyle's examination, which Kyle stated had been done toward the end of the examination period.

The Administration of Campus Discipline . . .

Before reporting the matter to her dean, the instructor met privately and individually with John and Kyle. Both asserted that they had not engaged in any form of cheating, and that the similarity of their short answer questions reflected the fact that they studied together. They also observed that their inferior performance on the essay portion of the examination was caused by the fact that neither has a history of doing well on essay examinations.

Finally, Kyle offered a number of reasons for his apparent determination to sit next to John during the examination. He asserted that the room was crowded, and vacant seats were not readily apparent. Furthermore, when he sat next to John a third time, he did so for "only two or three minutes" because he was "disoriented" and "not thinking or seeing clearly" due to "the pressure of the examination." His numerous erasures, in his view, proved his innocence, since they demonstrated that he was uncertain about his answers, and was concentrating on his own work.

The instructor told both students she was not persuaded by their responses. She told Kyle in particular that she was disappointed in him, since he had told her what she regarded as an obviously false and contrived story. She then referred the case for hearing, in accordance with campus policies.

Both John and Kyle appeared at the hearing, which was held six weeks after the instructor referred the charge. Since the instructor was on sabbatical at the time, her written statement was submitted into evidence. John and Kyle spoke for themselves, since their legal advisor was not allowed to address the hearing panel. The panel found both students guilty, by a "clear and convincing" standard of proof, although one panel member did vote for acquittal. Also, at the end of the hearing, one panelist reminded Kyle that they had been high school classmates, and expressed regret at having to meet again under such unfortunate circumstances.

John and Kyle were outraged! They raised the following issues in an appeal to the dean:

1. The case against them was based solely upon circumstantial evidence. No one had seen them cheating, nor was any crib sheet found.

2. The instructor's comments to Kyle about what she believed to be a contrived story were defamatory, insensitive, and abusive.

3. Due process standards were violated by:
   a. faculty member's failure to appear at the hearing where she would have been subject to cross-examination;
   b. College policies restricting the role of legal counsel;
   c. Absence of a "beyond a reasonable doubt" standard of proof;

d. A policy permitting students to be found guilty by anything less than an unanimous vote;

e. A biased hearing panel member, who had known Kyle several years before.

How should the dean respond?

Commentary

This case may provide some insight into the reluctance of many faculty members to report allegations of academic dishonesty. Such matters can become bitterly contested and very time consuming. Although the first obligation of the campus administration is to insure that the accused students are treated fairly and reasonably, it will also be important to create a climate in which faculty members believe that their efforts are appreciated.

Faculty members should not expect to "win" every case; not should they take an adverse finding as a personal affront. However, it would be reasonable for faculty members to expect that honest and diligent efforts to protect academic integrity on campus will be properly recognized as a component of their "service" obligation to the institution.

Circumstantial evidence that has probative value may be relied upon, even in a criminal case. For example, a hearing panel may properly draw inferences from the totality of evidence in order to conclude that "chance alone" would be "an extremely unlikely explanation" for suspicious patterns of answers on an examination (*McDonald v. Board of Trustees*, 1974, pp. 102, 104). It is true that care should be taken in relying exclusively upon statistical evidence. In the present instance, however, there are many other forms of evidence as well:

1. Virtually identical multiple choice answers, resulting in superior scores;

2. Contrasted with inferior responses to essays covering the same academic material;

3. Consistent and eventually successful efforts to sit in adjoining seats;

4. Such efforts being specifically prohibited by the instructor, requiring her repeated personal intervention;

5. Over a dozen answer sheet erasures by Kyle, which he admits were accomplished sometime after he sat next to John during the examination.

Taken separately, each of these factors might be insufficient proof of academic dishonesty. In the aggregate, however, they are more than adequate to support the finding of the hearing panel, especially when one considers reasonable assessments of credibility, and Kyle's implausible justifications for his repeated efforts to sit next to John.

The Administration of Campus Discipline ...

In reaching this conclusion, one might rely upon the aphorism, "when offered a number of different theories, start with the simplest." The facts outlined above are most simply and logically explained by a theory which would encompass a finding of academic fraud. By contrast, John and Kyle offer a somewhat baroque defense, based upon coincidence, improbable difference in performance upon the same examination, and Kyle's stress-induced visual impairment (which, remarkably, did not affect his performance on the multiple choice portion of the examination).

Essentially, it is reasonable to conclude that both students, having reportedly studied together beforehand, also found it necessary to collaborate during the examination. Kyle was almost certainly determined to sit near John in order to give or receive unauthorized assistance. Such assistance may have been prepared in advance, reduced in writing, designed to be shared, and initially held by John. This suggestion must remain a hypothesis, however, since the precise nature of the collaboration probably cannot be established with certainty. It is simply not possible to know "the intentions and thoughts" of individuals in these situations, "but such unattainable evidence is not required" (*Nash v. Auburn University*, 1985, p. 959).

The hearing panel came to the reluctant conclusion that John and Kyle were not telling the truth about the nature of their activities during the examination. Making a determination of this nature is difficult and painful in a collegial setting. Nonetheless, while members of hearing panels must not assume that a student who is accused of academic dishonesty is likely to be lying, it will be essential to maintain a capacity for critical judgement, and to allow an honest and rigorous assessment of the facts to determine the outcome of the case.

Experienced observers recognized the unpleasant reality that some individuals accused of academic dishonesty may seek to rely upon contrived and fabricated evidence, both to "prove" their innocence, and to discredit the accuser. Indeed, a number of current trends in our culture would appear to be exacerbating this problem.

A related problem which frequently arises in comparable cases is the hearing panel's ability to render a decision if some critical question depends upon assessment of "one person's word against another." Inexplicably, this issue seems to pose a special problem in the academic community, since faculty and staff members are occasionally paralyzed by indecision if a factual dispute cannot be resolved with mathematical certainty. Indeed, apparent violations of a wide variety of school regulations may go unreported, due to an assumption that more than one witness will be necessary.

It must be emphasized that it is possible to resolve a case even if two individuals give contradictory testimony about an issue in dispute. Members of the hearing panel should listen carefully, ask questions, consider the logical order and consistency of the testimony, evaluate the demeanor of the witnesses, and make a judgment.

College and university administrators need to understand that no judicial process can produce perfect justice. Indeed, even in a criminal case with a "beyond a reasonable doubt" standard of proof, there is a small risk that an innocent person may be convicted and punished. We reluctantly accept (and subject ourselves) to such a risk, because an even higher standard (e.g., proof of guilt "by a moral certainty") would make it virtually impossible for the community to protect itself. A careful balance between competing interests is necessary, and must be based upon a foundation of fundamental standards of fairness. The unavoidable fact is that close and difficult decisions simply cannot be avoided, even though we recognize the capacity for human error.

Kyle's argument about "defamatory" comments by the instructor does not appear to be accurate or relevant. Since Kyle and the instructor were speaking privately, the teacher's expression of concern about Kyle's "false and contrived story" cannot be defamatory, since it was not directed to or overheard by a third party. In any event, Kyle needs to be reminded that the scope of the hearing was limited to resolution of the allegation of academic dishonesty. The issue of the alleged defamation was simply not relevant at the hearing, or on appeal.

Furthermore, Kyle's concern about the instructor's comments reflects extraordinary and unjustified sensitivity. Complaints of this nature must not be allowed to inhibit staff members from speaking candidly with students. If the instructor believed Kyle was lying to her, it was reasonable to raise the issue privately, and to explain to Kyle why such behavior is likely to be self-defeating. Also, it would be appropriate for the instructor to report the underlying facts of the case to campus officials responsible for academic integrity and student conduct, as provided by institutional regulations. Even if it were subsequently determined that some or all of the facts in the instructor's report were inaccurate, it is unlikely that the instructor could be found liable for defamation, unless the report were reckless, or motivated by malice.

Engaging students in dialogue and discussion about ethical issues can generate complaints that faculty and staff members are "judgmental" and "insensitive." What is truly insensitive, however, is the aura of benign, undifferentiated benevolence that too many educators use to disguise the exercise of authority. The latter practice has become a sophisticated bureaucratic art of survival that often enables college and university officials to avoid confrontations and quarrels; unfortunately, it also fails to help students define the boundaries by which they may shape their character.

Most of John and Kyle's due process arguments are unsupported by caselaw. The courts are virtually unanimous in holding there is no legal right to the full and active participation of an attorney in a case involving academic discipline (*Nash v. Auburn University*, 1985). Likewise, neither the "beyond a reasonable doubt" standard of proof, not a unanimous verdict have been required by the courts in campus disciplinary proceedings. It is true, of course, that John and Kyle are entitled to an unbiased hearing panel. However, the simple fact that one of the panel members knew Kyle, does not constitute sufficient proof of bias.

It will be necessary for Kyle to establish that the panel member was motivated by some sort of animosity toward him. Even a panelist with a superficial knowledge of the background of the case need not be disqualified, provided that he or she can "judge the case fairly and solely on the evidence presented" (*Keene v. Rodgers*, 1970, p. 222). However, hearing panel members who know the accused student, or who may be familiar with the facts of the case, should reveal such knowledge at the outset of a hearing, rather than at the end. Generally, if the accused student objects to the panelist's participation, it would be prudent to find a replacement.

John and Kyle do raise a legitimate and important due process argument when they assert that they were unable to question the referring faculty member at the hearing. It is true that a series of cases have held that there is no constitutional right to cross-examination in college or university disciplinary proceedings (*Dixon v. Alabama State Board of Education*, 1961, *Jaksa v. Regents of the University of Michigan, Nash v. Auburn University*, 1985). Nonetheless, judges recognize the value of cross-examination as an "essential and fundamental requirement for [a] fair trial" (*Pointer v. Texas*, 1965, p. 405) and may require it if a college disciplinary case "resolved itself into a problem of credibility" (*Winnick v. Manning*, 1972, p. 550).

Application of the "Golden Rule" would be a useful guide in this context. If a faculty member or administrator would wish to cross-examine a person who had made a serious accusation against them, it would seem prudent and reasonable to accord a similar right to students.

In the present case, the inability of John and Kyle to question the instructor does not necessarily mean that the findings should be reversed, or a new hearing conducted. The dean needs to undertake an honest assessment of the potential value of cross-examination before making a final decision. For example, if John and Kyle do not deny the basic facts set forth in an affidavit by the instructor, cross-examination about unrelated issues (e.g., "defamation," or prior grading practices) would have "no bearing on the outcome of the hearing" and it would serve "no useful purpose" (*Winnick v. Manning*, 1972, p. 549). These are difficult decisions for administrators to make; if there is a substantial doubt, it is usually best to resolve it in favor of the student, and to conduct another hearing. The rehearing might be held by the original hearing panel, although it would be best to use a new panel, if at all possible. In any event, an important lesson to be learned from this situation is the need to conduct disciplinary proceedings promptly, when witnesses are most likely to be available.

> —*This case study and commentary was written by Gary Pavela, Director of Judicial Programs, University of Maryland-College Park. It appeared in* **Academic Integrity and Student Development: Legal Issues and Policy Perspectives** *by William L. Kibler, Elizabeth M. Nuss, Brent G. Paterson, and Gary Pavela. This edited case study is reprinted with the permission of College Administration Publications, Inc. which published the monograph in 1988.*

Case Study VII.
MISUSE OF UNIVERSITY COMPUTER RESOURCES

As the disciplinary hearing officer at a large state university in California, the security officer at computer and information services has recently brought to your attention that a particular student's Web page has been receiving a significant amount of activity. The immense amount of "hits" to the site has slowed down the university's server.

You view the Web page and discover that the excessive amount of activity is related to controversial material located on the Web page and numerous hot links leading to pornographic sites. You must notify the student by letter that he is in violation of misusing the computer resources and ask the student to immediately remove the link or disciplinary action may be taken. After receiving your letter, the student calls your office and asks you to help him understand what he has done wrong. An appointment is set for you to meet with the student later that afternoon.

The student, Showmee D'Moni, informs you that he really isn't "into all that controversial material" and only placed it there to draw attention to his Web page and encourage "surfers" to visit his sponsors. Showmee claims that "the main reason I included the links on my page was because through research I learned that by hosting links, I could receive a monetary kickback from the company." He further explained that the more hits he receives to his site, the greater the kickback from his sponsors, which assists in paying his school bills.

As a hearing officer, you have never encountered this type of situation in which a student is benefiting from usage of university computer resources through Internet links. You share with Showmee the following policy:

Computing resources are provided by the university to accomplish tasks related to the university's mission. Usage of computing resources for these purposes is "authorized." Computing resources are connected to the campus network for the performance of authorized tasks. Accessing or attempting to access resources to perform unauthorized tasks is not permitted and is "unauthorized usage." The following issues are noted in determining authorized use:

1. Computing resources may not be used for illegal activities.
2. Computing resources may not be used for commercial activities unless specifically authorized.

You further explain that if the university system becomes "bogged" down, an individual can be asked to alter his/her page in order to remedy the situation. Showmee acknowledges the inconvenience that he has caused and agrees to remove the links and clean up his Web page when he leaves.

The next issue you cover with Showmee is the issue of using university computer resources for personal gain. Showmee is a bit more defensive on this issue and tells you that in his freshman year, as part of a class assignment, he was required to create his own Web page. His professor also informed the class that detailed directions for creating a Web page were located on his own homepage. Showmee stated that while he was viewing his professor's homepage, he came across an online form to purchase a book that the professor had written. Deciding to purchase the book, Showmee completed and submitted the form. Showmee now questions you as to what the difference is between a professor using a computer for personal gain and a student utilizing a hot link to make some extra money.

Is there a difference between the two situations? If so, what?

What action, if any, should be taken by the university?

How can the university remain free from accusations of censorship?

What can the university do to prevent situations like this from occurring again?

Commentary

The only difference between the two situations lies in the fact that one situation has caused a drain on the network resources as opposed to the other has not. Aside from that, if the professor has not received authorization for commercial use, the two situations appear to be the same and must be addressed by the university in accordance with the computer usage policy. In both situations, computer system resources were used for personal gain, directly violating the policy that states:

Accessing or attempting to access resources to perform unauthorized tasks is not permitted and is "unauthorized usage." Computing resources may not be used for commercial activities unless specifically authorized.

In addressing Showmee D'Moni's situation, the university needs to educate the student on electronic resources. Since the student already stated that he would remove the material and clean up his Web page, the university has the discretion whether or not to implement a formal sanction.

In these two situations, it is important for both parties to note that regardless of whether or not a decision is made, the decision to sanction one or both of the individuals has nothing to do with the concept of censorship. Rather, the university is simply following their current rules regarding computer misuse. Also, the institution needs to be thorough in explaining their current rules regarding the policy to the professor as well as to the student. This explanation must make it clear that the content of the links is not a concern, and has nothing to do with censorship or content, but that the behavior violated the computer misuse policy!

> —*This case study and commentary were written by Jacqui Spevak & George Castorena, graduate students in the student affairs administration program at Texas A&M University.*

Case Study VIII.
COMPUTER USE AND MISUSE OF COMPUTERS

Mr. James Davis is a sophomore computer science major at the University of Southeastern North Carolina. He is employed as a student worker with the university's computer information services (CIS) office. He also runs a small, enterprising but private business that sells pirated commercial software to other students on campus that he "borrows" from his office. To duplicate the various software in a quick and easy manner, he uses the student worker computer at the CIS office to produce the copies and then discreetly replaces the software back into the case where it is stored. To advertise his software products, Mr. Davis posts his product sheet on his own web page that is located on the local university computer server.

On Wednesday, March 18, Mr. Davis is in his room when he receives a call inquiring about the purchase of a certain software program by a faculty member, Dr. Stan Parker, who works in the accounting department. Mr. Davis and Dr. Parker arrange for a meeting the following week to examine the accounting software and strike a deal. On Tuesday, March 24, Dr. Parker reviews the software, buys it with a check and installs the software on his office computer. Dr. Parker is aware that the software that he has just purchased is very expensive and only used by the university's business and finance department.

The following week, Dr. Parker presents his latest findings on his current research to his colleagues at the monthly department meeting. Everyone is amazed at the dramatic improvements that Dr. Parker has made on his usually "stagnant" research, especially the complexity of his accounting spreadsheets. After the meeting, the department head approaches Dr. Parker and inquires about the type of software that he has obtained to produce such complex and developmental accounting spreadsheets in such a quick and efficient manner. Dr. Parker replies that the "new" accounting formulas installed on the software are just part of his "top secret" research being conducted.

Suspicious, the department head goes to the university computer center and discusses the situation with the assistant director of CIS and finds out that this particular software is virtually impossible to get. The assistant director shares with the department head that she noticed that that particular software was missing on Thursday, March 19. However, the following morning, the expensive software was in its correct place.

Realizing that this problem was internal, the department head and the assistant director go to Dr. Parker's office to inquire about the source of the software. They explain to him that obtaining this software is very difficult to come by as well as very expensive. By obtaining it through inappropriate channels, it is illegal and it breaks the university's ethics policies. They inform him that with his cooperation, they would not press charges if he agrees to disclose the name of his supplier. Fearful of losing his professorship, Dr. Parker decided to reveal his source. A day later, university authorities come to the office where Mr. Davis works and informs him that he is under investigation for piracy of copyrighted software.

What issues exist in this case?

Why is the university concerned about the licensing issue of the software?

Is this act considered to be wire-fraud? If so, why?

What can the university do to avoid this situation in the future?

Commentary

There are several issues that are relevant to the case study. Mr. Davis is in violation of several laws and university ethical codes by copying and selling unauthorized copies of software, using the university's computer to produce the copies; and advertising his own business on the university web server. The Federal Copyright Statutes are designed to prohibit the unlicensed copying of copyrighted material and software. Regarding computer software, the statutes focus on the "rental, lease, or lending of unauthorized copies of computer programs." Mr. Davis did not have a license or authorization to make copies of the office software.

By using the computer at his student worker station and by posting his product sheet on the web, he was violating university ethics codes, that prevent a person from using a computer resource for personal gain, as well as the code of student conduct. The issues that surround Dr. Parker involve his knowledge of purchasing an unauthorized piece of software and using it for personal gain. The same ethics code that applies to Mr. Davis also applies to Dr. Parker. In addition, Dr. Parker may also have violated several personnel regulations and laws.

The university is the sole licensee of the various software items which Mr. Davis "borrowed." If a software corporation suddenly pursues the university for copyright infringements, the university may be held legally liable for the unauthorized copies of software and even receive substantial fines.

The acts committed by Mr. Davis are considered to be violations of the federal wire-fraud law because he sold his duplicated software for the purpose of private financial gain.

Colleges and universities must be more conscious of copyright infringements occurring on campus because they may be more responsible for violations of the copyright law than was previously the case prior to recent revisions in the law. Administrators must be more proactive in educating students, faculty and administrators. Finally, Computer Information Service offices should have their inventory checked regularly for compliance with software licensing procedures.

> —*This case study and commentary were written by Jennifer Jamieson and Karen Horn, graduate students in student affairs administration at Texas A&M University.*

Case Study IX. CRAZY ROGER

Roger Scully is a freshman at Shelbyville University. In October he began confiding in his resident director, Ricardo, about some problems he was having with his girlfriend that seemed to be interfering with his class work. Over the course of several conversations, Ricardo learned that Roger had had a rough time during his senior year of high school because of his parents' divorce. He was easily distracted during class, and that he was feeling listless and indifferent about classes and about life in general. Ricardo also had heard from some of the other residents that Roger was quick to start fights during touch football games when calls were made against him.

Ricardo has encouraged Roger to seek some counseling and has suggested the Student Health Center on campus, which was free to students. After talking to his mother, Roger decided to go see a psychiatrist in his hometown, because this could be covered by his mother's insurance. Roger was diagnosed with bi-polar disease and given a prescription for lithium. Roger was a little embarrassed by this, and when he got back to school the only person he told was Ricardo.

In December, at the end of the semester party in the residence hall, Roger was drinking alcohol with some friends when his now ex-girlfriend walked in. Roger got very upset and started a shouting match with her. When she called him crazy and accused him of being on drugs, he threw a chair across the room and hit the wall with his fist, putting a hole in the wall. By the time the RA on duty got to the room, Roger was sitting on the broken chair talking to himself about being out of control.

During Christmas break, Roger received a certified letter in the mail notifying him that he was being withdrawn from Shelbyville University for medical reasons. The letter stated that as a result of the incident in the residence hall on December 10, and the fact that Roger had been diagnosed with bi-polar disease, the university felt that Roger did not have the ability to function properly within the academic community. The vice president of student affairs and the director of the student health center signed the letter.

Upon reading the letter, Roger's father decided to sue Shelbyville University, the vice president for student affairs, and the director of the student health center for violation of section 504 of the Rehabilitation Act of 1973 and the Americans with Disabilities Act and for violating Roger's right to due process. Mr. Scully also decided to sue Ricardo for libel and violation of the Buckley Amendment of the Family Educational Rights and Privacy Act (FERPA).

Lawyers for the university started their inquiry into the allegations by studying the university's policy on involuntary withdrawal for medical reasons. The current policy states that the university has the right to involuntarily withdraw a student whose behavior it considers a manifestation of a serious psychological problem. In the policy, serious psychological problems include, but are not limited to:

1. Instances where a student engages, or threatens to engage in behavior which poses a danger of causing physical harm to self or others; or

2. Instances that would cause significant property damage, or would directly and substantially impede the lawful activities of others, or would interfere with the educational process and the orderly operation of the university.

Are Mr. Scully's allegations substantiated?

Would the situation differ if Roger had gone to the student health center for counseling?

Should this situation have been handled differently? If so, how?

Commentary

Roger should have been given the right to defend himself. One major flaw in Shelbyville University's policy is that is does not have the necessary due process steps prior to the actual withdrawal taking place. Roger was not referred for evaluation nor given the chance to show that the current treatment he was receiving was improving his ability to function within the academic community.

The university made no request for an authorization to exchange information between Roger's psychiatrist and the university. Roger was not given the right to a hearing. He was given no representation and no method of appeal. Roger was also not informed of the measures he could pursue to be re-enrolled in the university.

Section 504 of the Rehabilitation Act of 1973 and the Americans with Disabilities Act (ADA) do not prevent an institution from holding students accountable for their behavior. What both Section 504 and ADA do disallow is basing a decision to exclude a student from the university on the fact that the student has a mental disorder. Shelbyville University erred in the application of these acts because in the withdrawal letter one of the reasons stated for Roger's withdrawal was the fact that he had been diagnosed with bi-polar disease.

The issue of whether Roger's records were unlawfully obtained to determine that he was bi-polar is uncertain in this case. If Roger had been seeing a psychiatrist at the student health center, and the university had gained the information about his disease from that source without Roger's permission, the university would not have been in violation of the Buckley Amendment of FERPA. The university could have argued that the information was based upon a "legitimate educational need". Since the university had no real knowledge of Roger's illness other than second hand hearsay, it appears that the "evidence" was used improperly. Even if the "evidence" had been obtained from a legitimate medical source, it is questionable as to whether it would be an "education record" in the spirit of FERPA.

The allegation of libel against Ricardo is not substantiated because for libel to exist a falsehood had to be present. If, in fact, Ricardo had told the university about Roger's condition, this would not constitute libel because Roger does in fact have bi-polar disease. Ricardo's informing university officials would also seemingly be protected under FERPA.

Shelbyville University's primary error in handling Roger Scully's situation was the fact that they based the withdrawal on the school's policy of involuntary withdrawal for medical reasons. A better option would have been to use the student disciplinary process. Roger committed several violations in the residence hall including damaging property and illegal consumption of alcohol. If the university had followed the student disciplinary procedures, Roger would have received his due process and may have gotten the help he needed, as opposed to being withdrawn from the university and possibly having to endure an embarrassing and stigmatizing court case.

> —*This case study and commentary were written by Jennifer Hodges, a graduate student in student affairs administration at Texas A&M University.*

Case Study X. ALTERNATIVE DISPUTE RESOLUTION

Ruth and Kim have been good friends since high school and came to State University together. Their junior year, Ruth and Kim decided to move to University Towers, an apartment style living complex on campus. To fill the apartment, they asked another junior named Jeri, and Bridget, who was a sophomore, to share the apartment. Ruth, Kim, Jeri and Bridget have shared this apartment for the last three semesters. The apartment has four separate bedrooms with common kitchen, bath, and living areas.

Fall exams had just concluded when Kim suggested that they host an end of the semester party. It was intended to be a small get-together of some of their close friends before everyone left for the holiday break. Each of the roommates had agreed to share the expenses for the party, which included beer, soft drinks and a variety of snacks. Ruth, Kim and Jeri were all 21 years old, however Bridget was only 20. University policies permit students of legal age to consume alcoholic beverages in the privacy of their own rooms or apartments.

What began as a small get-together, quickly grew to over 20 people crammed into the small apartment with several people drinking and talking out in the hallway. The case of beer originally purchased for the party was emptied almost immediately. Kim and her boyfriend went to get more beer and returned with a keg. While Kim had talked with her roommates about getting more beer, they never discussed exactly how much to get.

Shortly after Kim returned with the keg, a fight broke out between Jeri's boyfriend and another one of the guests at the party. During the fight, one of the apartment windows was broken. University Towers staff responded to the disturbance. Due to the large number of people, the staff contacted university police for assistance. Both participants in the fight were charged with assault. Several guests, including Bridget, were issued citations for being in possession of an alcoholic beverage by a minor. University Towers staff have filed an incident report regarding the situation and estimated the cost of the broken window at $150.

This incident has caused considerable stress on the relationships between these roommates. In the few days since their return for the spring semester, the staff have already reported two conflicts between the roommates.

How should this situation be addressed, through mediation or the student judicial process?

What aspects of this case lend themselves to a mediated resolution?

How might a campus dispute resolution center assist in responding to a situation such as this?

Commentary

Mediation and the student judicial process are not mutually exclusive. Both processes can be used to address different aspects of the case. Mediation should not be used in the place of the normal judicial process. If alleged violations of the student conduct code have occurred, then these violations should be addressed through the judicial process as in any other case. Mediation provides an opportunity to resolve issues that may be the root cause of some violations, or as in this situation, address issues which may be the source of future problems.

The four women involved in this situation have been roommates for the past three semesters, and appear to have had a positive relationship prior to this incident. If they remain roommates, but fail to resolve the conflict that exists, problems are likely to continue and may escalate. However, separation of the roommates may not be feasible depending upon the availability of space, and would present a major disruption to their academic and personal lives when the majority of these women will be graduating at the end of the spring term. Mediation is a particularly good option for resolving the conflict between the roommates, because it allows individuals to focus on the problem while preserving their relationship. Issues that may be part of the mediated resolution include:

1. Distribution of expenses related to the beer purchased for the party may be a source of conflict since Kim never really discussed exactly how much beer she was going to get.
2. Jeri's boyfriend was involved in the fight that resulted in the broken window and there may be conflict over the level of responsibility the others feel they have for replacement of this window.
3. Bridget may be resistant to sharing responsibility for the beer and the window because of the added burden she is experiencing due to the citation she received.

Another aspect of this case which might lend itself to a mediated resolution is the fight which took place between Jeri's boyfriend and the other guest. While student conduct charges may be pursued because of the physical altercation, these incidents often occur because of some underlying conflict between the parties. If identified, this underlying conflict could be the focus a mediation session.

A campus dispute resolution center provides a variety of resources to address situations such as this. While the student judicial process may be able to address the student conduct violations in this case, the adversarial nature of the process is not conducive to resolving the interpersonal conflicts between the parties. Further, the student's needs for legal assistance in their criminal cases is not addressed.

A campus dispute resolution center can fulfill the institutional responsibilities for addressing student conduct, while providing an opportunity to address the interpersonal conflicts through mediation, and legal advice on the criminal matters through legal services. This combination of services addresses all facets of the incident and provides the students with the necessary support to truly make this situation an educational experience.

—*This case study and commentary were written by Eugene Zdziarski, Assistant Director of Student Life, Texas A&M University*

Case Index

Subject Index